Theoretical and Empiri Foundations of Critical Global Citizenship Education

In the first volume in the Critical Global Citizenship Education series, Carlos Alberto Torres combines theoretical and empirical research to present an original perspective on global citizenship education as a vitally important way of learning in a globalized world. In examining the requirements for effective global citizenship education and education reform, he investigates pathways to citizenship building at the local, national and global levels and urges development of teaching methods, teacher education and curriculum within a social justice education framework. Taking into account post-colonial perspectives, political realities at play and practical implications, Torres provides a succinct but comprehensive understanding of how global citizenship education can expand the concept of civic education in a global society and interrupt inequality.

This volume considers the ways that global citizenship education has been incorporated and is used by international institutions, governments and the academy, and provides a clear framework for anyone struggling to make sense of the tensions and complexities of global citizenship education today.

Carlos Alberto Torres is Distinguished Professor of Education at UCLA, UNESCO Chair in Global Learning and Global Citizenship Education and Director of the Paulo Freire Institute.

Critical Global Citizenship Education
Edited by Carlos Alberto Torres
University of California, Los Angeles, USA

1   Theoretical and Empirical Foundations of Critical
    Global Citizenship Education
    Carlos Alberto Torres

Theoretical and Empirical Foundations of Critical Global Citizenship Education

Carlos Alberto Torres

Routledge
Taylor & Francis Group

LONDON AND NEW YORK

First published 2017 by Routledge

2 Park Square, Milton Park, Abingdon, Oxfordshire OX14 4RN

52 Vanderbilt Avenue, New York, NY 10017

Routledge is an imprint of the Taylor & Francis Group, an informa business

First issued in paperback 2018

Library of Congress Cataloguing-in-Publication Data
A catalog record for this book has been requested

ISBN: 978-1-138-21162-9 (hbk)
ISBN: 978-0-367-19434-5 (pbk)

Typeset in Sabon
by Apex CoVantage, LLC

I dedicate this book to my three-year-old granddaughter, Madeline Lia McMullin, with the hope that she will grow up to be a great global citizen in a peaceful and sustainable world.

Contents

Social Movement?   104

11 Implementing Global Citizenship Education: Challenges   141

    Appendix   152
    Bibliography   158
    Index   167

Preface

This book provides a systematic analysis of global citizenship education, exploring theoretical and empirical foundations.

Citizenship education has been traditionally associated with "civic education," that is, the teaching of constitutional democracy and obedience to the nation-state. Three categories are linked to civics education. The first one is civic knowledge, which in the context of constitutional democracy entails the knowledge of basic concepts informing the practice of democracy such as public elections, majority rule, citizenship rights and obligations, constitutional separation of power, and the placement of democracy in a market economy that is used as the basic premises of civil society.

The second category associated with citizenship building is civic skills, which usually mean the intellectual and participatory skills that facilitate citizenship's judgment and actions.

The last category is civic virtues, usually defined in Western societies around liberal principles such as self-discipline, compassion, civility, tolerance and respect.

What will be the definition of citizenship building including global citizenship education (GCE)? How has the concept of GCE been incorporated into the contemporary discourses circulating and competing in the international system, governments and academia? What is the role of UNESCO and the United Nations in promoting GCE and education for sustainable development? These are some of the themes that I address in this book: themes that are connected with the dominant agendas in the multiple globalizations that we are experiencing and slowly but surely are altering the way we understand education and learning in the 21st century; themes that are also connected to the controversies around citizenship building, diversity and the dilemmas of multiculturalism; themes that interact with the responsibilities of universities and adult learning systems in promoting citizenship building.

I shall echo Paulo Freire when he said in *Pedagogy in Process* words that I will make mine: "Without exception, every book that I have written has been a report of some phase of the political pedagogical activity I have been engaged with ever since my youth."[1]

This volume attempts to reveal multiple layers for understanding the meta-theoretical, theoretical and empirical implementation of global citizenship education.[2]

Because this book is written with a political pedagogical purpose, I decided not to write only for the cosmopolitan elite but for anyone who is struggling to make sense of global citizenship education and education for sustainable development. This movement towards global citizenship education and education for sustainable development is beginning to impact the life, actions, policies and practices of ministries of education and ministries of foreign affairs the world over, and therefore impacting the way that teacher trainers and teachers are working in diverse environments.

I want this book to achieve multiple goals by reaching diverse audiences because this book is the first one in a new series on Critical Global Citizenship Education. I hope this volume will constitute a signpost for the books that will follow. My goals have been to outline the cornucopia of topics that should be addressed in this series incorporating multiple dimensions of human life, scientific specialties, political philosophies and political pedagogical projects as they relate to global citizenship.

Second, I also want to identify and discuss some of the conundrums of global citizenship education because by addressing global citizenship education and education for sustainable development, we are dealing with a confusing and difficult analytical and practical, not to mention political problem of implementation. In doing so I want to address, the Kantian dilemma that asks the appropriate question: "Can a state be fully democratic in a world that is not (as yet) democratic and vice versa?" This of course can be extended to a sort of Kantian dilemma by asking the question not only on democracy but on citizenship: Can we try to build a global citizenship education when so many nation-states have failed even to build national citizenship education, or when national citizenship building is still an abysmal work in progress?

Third, if we can build global citizenship education, what are the conditions to build this model globally, what is the added value to national citizenship, what are the challenges, and how may global citizenship education interact with national citizenship?

What follows is the ecology of this book and its chapters. The first chapter discusses some of the recent developments in Global Citizenship Education or what I have called the realpolitik of GCE.

The second chapter asks the question of why global citizenship and why now, and advances some of my theses fully documented in the following chapters.

Chapter 3 is a modified version of my keynote presented at the First Global Citizenship Education Forum organized by UNESCO in Bangkok, Thailand in 2013 and discusses the tensions between collaboration and competition in the world system, a tension that surely impacts both national citizenship education and the project of global citizenship education per se.

Chapter 4 analyzes three dominant agendas of globalization that includes hyper-globalists, skeptics and transformationists. These developmental agendas by definition play a role in how people, institutions, corporations and governments, with their political agendas, position themselves in the debates about global citizenship education. This chapter was originally presented in a meeting in Canada and a few sections were published in an article published in the *European Journal of Education*.[3]

Chapter 5 discusses the new common sense of neoliberalism and how it impacts the university and by implication citizenship building. Organized around seven iconoclastic theses, this chapter offers a foundation or building blocks to understand the interaction of universities and their role in citizenship building.[4]

Chapter 6 offers a typology of national universities and global universities that is both analytical and provocative, linking universities and public spheres as well as global and local imaginaries affecting citizenship building.[5]

Chapter 7 written in collaboration with Massimiliano Tarozzi and is tributary of our joint book just published[6] discussing the question of multiculturalism in the world system with a particular emphasis on social justice education. This discussion has implications for citizenship building in general and global citizenship education in particular.

Chapter 8 is entitled "Global Citizenship Education and Global Peace: *Vive la Liberté!*" and was written for the Second Global Citizenship Education Forum and presented at the UNESCO headquarters in Paris, just weeks after the massacre of Charlie Hebdo.

Chapter 9, entitled "Adult Learning and Global Citizenship Education," written with Jason Dorio, offers commentaries aimed at the practitioners working in the difficult trenches of adult learning education.

Chapter 10 asks the question: Could Global Citizenship Education became a global social movement?

Chapter 11 offers some commentaries in the guise of a conclusion.

Notes

1. Paulo Freire, *Pedagogy in Process*, Freire, 1978, p. 176. See also his statement in my interview with him in *Aurora Review*: "My books are as if they were theoretical reports of my practice." http://aurora.icaap.org/talks/freire.html
2. What I have done in this book is link my ongoing research agenda with specific public presentations and keynotes that I have made over the last three years, and have included some of this work here. Inevitably, there is some repetition in some of the chapters, but I decided to leave them as is for a simple reason: Some of the chapters are written for popular audiences, some are written for academic audiences, and all of them could be read independently from each other. Put in another way: There is no need to read the book in a sequence. So the reader can choose to read this book from front to back or simply read individual chapters as they need.
3. Paper presented at the Canada Society for the Study of Higher Education (CSSHE) Conference in Ontario, Canada, 22–24, 2014. Some parts of this chapter belong

to the article published in the *European Journal of Education*, volume 50, number 3 (2015), pp. 262–279, reprinted with permission.

4. Published as "Public universities and the neoliberal common sense: Seven iconoclastic theses" in *International Studies in Sociology of Education*, volume 21, number 3 (2011), pp. 177–197. A follow-up article, which will be reprinted in a book edited by Carlos Alberto Torres and Gabriel Jones and to be published by Routledge, is entitled "Neoliberalism as a new historical bloc: A Gramscian analysis of neoliberalism's common sense in education" and was published in *International Studies in Sociology of Education*, volume 23, number 2 (June 2013), pp. 80–106.

5. Also partially published in the *EJE*, reprinted with permission.

6. Massimiliano Tarozzi and Carlos Alberto Torres, *Global Citizenship Education and the Crises of Multiculturalism Comparative Perspectives*. London: Bloomsbury, 2017.

Acknowledgements

This book could not have been written without my participation in a number of UNESCO meetings over the last three years. Dialogues with several colleagues deserve special recognition. I am grateful for conversations with Soo Hyang Choi, Lydia Ruprech, Utak Chung, Alexander Leicht, Cristopher Castle, Anantha Kumar Duraiappah, Jason Dorio, Daniel Schugurensky, Massimiliano Tarozzi, Ana Elvira Steinbach Torres, Robert Rhoads, Luis Miguel Lazaro, Tuan Anh Nguyen and Lynette Shultz. While I learned immensely from their experience and wisdom, I am solely responsible for what is being said in this book.

1 The Realpolitik of Global Citizenship Education[1]

Introduction

One could trace the current developments in global citizenship education at two different levels. The first one is well articulated in the opening chapter of William Gaudelli's book speaking about Diogenes of Sinope, "the ancient Greek cynic who once declared 'I am a citizen of the world.'"[2] This narrative strategy situates the beginnings of the conversation about global citizenship in the context of a traditional history of philosophical thinking hundreds of years ago. In other terms, the realpolitik of the concept can be traced back academically centuries ago and through diverse philosophical currents, traditions and thinkers. This strategy, as valuable as it is, will not be followed in this book.

There is another way to trace the realpolitik of the concept and how it reached its current development, and it is to trace the emergence, definition of the main phases of implementation and its relevance in the international system, in the United Nations and its specialized institutions, specially UNESCO. To trace these developments, we will be well served if we focus on the 1990 Education for All initiative and its aftermath.

[handwritten margin note: Tracing UNESCO & its development of the "citizen of the world" idea]

1990—EFA, Thailand

The contemporary origin of the movement was a global commitment to provide basic education for children, youth and adults; it was above all an attempt to increase access. It was launched at the World Conference on Education for All in Jomtien, Thailand, on March 5–9, 1990. Sponsored by key educational stakeholders including UNESCO, UNDP, UNICEF and the World Bank, the conference was attended by delegates from 155 countries and representatives from 150 governmental and non-governmental organizations. As a first attempt to connect donors with operative institutions, this conference may be considered the first global education initiative in the last decade of the 20th century. The goal was to define an expanded vision of learning and to pledge to universalize primary education, massively reducing illiteracy by the end of the century. The focus was on access, and these lofty goals were adopted in a *World Declaration on Education for All* urging the countries to adopt the *Framework for Action to Meet the Basic Learning Needs.*

As articulated by Dr. Soo-Hyang Choi, Director of the Division for Inclusion, Peace and Sustainable Development Education Sector at UNESCO: "All means and modes of delivery, including formal, non-formal and informal, were advocated to expand learning opportunities. The scope of basic education was broadened to start from birth. Equity was the paramount policy principle, and stakeholders were urged to reach the unreached. Major global investment in education was directed to the universalization of primary education, which was also one of the millennium development goals."[3]

EFA Revisited: 2000—Dakar, Senegal

A decade later, at the beginning of the 21st century, it was clear that the goals had not been met in many countries of the world. The *Dakar Framework for Action, Education for All: Meeting Our Collective Commitments,* which included six regional frameworks for action, was adopted by the World Education Forum in Dakar, Senegal, April 26–28, 2000. In this meeting, the stockholders reaffirmed their commitment to achieving *Education for All* by the year 2015, but they added a new focus that was not previously evident: quality of education as crucial to achieve learning opportunities.

Table 1.1 Education for All Goals

Goal 1

Expanding and improving comprehensive early childhood care and education, especially for the most vulnerable and disadvantaged children.

Goal 2

Ensuring that by 2015 all children, particularly girls, children in difficult circumstances and those belonging to ethnic minorities, have access to, and complete, free and compulsory primary education of good quality.

Goal 3

Ensuring that the learning needs of all young people and adults are met through equitable access to appropriate learning and life-skills programs.

Goal 4

Achieving a 50 percent improvement in levels of adult literacy by 2015, especially for women, and equitable access to basic and continuing education for all adults.

Goal 5 ·

Eliminating gender disparities in primary and secondary education by 2005, and achieving gender equality in education by 2015, with a focus on ensuring girls' full and equal access to and achievement in basic education of good quality.

Goal 6

Improving all aspects of the quality of education and ensuring excellence of all so that recognized and measurable learning outcomes are achieved by all, especially in literacy, numeracy and essential life skills.

In addition, the focus shifted from the system providers to the receivers, the learners.[4]

UNESCO as the lead agency was mandated to coordinate the educational efforts to reach *Education for All*. While the EFA goals were seen as contributing to the eight Millennium Development Goals (MDGs), adopted by 189 countries and leading development institutions in 2000, the Dakar meeting identified six key education goals to meet the learning needs of all children, youth and adults by 2015.

2012 Global Education First Initiative (GEFI)

Putting every child in school, improving the quality of learning and fostering global citizenship are the three principles of the Global Education First Initiative (GEFI) launched by the United Nations in 2012. The three principles are intimately interrelated, and constitute the soul of the post-2015 development model advocated by the United Nations and its specialized agencies, particularly UNESCO, to be implemented until 2030.

UNESCO provides the following definition of global citizenship: "Global citizenship refers to a sense of belonging to a broader community and common humanity. It emphasizes political, economic, social and cultural interdependency and interconnectedness between the local, the national and the global."[5]

Global Citizenship Education (GCE) is one of the three pillars of the 2012 UN Global Education First Initiative (GEFI),[6] promoted internationally by the support and work of UNESCO. The aims and ambitions are set high: "Global Citizenship Education aims to equip learners of all ages with those values, knowledge and skills that are based on and instill respect for human rights, social justice, diversity, gender equality and environmental sustainability and that empower learners to be responsible global citizens. GCE gives learners the competencies and opportunity to realize their rights and obligations to promote a better world and future for all. GCE builds on many related fields such as human rights education, peace education, education for international understanding and is aligned with the objectives of education for sustainable development (ESD)."[7]

The previous point is well argued by Dr. Soo-Hyang Choi: In 2012, the UN Secretary-General launched the *Global Education First Initiative* (GEFI). Introduced before the dawn of the era designated "post-2015," GEFI aimed to give a boost to the EFA frameworks, goals of which were set to be achieved before 2015. Access and quality of education, emphasized in the Jomtien and the Dakar frameworks for more than two decades, were reiterated as two of the three priorities. The long-lasting impact of GEFI, however, has to do with its third priority, global citizenship education, which was mentioned in neither of the two EFA frameworks. Many pondered the addition of this particular thematic area, the importance of which was elevated to that of access and quality, the two supreme policy agendas of EFA. The message the UNSG wished to convey by introducing the GEFI that included global citizenship education was clear. He said: "Education is about more than literacy and numeracy. Education must fully assume its essential role in helping people to forge more just, peaceful and tolerant societies." The implications of this simple statement are not negligible. No longer is it sufficient to speak of the benefits of education only in terms of realizing individual rights or fulfilling national aspirations. With GEFI, the world education community entered an era in which education is expected to contribute also to the wellbeing of humanity and the global community. The perspective on the utilitarian role of education remains unchanged, but the idea of what education should aim to achieve has clearly evolved.[8]

Dr. Choi offers a frank analysis, arguing: "The advocacy for learning to live together existed for a long time, even before the announcement of GEFI. UNESCO itself was created in 1947 with the mandate of 'since wars begin in the minds of men, it is in the minds of men that the defenses of peace must be constructed.' In the past, the idea was expressed through such concepts as international understanding, international cooperation, tolerance, etc. Peace education or education on the culture of peace also shares many conceptual properties with global citizenship education. The concept of global citizenship itself is thus not new."[9]

2015, Incheon

In Incheon, Republic of Korea, the World Education Forum took place on May 19–22, 2015. This conference pointed to linking education with the Millennium Development Goals, connecting as well with Education for Sustainable Development, which was the key motif of the UNESCO development decade.

The meeting had two parts. The first one was a discussion of NGOs that I attended as president and representative of the World Council of Comparative Education Societies (WCCES), an NGO associated with UNESCO, and a second part with the participation of government representatives—I participated in this second meeting as invited expert.

The *Education 2030: Incheon Declaration and Framework for Action* marks an important departure from the previous declarations, with a strong emphasis on gender disparities, and emphasizing that post-secondary and tertiary education play a major role in lifelong learning. The unfinished business of EFA was revisited critically and the commitment reaffirmed. Yet:

> . . . the place for a newest development vis-à-vis the two previous EFA frameworks is reserved for its Target 4.7, devoted to specific thematic areas, such as education for sustainable development, gender, human rights, cultural diversity and global citizenship, etc. Inclusion of the Target 4.7, which is often referred to as one of the "messy" targets when it comes to measuring and monitoring, changes the kinds of question we are to pose on education. Questions about school attendance or

learning achievements are no longer considered sufficient to address the emerging challenges of the world. The questions on access and quality now need to be complemented with our question about content.[10]

The new trends that are identified focus on what is termed "soft" skills, or to put it in the traditional analysis of the Delors Report's proposal, "learning to live together."[11]

All these developments translate into a number of trends: a trend marked by an effort to complement the discourse of access and quality with that of content; an effort to complement the discourse of cognitive skills with that of socio-emotional skills; a trend to complement the discourse of skills and competencies for employment and job market with that of skills and competences for learning to live together; and a trend to complete an education that measures with an education that matters. The fact that the Republic of Korea, a country which has seen education from the economic perspective of human resources development, is now requiring, by legislation, that schools teach soft skills of learning to live together, as an effort to counter the rising violence in schools, is one telling example.[12]

2015 Sustainable Development Goals

The conclusion of the decade of Education for Sustainable Development (2005–2014) was celebrated in 2014 with the 2014 UNESCO World Conference on Education for Sustainable Development which took place November 10–12, 2014 in Aichi-Nagoya, Japan.

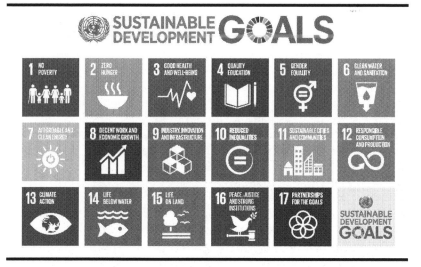

Figure 1.1 Sustainable Development Goals

The location for this conference was no accident. The government of Japan has been the most enthusiastic and committed government in the world promoting education for sustainable development and providing abundant resources to achieve substantial goals. The conference launched the *Aichi-Nagoya Declaration on Education for Sustainable Development* (ESD) and the *UNESCO Roadmap for Implementing the Global Action Programme on Education for Sustainable Development*.

This Global Action Program was endorsed by UNESCO's 37th General Conference and the 69th session of the UN General Assembly, which was intended to contribute to the post-2015 agenda. For a complete narration of the main goals and plans for development, see the *Sustainable Development Knowledge Platform*.[13]

2013–2017 GCE Forums

The GEFI initiative announced by UN Secretary-General Ban-ki moon in 2012 caught the world by surprise. Linking access with quality of education in quality schools was a long-sought goal by experts and educational pundits, but bringing the third pillar of global citizenship as a prerequisite to obtain such lofty goals created turmoil in some quarters and satisfaction in others.

What exactly is global citizenship? How could it be implemented? What are the pros and cons of global citizenship education? Who should be in charge of implementing GCE? How different is this model of citizenship building from national citizenship that emerged with the constitution of the nation-states in the last two centuries? What is the role of the UN as a kind of supra-national state in achieving this trilogy of goals that seemed so interconnected in the perspective of the UN Secretary-General? Is this global citizenship a kind of civic education for the 21st century? Moreover, how is it connected with global education, peace education, education for sustainable development and a host of other terms and eventually the ideology and practice of transnational social movements that already established their credentials in the world system, or how is it represented among specialized units of the UN as well as governments and professional associations?

A great deal of enthusiasm and interest was concocted around this trilogy of pillars, but what is very challenging is to define exactly what is the role of global citizenship, and what specialized institution in the United Nations system should be in charge.

Shortly after the GEFI initiative was launched in 2012, UNESCO was designated as the site for building this project, and naturally, it was connected to education—hence Global Citizenship Education.

Let me go back to the preparatory work for implementing Global Citizenship Education (or GCE) in the realm of UNESCO, a true process of mutual learning between UNESCO officers, invited experts and governments as well as NGOs and civil society.

The eighth Secretary-General of the United Nations, Mr. Ban ki-moon, who launched the first-ever educational initiative in the United Nations, is a Korean diplomat who at the time of his election was Minister of Foreign Affairs and Trade in Korea. He took office on January 1, 2007. On June 21, 2011, he was unanimously re-elected by the General Assembly and served through December 31, 2016.

His biography states: "I grew up in war . . . and saw the United Nations help my country to recover and rebuild. That experience was a big part of what led me to pursue a career in public service. As Secretary-General, I am determined to see this Organization deliver tangible, meaningful results that advance peace, development and human rights."[14]

Not surprising, one of the most important advocates for GCE has been the government of Korea. The South Korea ruling conservative Saenuri Party (roughly the equivalent to the Republican Party in the United States) and South Korean President Park Geun-hye, elected in 2013, have been pushing for a new policy model with a strong emphasis on GCE and public diplomacy. Perhaps Mr. Ban ki-moon might compete for the presidency in the elections planned for December of 2017. Whatever the vicissitudes of Korean politics today, the concept of GCE is a topic that is embraced and deeply rooted in both key political parties, the conservative Saenuri Party and the liberal Minjoo Party, which has recently made enormous gains in the National Assembly.[15]

A key institution in Korea to promote GCE is *The Asia-Pacific Centre of Education for International Understanding* (APCEIU), established on August 25, 2000 by the Agreement between the Government of the Republic of Korea and the United Nations Educational Scientific and Cultural Organization on the Establishment of the Asia-Pacific Centre of Education for International Understanding (August 25, 2000) in accordance with the Resolution of the 30th UNESCO General Conference (30C/Resolution 17).

APCEIU under the auspices of UNESCO is UNESCO's Category II institute to promote International Understanding and Peace through Education as stated in the Recommendation concerning Education for International Understanding, Cooperation and Peace and Education relating to Human Rights and Fundamental Freedoms (adopted at the 18th UNESCO General Conference on 19 Nov. 1974), and also the Declaration and Integrated Framework of Action on Education for Peace and Education relating to Human Rights and Fundamental Freedoms (adopted at the 18th UNESCO General Conference on 19 Nov. 1974), as well as in the Declaration and Integrated Framework of Action on Education for Peace, Human Rights and Democracy recommended by the 44th International Conference on Education in 1994. Its inception is a significant step forward to promote a Culture of Peace through Education and to renew the commitment and cooperation of UNESCO Member States and all stakeholders involved in the Asia-Pacific region.[16]

As described in their mission and mandate, APCEIU is working in close collaboration with UNESCO offices, national commissions of Member States, related educational institutes and civil society to promote Education for International Understanding (EIU) towards a Culture of Peace in the Asia-Pacific region.

With the important role to play by UNESCO soon after the GEFI initiative was launched, and the complexities associated with building GCE, APCEIU was chosen as one of the key institutions to lead the beginning of conversations leading to the establishment of a solid GCE narrative—specific actions that may contribute to network building among and within government institutions worldwide.

The first GCE foundational meeting took place on APCEIU's main campus in Seoul as the site of the UNESCO Technical Consultation on Global Citizenship Education on September 9–10, 2013 in Seoul, Republic of Korea. There were four sessions established to digest and discuss exactly what was the task at hand and how could it be implemented. The titles of the sessions speak for themselves:

> **Session 1: Why Global Citizenship Education?** Including a discussion of Education for All, Global Education First Initiative, Education for Sustainable Development and other post-2015 processes, latest discourses on quality education, civic education, etc.
>
> **Session 2: Mapping Initiatives** and trends consisting of a synthesized presentation of initiatives identified by the participants.
>
> **Session 3: Conceptual, definitional and measurement issues** with the goal of addressing conceptual issues, measurement issues and definitional issues.
>
> **Session 4: An operational guiding framework** that helped discussions and future activities.

This foundational meeting was very important because it not only included a great variety of people mostly from institutions of civil society, some representatives of government and academia, but because the UNESCO personnel were seeking orientations and clarity on a very large mandate—a mandate that was not only challenging but analytical, political and semiotically difficult, perhaps even elusive.

As one of the invited experts, I discovered the power of interaction among people selected for a variety of reasons and not necessarily in agreement with each other, which is not uncommon for events of the United Nations' specialized institutions. But there was a sense of hope, perhaps even a secular spirituality being practiced by many people who have devoted an important part of their lives, whether in international institutions, government or academia, to pursue answers to troubling times, particularly when many of us have lived our lives seeking how to build consensus when it is almost impossible to do so, how to promote a culture of peace in the midst of conflict, and how to preserve hope when despair seems to prevail everywhere.

As a natural outcome of this meeting, the conceptualization of the First Global Citizenship Education Forum was conceived in the spirit of the Roman Forums, which not unlike a Greek Agora, represented a public gathering for debate and discussion. The Agora or the Forums were a public arena for all sorts of public activities, from commerce to religious, economic political or social exchanges. If one were to extrapolate this concept a bit, it is a sibling of the concept of public sphere with the sophisticated analyses provided by Habermas and some of the critical theorists in the 20th century.[17]

The First Global Citizenship Education Forum took place in Bangkok from December 2–4, 2013 under the theme of Global Citizenship Education, with the goal of preparing learners for the challenges of the 21st century, and coordinated by the UNESCO Bangkok office. Perhaps it was a sign of the times that we met in a hotel downtown in one of the areas of the city considered safer at the moment with the strong presence of United Nations security. Bangkok at the beginning of December 2013 was undergoing a most turbulent period with violent and deadly demonstrations that some considered the "people's revolution." There were massive demonstrations that eventually forced the ousting of Prime Minister Yingluck Shinawatra; after months of political agitation and massive demonstrations, the Constitutional Court of Thailand declared in 2014 that she had abused power and was removed from office.[18]

"Empowering young learners with the skills and competencies they need to meet the challenges of a rapidly changing and interconnected world" was "the focus of the first international UNESCO Forum on Global Citizenship Education (GCE) in support of the Global Education First Initiative (GEFI) launched in September 2012 by the UN Secretary-General."

The objectives of the UNESCO forum on GCE included the following:

- Share experiences of policies, research and practice relating to the emerging area of GCE including trends, innovations and current debates from the perspective of a range of key stakeholders
- Advance conceptual thinking, content, definitional and measurement issues and characteristics of good-quality GCE that can provide leadership and support for action by the education sector's strengthened engagement
- Provide a platform for intellectual debate among education professionals that will support future interactions and efforts to advance the GCE agenda[19]

The Second Global Citizenship Forum took place at the Paris UNESCO headquarters in Paris, France from January 28–30, 2015. The goals of this second Forum were embedded in multiple activities going on at UNESCO Headquarters, celebrating its 70th anniversary in 2015, coinciding with the end of the Second World War and highlighting the importance of human rights, with discussion on the one of the most important genocides of the 20th century, the Holocaust, which took 6 million lives in the hands of the Nazi concentration camps.[20]

As I have indicated in the paper I presented in the introductory presentation of the Forum on "Overview Opportunities in achieving peace through GCED" and that it is included in this book with few modifications (see Chapter 8), the macabre paradox is that we held a meeting in Paris devoted to global citizenship education and peace, just weeks after the Charlie Hebdo massacre on January 7, 2015.

Building on the lessons and achievements of the First Forum held in Bangkok in 2013, the goal of this meeting was to:

- Set global policy directions for Global Citizenship Education in the context of ongoing discussions around the post-2015 development agenda
- Develop innovative implementation strategies for GCE looking at cutting-edge research and practice, with a particular focus on GCE and peace
- Expand and reinforce partnerships and networking opportunities

The Third Global Citizenship Education Forum will take place in Ottawa, Canada, March 6–10, 2017 in association with a meeting that will take place just before this on Education for Sustainable Development, showing the close association between these two social movements.

Conclusion

This chapter has traced the different activities to implement the GEFI project and its dual goals of global citizenship education and education for sustainable development, goals that are of particular relevance to UNESCO and other United Nations specialized units.

UNESCO is not in charge of conducting research. That is work that should be conducted in our universities, and one of the fundamental principles of the UNESCO UCLA Chair in Global Learning and Global Citizenship Education that I have the honor to occupy. Despite not having been able to conduct empirical research, UNESCO over the last decades has produced knowledge and thinking of great impact. This is exemplified in remarkable documents like *Learning to Be*, which marked the pedagogical discussions in the 1970s, or the *Delors Report*, which did the same in the 1990s. The title of the Delors Report's introduction to the volume, *The Treasure Within, Report to UNESCO of the International Commission on Education for the Twenty-First Century*, speaks of education as the necessary utopia.

While writing this book on Global Citizenship Education in the year that we celebrate the 500 years of publication of the famous work of fiction and political philosophy of Thomas More, *Utopia*, the reverberations of the calling of *Learning to Be, The Treasure Within* and *Education for All* are an invitation to a new utopia of the 21st century. No word than better than "utopia" will define the goals of education for sustainable development in the context of global citizenship education.[21]

At the time of writing this book, a major meeting is planned at the Mahatma Gandhi Institute for Peace and Sustainable Development (MGIEP), a Title I UNESCO Institute, on violent extremism in New Delhi for September 20–21, 2016.[22] Per the request of many countries, UNESCO has been thinking how the work on education for sustainable development and global citizenship education requires figuring out how education may help to prevent violent extremism, a topic intimately associated to national security and the identity of the nation-state.

Recent UNESCO work in knowledge production offers two titles of interest for people concerned with these topics. One of them is entitled *Global Citizenship Education: Topics and Learning Objectives*. This short book is a condensation of some of the learning accrued in the meetings mentioned above. As such, this book constitutes a very useful guide for implementing global citizenship education in the world's classrooms.[23] Most recently, while attention on global citizenship education has not shifted or diminished, the growing presence of violent extremism and specific requests from many nations for UNESCO to address the issue, a teacher's guide has been published that deserves serious academic, pedagogical and political attention.[24]

As part of its work on Education for Sustainable Development, UNESCO is currently preparing a publication that will provide guidance on the integration of the Sustainable Development Goals (SDGs) into education. At its core, the publication will spell out learning objectives for each of the 17 SDGs. It will also address implementation policy, curriculum, teacher education, classroom practice and assessment. The publication will be addressed to policy makers, curriculum developers, teacher educators and educators (from pre-primary to upper secondary levels). It is hoped that this publication will help shape the discourse around education for sustainable development and by implication global citizenship education.[25]

Notes

1. Realpolitik is a term that has been widely adopted to indicate that politics or diplomacy should be based primarily on specific circumstances and factors, rather than explicit ideologies or moral and ethical premises. I choose the term to indicate the dialectics of the global and the local in citizenship building. If one assumes that the human rights regime is the bedrock for the constitution of any form of citizenship and more so of global citizenship education, there are surely moral questions that cannot be ignored. On the other hand, we shall accept a certain pragmatism that not all the moral and ethical goals that are projected through the 'soft power' of the United Nations or UNESCO can be achieved.

In fact, there is an uneasy tension between the agendas that are advanced by international organizations like UNESCO and the demands from governments whom UNESCO must serve. It is indeed a difficult dance that requires skills, dexterities and knowledge, not to mention elegance and poise. Not all actors possess these qualities. It should not be a surprise then that the most extreme or radical positions are not represented in the international arenas seeking compromise and viable options for policy implementation.

2. Gaudelli, 2016, p. 2.
3. Soo-Hyang Choi, "From Jomtien and Dakar to Incheon: The Evolving Landscape of Global Education and Its Implications for Education Investment", Prepared for a panel discussion of the *International Conference on More and Better Investment in Global Education* organized by *the Korea Development Institute and the Int'l Commission on Financing Global Education Opportunity*, June 14, 2016, Seoul, Republic of Korea.
4. Ibid., p. 1.
5. UNESCO, 2014, p. 14, 2015, p. 14.
6. www.unesco.org/new/en/education/global-education-first- initiative-gefi/
7. www.unesco.org/new/fileadmin/MULTIMEDIA/HQ/ED/pdf/ questions-answers-21jan-EN.pdf
8. Soo-Hyang Choi, "From Jomtien and Dakar to Incheon", pp. 2–3.
9. Ibid., p. 3.
10. Ibid., p. 4.
11. Delors Report, *Learning the Treasure within*. Report to UNESCO of the International Commission on Education for the Twenty-First Century. UNESCO, 1996.
12. Soo-Hyang Choi, "From Jomtien and Dakar to Incheon", p. 6.
13. https://sustainabledevelopment.un.org/
14. www.un.org/sg/biography.shtml
15. www.worldpoliticsreview.com/articles/18622/election-defeat-complicates-park-s-plans-in-south-korea
16. www.unescoapceiu.org/en/m16.php?pn=1&sn=6
17. Habermas, 1992; Torres, 1998b.
18. www.theguardian.com/world/2013/dec/01/thailand-protest-yingluck-shinawatra-violence
19. www.unescobkk.org/education/news/article/unesco-forum-on-global-citizenship-education/
20. Per the United Nations Genocide Convention, prevention of genocide is one of the most important activities of the United Nations since its creation. Discussions about the Holocaust have dominated the mass media for more than half a century, constituting one of the key topics in teaching and learning about human rights. Unfortunately, the history of genocide is still haunting our civilizations, including Bosnia Herzegovina with 200,000 deaths between 1992 and 1995; Rwanda, in 1994 with 800,000 deaths in less than six months of a Tutsi minority and moderate Hutu majority; Pol Pot in Cambodia (1975–79) with more than 2 million deaths; the Nankim Japanese invasion with close to 300,000 Chinese soldiers and civilians dead between 1937–38; Stalin's Ukraine famine in 1932–33 with 7 million deaths; and the Armenian genocide in Turkey with 1.5 million deaths. In the recent First Global Capacity-Building Workshop on GCE at APCEIU, June 19–July 2, 2016 in Seoul, Republic of Korea, discussions about the Holocaust among other genocide experiences took a central role.
   http://natethayer.typepad.com/blog/2012/04/an-atol-investigation-all-of-kim-jong-euns-men-by-nate-thayer.html; http://endgenocide.org/learn/past-genocides/; www.genocidewatch.org/aboutgenocide/8stagesofgenocide.html

21. The number of organizations that are working in this realm is too large to cite here. Yet just few of them will suffice to exemplify, including the UNESCO guide for policy makers in educating to prevent violent extremism, the work of The Tim Parry Johnathan Ball Foundation for Peace in the United Kingdom, concerned with understanding the drivers of violent extremism and the role of education; the Tony Blair Faith Foundation, working in 30 countries with goals to promote dialogue, understanding religion, conflict and extremism, and trying to help young people to navigate difference; or the work of the NGO Think Equal, a Global Resource for Educating Hearts Empowering Change through Education.

21. http://mgiep.unesco.org/

23. UNESCO, *Global Citizenship Education: Topics and Learning Objectives.* Paris, France: UNESCO, 2015.

24. UNESCO, *A Teacher's Guide on the Prevention of Violent Extremism.* Paris, France: UNESCO, 2016.

25. Private letter to the author.

2 Why Global Citizenship?

An Intervention in Search
of a Theory

A central premise of my analysis is that global citizenship is an intervention in search of a theory. Global Citizenship Education is seen as an intervention dealing with:

> . . . a new class of global challenges which require some form of collective response to find effective solutions. These include increasingly integrated and knowledge-driven economies; greater migration between countries and from rural to urban areas; growing inequalities; more awareness of the importance of sustainable development and including concerns about climate change and environmental degradation; a large and growing youth demographic; the acceleration of globalization; and rapid developments in technology. Each of these elements carries far-reaching implications, and taken together, these represent a period of transition of historical significance. Education systems need to respond to these emerging global challenges which require a collective response with a strategic vision that is global in character, rather than limited to the individual country level.[1]

good quote

Theories of global citizenship have formed part of diverse knowledge fields for a long time, including comparative and international education, civic education, political sociology of education, political science and political philosophy, to name a few. Still there is a need for a theory to underwrite the concept of global citizenship and its intervention in education: " . . . no clear definition of global citizenship—or as otherwise referred to, cosmopolitan or world citizenship—have been concisely articulated."[2]

Raising the stakes by launching the Global Education First Initiative, and linking education for all with quality of education, the UN Secretary-General Ban Ki-moon spoke of global citizenship as a new model of intervention in securing peace and sustainable development in the global system.

Global citizenship is a form of intervention searching for a theory and an agency for implementation because the world is becoming increasingly interdependent and diverse, and its borders more porous.[3] There is "a deterritorializing of citizenship practices and identities, and of discourses about loyalty and allegiance."[4]

Any definition and theory of global citizenship as a model of intervention to promote global peace and sustainable development should address what has become the trademark of globalization: cultural diversity. That explains the emphasis of many scholars in looking at multiculturalism and interculturalism as specific interventions and even educational paradigms to help social cohesion, the redressing of inequalities, and ways and means of facilitating new pedagogical models which are culturally sensitive and respectful of the diversity of identities we confront in our schools and society.

Therefore, global citizenship should rely on a definition of *global democratic multicultural citizenship*. It is imperative that global citizenship adds value to national citizenship! Yet the expansion of a universalistic claim of world solidarity rests on the concept of cosmopolitan citizenship nested in a model of cosmopolitan democracies.

Two key elements of citizenship should be defined at the outset: First, civic minimums, because full participation in citizenship as argued by T. H. Marshall rests ultimately on material bases. A second important concept is civic virtue. Amy Gutman has persuasively argued that "education for citizenship should focus on the justification of rights rather than responsibilities, and, at the same time, that schools should foster general virtues (courage, law-abidingness, loyalty), social virtues (autonomy, open-mindedness), economic virtues (work ethic, capacity to delay self-gratification) and political virtues (capacity to analyze, capacity to criticize). Though these values are defined and defended in the context of Western philosophies, the question that one could raise is whether these values are shared by other civilizations such as the African, Arab or Asian civilizations.[5]

Despite important questions about values underscoring the human rights regime which is the bedrock of global citizenship education, I see global citizenship as being marked by an understanding of global ties and connections, and a commitment to the collective good. Robert Rhoads and Carlos Alberto Torres advanced the idea of "democratic multicultural citizenship," in which education helps students to develop the dispositions and abilities to work across social and cultural differences in a quest for solidarity. They argued that such skills are essential to citizenship in a multicultural global environment.[6]

In their compelling book Rhoads and Szelényi have advanced this thesis onto another level of understanding, claiming that we should advance a view of citizenship in which the geographic reference point for one's sense of rights and responsibilities is broadened, and in some sense, complicated by a more expansive spatial vision and understanding of the world.[7] The engagement of individuals as citizens reflects understandings of rights and responsibilities across three basic dimensions of social life: the political (including civic aspects), the economic (including occupational aspects), and the social (including cultural aspects). In this vein, Soysal advanced a "post-national" definition of citizenship in which one's rights and responsibilities are rooted not in the nation-state, but instead are tied to one's personhood: "What were previously defined as national rights become entitlements legitimized on the basis of personhood."[8]

Global citizenship is not seen as an alternative to national citizenship. On the contrary, it may be a supplement to reinforce the robustness of representative and participatory democracies worldwide, ultimately seeking to guarantee the social democratic pact on the rights of persons, not only the rights of property.[9] In other words, global citizenship adds value to national citizenship.

The construction of national citizenship could be considered unfinished business; henceforth the value added of global citizenship may be another layer of support for a process of transforming citizenship making and citizenship education into models based on principles of liberty and equality for all.

I have advanced in my own work the idea of "democratic multicultural citizenship" in which education helps students to develop the dispositions and abilities to work across social and cultural differences in a quest for solidarity. Such skills are essential to citizenship in a multicultural global environment. Rhoads and Szelényi developed this idea by focusing on the responsibilities of universities.

There are multiple claims made in this book about the value added of Global Citizenship Education to citizenship building at the regional, national and local levels and how Global Citizenship Education interrupts inequality. To clarify my intent, it is important to summarily present the meta-theoretical, theoretical and empirical foundations of my analysis, which will be developed further and substantiated in this book.

> *First claim*: Though not a precondition to implement global citizenship education, it is clear that we need to remove ambiguities in the use of the concept Global Citizenship Education, which involves fundamental theoretical work in citizenship building at the local and global levels. This theoretical work is not only about concepts or theories but about policy and practical implications for educational reform. For example, a concept that has been usually associated to GCE is Global Education. In the perspective of the North-South Centre of the Council of Europe an important source for GCE, **Global Education** aims at enabling learners to understand world issues while empowering them with knowledge, skills, values and attitudes desirable for world citizens to face global problems. It brings cultural, artistic and ethical knowledge and competences into curricula too often subordinated to the adaptation of learners to the demands of the national or international labor markets. By bringing these human-based competences, it becomes a process of individual and collective growth which allows transformation and self- transformation, in which the acquisition of

operative and emotional competencies for analyzing and thinking critically about the reality makes it possible for learners to become active social agents.[10]

Second claim: From a critical theory perspective, GCE should be framed within a social justice education framework. Without bare essentials we cannot fully accomplish citizenship building and particularly global citizenship education, and by implication, the impact of multiculturalism and interculturalism in the lives of communities, individuals, families and nations will be very limited, merely rhetorical or academic in the worst sense of the word, but not practical, political and transformative. Bare essentials include economic citizenship—that is, the right to a job, education, health care, affordable housing and retraining over the course of life.

Third claim: GCE has to deal with difference and diversity and never impose a 'neutral' and 'universal' ideal of citizenship. Cultural diversity, indigenous knowledge, critical post-colonial perspectives are embedded in our conceptualization of GCE. There are fundamental principles that articulate the conversation between global citizenship education and multiculturalism/interculturalism. They include respect for human rights, social justice education, planetarian citizenship for sustainability, migration and diversity, and enhancing the proliferation of public spheres and school reform promoting global citizenship education.[11]

Fourth claim: There are multiple agents participating in this process of furthering global citizenship education; as agents they are also arenas for confrontation and negotiation, and they include the international system, NGOs, social movements, national governments, local or regional authorities, school systems, non-formal education systems—including mass media.[12]

Fifth claim: It is imperative to develop teaching methods, teachers' education and curriculum that facilitate global citizenship education, including new models of teaching social justice education and peace education, linking these concepts with the growing theoretical and political as well as curriculum developments in the realms of multiculturalism and interculturalism.[13]

Sixth claim: As professional educators it is imperative that we use international forums to advance the institutional recognition of Global Citizenship Education in the school systems and adult and lifelong learning environments. Particularly important is teacher education, which represents a strategic action to integrate GCE in formal education.

Seventh claim: Global Citizenship education is a way of learning. As Werner Wintersteiner et al argue in a book conceived from the Austrian perspective, global citizenship education "responds to globalization by expanding the concept of civic education to global society"; adopts the ethical values of peace education and human rights education; draws upon the "global society" perspective provided by global education, which not only investigates global topics, but more specifically merges the global and the local into the *glocal*; combines mainly these three pedagogical fields through the concept of *global citizenship* in terms of political participation as such, but particularly on a global scale."[14]

I could not agree more with distinguished Austrian peace educator Werner Wintersteiner that GCE as a way of learning is "not entirely new, but builds on the pedagogies mentioned above; it combines them or some of their essential components and thereby gives them a new and unique focus. *Global Citizenship Education*, in any case, constitutes an original, necessary and forward-looking mental framework, which seems to be indispensable to education in times of globalization and a global society."[15]

- Terminological or semantic debates aside, global citizenship education is an intervention in search of a theory. Alas, it has a long way to go before it is widely adopted worldwide, and perhaps it will never be adopted by some countries.
- It could be conceived as a mental framework, as a framework for action, as an expression of pedagogies for peace education, as global education or civic education for the 21st century, and as a multitude of other concepts or definitions. The urgency, however, to incorporate into the world system a model of global citizenship that adds value to national citizenship cannot be denied.

Notes

1. UNESCO, *Concept Note UNESCO Forum on Global Citizenship Education: Preparing Learners for the Challenge of the 21st Century*. Bangkok, Thailand: UNESCO, 2–4 December 2013.
2. Rhoads and Szelényi, 2011, p. 22.
3. Benhabib, 2005.
4. Sassen, 2002, p. 6.
5. Carlos Alberto Torres, *Democracy, Education, and Multiculturalism: Dilemmas of Citizenship in a Global World*. Lanham, MD: Rowman and Littlefield, 1998, pp. 110–111.
6. Rhoads and Torres, 2006.
7. Rhoads and Szelényi, 2011.
8. Soysal, 1994, p. 7.
9. Bowles and Gintis, 1986; Torres, 1998b.
10. See www.coe.int/t/dg4/nscentre/default_en.asp
11. Tarozzi and Torres, 2016.
12. The North-South Centre of the Council of Europe has developed what they call the Micro-Macro Approach, involving *From local to global*, e.g. from pollution to poverty in our area we are led to the global dimension of these problems and back to the local level (*glocalization*); *From personal to collective*, e.g. from personal stories and experiences presented by the participants in a multicultural

global education program, we are led to confront the migration problem on a collective basis; *From emotional to rational*, e.g. from the emotions raised on an individual level after the above migration stories, we are led to explore the general aspects of the migration problem.

13. The North-South Centre of the Council of Europe has prepared important pedagogical material. They work with key principles including democratic dialogue, cooperative-based learning and problem-based learning. Their approach is based on defining and understanding the learning group, choosing the appropriate learning environment, developing critical thinking and stimulating curiosity and creativity.

14. Wintersteiner et al., 2015, p. 4.

15. Wintersteiner et al., 2015, p. 3.

3 Global Citizenship Education: Competitiveness versus Solidarity?

Liminal: Education and Citizenship

Education has in modern times been situated within the nation-state. It has been shaped by the demands within the state to prepare the labor force for participation in the economy and to prepare citizens to participate in the polity. This approximate congruence of nation-state and formalized education becomes problematic as globalization blurs national sovereignty and puts limits on state autonomy. We must move beyond assumptions about national boundaries and goals internal to national agendas.

Discussions on citizenship must address straightforward questions: Will globalization make human rights and democratic participation more universal, or will globalization redefine human enterprise as market exchanges invulnerable to traditional civic forms of governance? Whether education as a publicly shared invention contributing to civic life and human rights can thrive depends on the future of globalization—a future that may offer the internationalization of the ideals of a democratic education or may reduce education, and civic participation, to narrow instruments of remote and seemingly ungovernable market forces.

In several works[1] I have suggested that multiple and intersecting globalization processes do place limits on state autonomy and national sovereignty. These limits are expressed in tensions between global and local dynamics in virtually every decision and policy domain in the social, cultural and economic spheres.

Multiple globalization therefore not only blurs national boundaries but also shifts solidarities within and outside the national state. Globalization cannot be defined exclusively by the post-Fordist organization of production, but emerges as a major characteristic of a global world economy. Issues of human rights, regional states and cosmopolitan democracy will play a major role affecting civic minimums at the state level, the performance of capital and labor in different domains, and particularly the dynamics of citizenship, democracy and multiculturalism in the modern state.[2] To understand the issues at stake in education, we have to consider these tensions within globalization and their implications for reshaping the limits or potential for civil society.

I have defended a thesis that it is imperative to consider the connections of globalization with the concerns with worldwide markets and free trade, and how market competition in the context of neoliberalism affects the notions of citizenship and democracy at national, regional and global levels. In the same vein but from the very different political-ideological standpoint of universal human rights, we should understand the limits of citizenship. Two principles become antagonistic, namely, national sovereignty and universal human rights. For Nuhoglu Soysal "these two global precepts simultaneously constrain and enhance the nation-state's scope of action."[3] This creates an incongruity between the normative and the organizational bases of rights, as well as between constitutional prescriptions and laws.

Nuhoglu Soysal has argued that

> The state is no longer an autonomous and independent organization closed over a nationally defined population. Instead, we have a system of constitutionally interconnected states with a multiplicity of membership. [Hence] . . . the logic of personhood supersedes the logic of national citizenship, [and] individual rights and obligations, which were historically located in the nation-state, have increasingly moved to an universalistic plane, transcending the boundaries of particular nation-states.[4]

Nuhoglu Soysal's analysis has multiple implications, first at the level of citizenship, where notions of identity and rights are decoupled, and second, at the level of the politics of identity and multiculturalism, where the emergence of membership in the polity "is multiple in the sense of spanning local, regional and global identities, and . . . accommodates intersecting complexes of rights, duties and loyalties."[5] Third, at the level of what could be termed *cosmopolitan democracies,* which Soysal highlights as emerging from the importance of the international system for the attainment of democracy worldwide. Cosmopolitan democracies constitute a system relatively divorced in its origins and constitutive dynamics from codes of the nation-states.

In neoliberal times the main questions are how globalization is affecting organized solidarity and how citizenship is being checked by market forces and globalization dynamics. This is so because the unstable linkage between democracy and capitalism has been blurred to levels rarely seen before. What follows is an analysis of the concept of global citizenship education caught in the web of proposals to instill solidarity at a global level to support our common humanity, and proposals that global citizenship education will propel more competitiveness of the labor forces in the global markets. Clearly one may question whether both concepts—solidarity and competitiveness—are comparable concepts in global citizenship education.

Global Citizenship Education: Competitiveness versus Solidarity

A main thesis of this chapter is that solidarity versus competitiveness is an irresolvable tension in the world system. They could be seen in its more generic form as two extremes of a continuum. There are comparable concepts in global citizenship education only because in their most extreme definition they are antagonist concepts. Together they confront us with several conundrums.

First, to assume that human nature will be fully tamed by cultural nurturing is a wonderful assumption that we inherited from the Enlightenment. It is a goal and a dream that justifies our educational efforts. Yet, it is not reflected in reality because there are plenty of conflicts related to local and global identities; some are nationalistic in nature, others are ethnic or religious, or a mixture of all three, undermining all forms of citizenship. Moreover, everywhere there are deep fractures between goals of political unity versus goals of cultural unity. Solidarity rather than competition may help cultural nurturing.

Second, to assume that oppressors and oppressed can co-exist (compete and have degrees of solidarity) harmoniously in the world system is also a wonderful hope, but, unfortunately, not represented in actual data or critical theoretical traditions. Consider, for instance, the analysis provided by post-colonialist traditions, those provided by critical traditions in gender studies or race/and ethnic studies or class analyses, or consider the growing bibliography signaling that there are too many inequalities within and among nations for this co-existence to be realized.

Third, competition is the essence of sports. Is the impetus for global citizenship education comparable to the World Cup or the Olympic Games? An assumption in the Olympic Games or world soccer competition is that people and countries conduct themselves within a code of fair play, not cheating in their desires to win. 'Let the best win' is the motto of these competitions. This aphorism, which could be translated into global citizenship education, can it truly help us further global citizenship education so we can create a better world where we all can win, where all of us recognize our own humanity?

There are many examples which break down the fallacy of a level playing field in sports and contradict the false image of the prevalence of honesty in athletics. For example, cycling is particularly problematic because since 1988 more than one-third of the top finishers have been busted for doping, with the most egregious case being the seven-time winner of the Tour de France, Lance Armstrong.[6]

Conceivably, if we want to implement world citizenship education in a world system built on profit taking, like in world sports, we may face similar problems. In the 1987 movie *Wall Street*, Michael Douglas playing the role of a Wall Street tycoon Gordon Gekko provides us the answer of how economic competitiveness may not dovetail nicely with human solidarity, particularly when competition is based solely on greed.

Gordon Gekko, speaking to stockholders of a company he bought shares in, argues: "I am not a destroyer of companies. I am a liberator of them! The point is, ladies and gentleman, that greed, for lack of a better word, is good. Greed is right, greed works. Greed clarifies, cuts through, and captures the essence of the evolutionary spirit. Greed, in all of its forms; greed for life, for money, for love, knowledge has marked the upward surge of mankind."[7]

Fourth, assuming that solidarity and competitiveness can live together harmoniously implies that there is no incommensurability of political, scientific or ideological discourses. Solidarity speaks of cooperation and collaboration. This can be done at the level of distributional and humanitarian policies. Competition in the economic extreme speaks of contest and survival of the fittest, eventually creating conflict. Competition in the economic arena refers to production, accumulation and profit taking in wealth creation. Growing levels of solidarity may enhance the legitimacy of systems, but in a cutthroat neoliberal capitalist society, though monopolies thwarting competition exist, market competition is seen as one of the keys to productivity, profit taking and success.

In fact, we may argue that the two terms that work more closely and should be key in the construction of global identities in global citizenship education are coordination that leads to cooperation. Yet, the problem is how to coordinate divergent interests. Obviously all participants in processes of coordination try to have an agreeable rule or convention in place. But, "the typical case of cooperation, however, is one in which preferences differ as to what the rule should be, and also the cost and efforts required for complying with that rule are not the same for all players involved, as some may have to make more painful adjustments than others."[8]

Solidarity, Competition and Global Citizenship Education

There are more complications to this continuum between solidarity and competition. First, there is world inequality. From 2000 to 2007, incomes for the bottom 90 percent of earners rose only about 4 percent, once adjusted for inflation. For the top 0.1 percent, incomes climbed about 94 percent.[9] For instance, OECD reports the growing inequality in the UK, where the top 10 percent have incomes that are 12 times greater than bottom 10 percent, and this is up from eight times greater in 1985.

Second, competition for jobs undermines forms of solidarity.[10] The crisis of 2008 has made even more evident the importance of the growing inequality that has deeply affected market democracies.[11] A casualty of these crises in the global economy has been the loss of jobs, which has in turn increased inequality and poverty. Jim Clifton, chairman of Gallup Corporation argues that of the 7 billion people in the world, 5 billion are over 15 years old. Three billion said they currently worked or wanted to work, yet only 1.2 billion have full-time formal jobs. Hence there is a shortfall of 1.8 billon jobs worldwide. This does not include those that currently underemployed, working in jobs below their skill levels.[12]

Third, in the last century, the principal source of institutional and organized solidarity in the world has been the presence of various of forms of the welfare state, which guarantees individuals minimum levels of welfare, education, income, health care, affordable housing and transportation as a political right and not as charity. As Offe declares, "The welfare state is an accumulation of rights that the worker doesn't not have to earn, but which come as an original endowment of 'social citizenship.'"[13]

The inception of neoliberalism in the early 1980s and the workings of neoliberal globalization have led to a decline of the state and organized forms of solidarity. With neoliberalism, we find a drive towards privatization, marketization, performativity and the enterprising individual exemplified by Canadian political scientist Macpherson's concept of 'possessive individualism' in which individuals are conceived as sole proprietors of their own skills and owe nothing to society. In the political philosophy of possessive individualism there are multiple reasons for competition and virtually no reason for solidarity or collaboration with less fortunate people, communities or countries.

Fourth, war is a public policy option for the state more so in the geopolitics of powerful nation-states in the global system. War could be advanced to pursue the goals of competition more often than solidarity. The global defense budget (in 2012 US dollars) shows there is only reigning military superpower, the US spending $682 billion, this amount is more than the combined amount of $652 billion from the subsequent nine nation-states with the largest defense budgets.[14] One could only imagine what would happen if a fraction of these defense budgets could be devoted to public services that sustain solidarity policies.

There are plenty of discontents with neoliberal globalization, as there are serious misgivings about the geopolitics of the strongest nations on Earth guiding solidarity and philanthropy. Occasionally, in the name of human rights, we witness the imperialism of human rights being projected by Western countries to justify intervention in order to prevent atrocities of genocide and other ills, but also to justify intervention for the benefits of their own competitiveness and interest.

I have spoken of competition confronting solidarity as two ends of a continuum, and I have been quite skeptical that business-like competition could be very useful in the dictionary of furthering global citizenship education. Yet there are few experiences in which competition and solidarity may intersect.

Universities compete for the best undergraduate and graduate students, the services of the best professors, and, particularly, global universities compete for securing employment of the 'best brains' around the globe. They compete for research resources, growing endowments or better positioning in the rankings, and there is a civilized competition for advancing new knowledge and technologies.

This cultural competition is healthy, and is part of an educational utopia for 21st-century education, particularly when it is present in our schools, universities and lifelong learning systems which seek to build global citizenship through a new paradigm of education well defined by Súarez-Orozco and Sattin-Bajai when they seek an education: "privileging disciplined curiosity, the beauty of discovery, a ludic engagement with the world, and an ethic of care and solidarity will be less a luxury and a rarity than an essential requirement for the next generation of children to thrive. We must continue to cultivate, replicate, modify, and improve models of education that are built on these powerful and indispensable architectures."[15]

The quest for global citizenship education should be understood in the context of multiple processes of globalization, which are drastically changing our collective and individual worlds and consciousness. While globalization provides the backdrop for any conversation about global citizenship education, we are entering new frontiers and we need new narratives in education that confront the traditional positivist epistemology in education.

We should view citizenship marked by an understanding of global interconnectedness and a commitment to the collective good. We should advance a view of citizenship in which the geographic reference point for one's sense of rights and responsibilities is broadened, and in some sense, complicated by a more expansive spatial vision and understanding of the world.

In this book I argued that there are three main trends underscoring the need for global citizenship education. First, it should be noted that the world is changing, cultures are intersecting, and borders are more permeable than ever. Hybridity is the quintessential nature of contemporary societies. The second reason is that we have moved from a concept of citizenship in a city to a concept of citizenship in a nation-state and now we are at the sunrise of global citizenship in what I call the Age of Global Interdependence and Cosmopolitanism. Historically, education has played a major role in these transformations, hence the quest for global citizenship education. The third main reason for global citizenship education is that the different forms of globalization are confronting cosmopolitan democracies as emerging models of political organization of citizenship.

Notes

1. Tarozzi and Torres, 2017; Torres, 2009a, 2009b, 2013.
2. Torres, 1998b.
3. Nuhoglu Soysal, 1994, pp. 7–8.
4. Ibid., pp. 164–165.
5. Ibid., p. 166.
6. www.nytimes.com/interactive/2012/08/24/sports/top-finishers-of-the-tour-de-france-tainted-by-doping.html?_r=0
7. From the script of the movie, *Wall Street* (1987).
8. Claus Offe, 2006, p. 59.
9. Saenz and Piketty. Saenz, Emmanuel and Thomas Piketty. http://gmond.pariss choolofeconomics.eu/topincomes
10. Most analysts document that the gap between the US rich (1 percent of the population) has been growing markedly by any measure for the last three decades. There are a number of "teach-ins" on the matter, www.youtube.com/watch?v=FIKgApqgGgU (retrieved May 5, 2012). The press has also indicated several reasons for this growing disparity, see Dave Gibson and Carolyn

Perot, "It's the Inequality, Stupid: Eleven Charts that Explain What's Wrong with America", www.motherjones.com/politics/2011/02/income-inequality-in-america-chart- graph, March/April, 2011.

11. As early as February 5, 1984, Lester C. Thurow had stated, "By if Our Conventional Wisdom Is Right and the Middle Class Really Is the Social Glue that Holds Society Together, then America Is in the Process of Becoming Unglued", *Business Forum; The Disappearance of the Middle Class*, www.nytimes.com/1984/02/05/business/business-forum-the-disappearance-of-the-middle-class.html. This argument about inequality, as a result of technological innovation, was coupled a decade later with an argument about a possible trade war in the capitalist system. In one of his most famous books, *Head to Head*, he predicted after the failure of the Soviet regime an economic war between Japan, the European Union (with the economic engine of Germany) and the United States. Though his prediction didn't come true, the arguments about trade competition have been recently revisited with the reactions to trade pacts and the fact there are more losers than winners in the context of globalization. Not by chance, Thurow's casual comment in 2004 on technology displacing labor is coupled with competitive international behavior displacing workers. Lester Thurow, *Head to Head: The Coming Economic Battle among Japan, Europe, and America*. New York: Warner Books, 2013.

12. Jim Clifton, *The Coming Jobs War*. New York: Gallup Press, 2011.

13. Offe, 2006, p. 44.

14. States including Russia, Japan, UK, Saudi Arabia, France, Germany, China, India and Italy. www.mapsofworld.com/world-top-ten/world-top-ten-countries-with-largest-defence-budget-map.html

15. Suárez-Orozco and Sattin-Bajaj, 2010, p. 198.

4 Global Citizenship Education Confronting Hyper-Globalist, Skeptic and Transformationist Agendas[1]

1. Introduction

Globalization is the buzzword of the day and provides the backdrop for this keynote. There are many definitions of globalization as there are many faces of globalization. For example, globalization has been defined as "the intensification of worldwide social relations which link distant localities in such a way that local happenings are shaped by events occurring many miles away and vice versa."[2] Another view sees globalization as "a feature of late capitalism, or the condition of postmodernity, and, more importantly, . . . the emergence of a world system driven in large part by a global capitalist economy"[3] Others see globalization as the transformation of time and space in which complex interactions and exchange once impossible become everyday activities.[4] And still others see globalization as an assault on traditional notions of society and nation-state, whereby the very nature of citizenship and social change are dramatically altered.[5]

Globalization takes different forms and we really should talk about globalization's processes, in the plural. Here I would like to call attention to predominant forms of globalization, which are better described in Chapter 6, but for the purposes of this chapter I will provide a succinct analysis of the different forms or faces of globalization. One form of globalization, often seen as *"globalization from above,"* is framed by an ideology of neoliberalism and calls for an opening of borders, the creation of multiple regional markets, the proliferation of fast-paced economic and financial exchanges, and the presence of governing systems other than nation-states.

Another form of globalization represents the antithesis of the first. This form of globalization is often described as *"globalization from below,"* or anti-globalization. Globalization from below is largely manifest in individuals, institutions and social movements actively opposed to that which is perceived as corporate globalization. For these individuals and groups, "no globalization without representation" is the motto.

There is a third form of globalization, which pertains more to rights than to markets—the *globalization of human rights*. With the growing ideology of human rights taking hold in the international system and in international law, many traditional practices endemic to the fabric of particular societies or cultures (from religious to esoteric practices) are now being called into question, challenged, forbidden or even outlawed. The advancement of cosmopolitan democracies and plural citizenship is the theme of this version of globalization.

There is a fourth manifestation of globalization. This form extends beyond markets, and to some extent is against human rights. It is *globalization of the international war against terrorism*. This new form of globalization has been prompted in large part by the events of September 11, 2001—which were interpreted as the globalization of the terrorist threat—and the reaction of the United States to the event. This form of globalization is represented by the anti-terrorist response, which has been militaristic in nature, resulting in two coalition wars led by the US against Muslim regimes in Afghanistan and Iraq, under the auspices of the "Global War on Terror" (GWOT). Islamophobia is also a theme of this globalization. Terrorism and the terrorist threat were made synonymous with Islam and Muslims and became a global norm. Yet, the overall theme of this process was not only its military flavor, but also the emphasis on security and control of borders, people, capital and commodities—that is, the reverse of open markets and high-paced commodity exchanges. Security as a precondition of freedom is the theme of this form of globalization.

How do we analyze the complex theoretical frameworks associated with the globalization processes? I will propose an analysis from the political sociology of education based on the dialectics of the global and the local, and the implications for different stakeholders.

2.   The Dialectics of the Global and the Local: A Sociological Framework

Sociological studies of role theory have for a long time considered the tension between cosmopolitans and locals crucial for role differentiation and identity formation. Alvin W. Gouldner, studying organizational behavior, discusses how reference groups and value commitments conflict with those prescribed by organizations.

In two articles on organizational sociology published in the 1950s,[6] Gouldner finds important differences between cosmopolitans and locals in terms of degrees of influence, participation, and propensity to accept or reject organizational rules and informal relations.

Following the work of Robert K. Merton and conducting empirical work in a small private liberal arts college, his thesis is that members of formal organizations may have two latent social identities. Focusing on group membership, he created a typology of two groups, calling them cosmopolitans and locals.

Speaking of two latent organizational identities, he poses that there are **cosmopolitans**, "those low in loyalty to the employing organization, high on commitment to specialized role skills, and likely to use an outer reference group orientation, and the **locals**, those high in loyalty to the employing organization, low on commitment to specialized role skills, and likely to use an inner reference group orientation."[7]

While the logic of organizational analysis may not be wholly pertinent to discuss questions of global citizenship, the parallels in terms of loyalty, commitment, group orientation and values may apply to discuss the connections between individuals and their nation-state.

Gouldner concluded that: "It would seem reasonable to expect that persons manifesting two such different combination of variables would have different self-conceptions and identities, as well as being differentially perceived and identified by others in their group."[8] Against a rigid binary distinction, Gouldner argues that "there might be different kinds of cosmopolitans as well as different kinds of locals."[9]

He identifies four types of locals and two types of cosmopolitans, rendering the tendency to binary representations somewhat muted. Among the *locals* Gouldner identified "the dedicated," the "true bureaucrat," the "homeguard," and "the elders." Among the *cosmopolitans*, he identified "the outsiders" and the "empire builders."

Just to illustrate, the "dedicated" are "true believers" "who are identified with and affirm the distinctive ideology of their organization."[10] The true bureaucrat is loyal not so much to the organization's distinctive values but to the place itself, and they are concerned about the security of the organization and seek to accomplish that through authoritarian and formal regulations to control the behavior of others.[11] The homeguards tend to be administrators whose personal histories are intimately interwoven with the organization. The elders tend to be the oldest people in the group and tend to have been with the organization for a long time.

Cosmopolitans are distinguished between the outsiders and the empire builders. Outsiders have "little loyalty to the organization and do not intend to remain with it permanently," and tend to be oriented toward an outer reference group. The empire builders have a sense of economic independence and tend to have a "strong pull towards increased departmental autonomy."[12]

Though ultimately this study and the ideal types that resulted from the study are a Weberian analysis of bureaucracies, Gouldner's work yields light in one important element that could be translated to the local imaginary of politics: Despite differential cleavages and conflicts within and across them, cosmopolitans tend to have less loyalty to local institutions than locals.

The most generic conclusion of Gouldner is that "It may be that the study of the relations between cosmopolitans and locals in the modern organization provides clues for the analysis of conflict within educational, governmental, hospital, and other bureaucracies."[13] Let us explore the dichotomy between locals and cosmopolitans in the context of globalization's processes in the world system.

3.   Globalizations and Global Citizenship Education:
     Hyper-Globalizers, Skeptics and Transformationists

Reading the academic, political and journalistic bibliographies on globalization, and assuming that there is somewhat of a continuity between locals
and cosmopolitans, there are at least three different positions to the limits
and possibilities of globalizations and their impact on our lives. There are
the *hyper-globalizers* who believe globalization understood as a singular
process encompassing all regions of the world and all aspects of human and
planetary life is the solution to poverty, inequality and all other social ills.
Therefore, Thomas Friedman implied that the quicker we move to make this
world a flatter world, the better.[14] This is certainly the dominant view in the
mass media, and is well represented in a number of international organizations such as the World Bank, the Import-Export Bank, the IMF, the World
Trade Organization, some sectors of the United Nations, many Western and
non-Western governments and is reflected in many reports of the OECD.

At the opposing end are the *skeptics*, who could in their most extreme
form, become anti-globalizers. Somewhere in the middle of this pendulum,
always struggling to make sense of the limits and possibilities of the new
realities, are different varieties of what I could call the *transformationists*.

There are several economic reasons that prompted the *hyper-globalizers*,
and particularly those connected with corporations, neoliberal governments
and some academics, to argue that globalization is a powerful tool to reduce
inequalities within and across nations.

Looking at the intersections between globalization and egalitarian distribution, Pranab Bardhan, Samuel Bowles and the late Michael Wallerstein
argue that "The freer flow of information, goods, and capital from the
richer to poorer nations should raise productivity and increase the demands
for labor in the labor-abundant and technologically lagging nations, induc-
ing tendencies toward convergence of wage rates for equivalent labor
throughout the world . . . . Globalization might also induce more competitive product markets, reducing profit markups—the discrepancy between
prices and marginal costs—and thus raising real wages. Finally, competition
among nation-states and the ability of citizens to compare institutional performance across nations might also provide greater popular accountability
for state and para-statal institutions often dominated by elites."[15]

The symmetrical counterpoint to an economist's position is built on a
critique of globalization as enhancing rather than reducing the power of
elites worldwide (within and across nations) and also affecting—some will
even argue obliterating—culture and ways of seeing and living for individuals, families and communities who find themselves deeply affected by the
changes in the world system. Of great importance is the way these changes
are affecting democracies and nation-states, particularly the welfare state
models. Without entering into the debates of whether or not the multiple
processes of globalization have withered away the nation-state and its

autonomy and ability to actually control its own territories and policies, it is clear that the skeptics point to the crises of 2008 as another indicator not only of the maliciousness of global processes but also the failure of neoliberalism as an economic model. They argue that the economic debacle resulted from the voracious, greedy and irresponsible actions of financial capitalism that brought the capitalist world system to the brink of its own dissolution.

One of the key elements for the skeptics in condemning globalization is that it has unleashed a wave of inequality worldwide that is without precedent. A well-known OECD inequality report shows how countries across the developed world are getting less equal, giving the skeptics fodder for their criticism.[16] For skeptics, globalization has been deleterious not only because of the increase in inequality, but also because technological change has generally favored skilled workers.

Similarly, as Michael Wallerstein has suggested, there is a decline in unions, which are known to defend income and wages and therefore a barrier to inequality, in addition to defending the fundamentals of democracy.[17] Because of the decline of unions, there is a falling minimum wage (one of the key reasons for inequality) and a rise in immigration (legal and illegal), producing brain drain of poor nations towards richer nations. Furthermore, some point to the rise of single-parent families, which are by definition one of the reasons for family impoverishment, (as an adverse impact of globalization). Finally the skeptics will point their finger to the voraciousness of elites who have taken control with the presence of neoliberalism in governments and international organizations and have created even greater levels of inequality.

Documented top income shares over the last 30 years show that top income shares have increased substantially in English-speaking countries and in India and China, but not in continental European countries or Japan.[18] Newspaper reports of growing inequality in the UK for instance, show that the OECD reports that top 10 percent have incomes that are 12 times greater than bottom 10 percent, and this is up from eight times greater in 1985. There is no question that the skeptics have powerful arguments against the impact of globalization in our lives and still consider the nation-state a lynchpin in articulating responses to globalization, but may not have great expectations for the successful performance of a democratic state.

The *transformationists* would " . . . argue that sovereignty, state power, and territoriality . . . stand today in a more complex relationship than in the epoch during which the modern nation-state was being forged."[19] There are many varieties of transformationists, pursuing different venues, political agendas and aggregated interests. On the left there are the *social democrats* who want to preserve the welfare state and its intervention in the economy, despite the fiscal crises of the state that they realize needs to be solved. There are traditional social democratic varieties, mostly in Europe, Canada, Australia and New Zealand, and populist social democratic varieties in Latin America and the United States. Here the key element is how the nation-state can control the behavior of the markets, and how to move beyond the class conflict model, assuming that the state could tax the earnings of capital and transfer the revenue to workers. This has been studied by Adam Przeworski[20] in several of his works, and has been advocated by Berkeley University Professor Robert Reich who was Secretary of Labor in the Clinton administration.[21]

On the right, there are the *market liberals* who argue that the state should work around basic principles of privatization and deregulation. However, they do not go as far as the hyper-globalizers in demolishing the welfare state, undermining the nation-state or thwarting state interventions in sensitive areas of state policies—mostly connected with capital accumulation and political legitimation. Many of these market liberals are truly provincials and occasionally their interest will be at odds with multinational corporations. Against both positions emerges a group that for the lack of a good term I will call an *authoritarian libertarian* segment that could be easily characterized as protectionists or ethno-nationalists. They have proliferated in Europe in the last two decades and with the electoral campaign in the United States seem to be highly represented in the fraction of individuals who follow the incendiary narrative of Mr. Trump, but there are representatives of this variety on many continents. Their ultimate goal is to seal national borders, preventing immigrants from coming into their territory, controlling capital influx, and outlawing outsourcing of jobs overseas and even cancelling trade pacts. In a very authoritarian manner, they want to exercise the full power of the state to control various issues within national borders, from crime to culture to capital accumulation. They are against free trade and the radical forms of globalization proposed by the hyper-globalizers. The recent experience of the Brexit indicates that this group is gaining traction in the United Kingdom and eventually may affect the European Union.

Finally, I argue that there is another variety that I will call New *Democrats*, who confront capitalism in terms of ways in which the capitalist system could be challenged around key elements of class, race/ethnicity, gender, sexual preference or disability discrimination. Depending of whether these New Democrats espouse a strong or weak critical feminism, critical race theory or any other critical theoretical and political orientations, including Neo-Marxism and socialism for the 20th century à la Heinz Dieterich Steffan,[22] they are usually immersed in domestic, regional, provincial and national-oriented politics, and find themselves confronting some version of the globalization processes at several levels in their own localities.

They are very prominent and linked to multiculturalist traditions in the United States, Canada, Australia, New Zealand and Western Europe, but they are present within a diversity of orientations in many other regions of the world, from Latin America to Sub-Saharan Africa to the Asia-Pacific region. They may overlap with some social democratic, populist or socialist (or post-socialist) traditions, but by and large they do not pay enough attention to the international developments regarding an emerging democratic cosmopolitanism.

Most varieties of New Democrats fall decisively within one of the ends of the spectrum or pendulum between *cosmopolitanism* and *localism* (or *provincialism*). They are deeply committed and unabashedly *provincial* in the defense of their learning and political communities, and their confrontation and engagement with the many processes of globalization is usually territorially, national or regionally based. With an important exception, solidarity matters to New Democrats. And international solidarity matters a great deal! While mostly provincial rather than cosmopolitan, New Democrats actively intervene in the international arena when they try to prevent wars, lending a hand to people who experienced distressing natural or manmade catastrophes, or struggling to find ways to help the planet by promoting sustainable development.

One of the principles connected with global citizenship education is its cosmopolitan nature, which relates to a formal model of democracy. *Cosmopolitan democracy* entails "a model of political organization in which citizens, wherever they are located in the world, have a voice, input, and political representation in international affairs, in parallel with and independent of their own governments."[23]

From a perspective of cosmopolitan democracy, Richard Falk delineated five categories of global citizens: (1) the "global reformer" and supporter of supranational government, (2) the elite class of globe trotters engaged in global business activities, (3) individuals committed to global economic and ecological sustainability, (4) supporters of regional governance structures as in the example of the European Union, and (5) transnational activists involved in grassroots organizations fighting for human rights and democracy.[24] Yet one may classify many of the representatives of democratic cosmopolitanism as a variety of New Democrats at a global level.

The dialectics between cosmopolitans and provincials cannot simply be put into a dichotomist taxonomy of strict binary classifications. I would argue that among the supporters of cosmopolitan democracy and by implication global citizenship, we may find all the varieties represented above, from the hyper-globalizers to mild forms of skeptics that still seek a way out of their own conundrums, to the many varieties of New Democrats, particularly those embracing models of global citizenship. This option of global citizenship is not seen as an alternative to national citizenship, but as supplement to reinforce the robustness of representative democracies worldwide, ultimately seeking to guarantee the social democratic pact on the rights of persons, not the rights of property.[25]

The gist of this argument throughout this book is that global citizenship adds value to national citizenship. Moreover, because the cause of national citizenship could be considered unfinished business, the value added of global citizenship may add another layer of support for a process of transforming citizenship-making and citizenship education into models based on principles of liberty and equality for all.

The world is complex. It would be nice to find categorizations that will line up in discrete boxes (or concepts) encapsulating each and all the agendas, agents, stockholders, ideologies or policy orientations, to mention a few critical issues affecting social action. But it is impossible. My attempt in this section is to throw some analytical light onto immense cones of shadow we face around us. Yet my goal is not only analytical, but also practical, seeking to provoke a conversation that goes beyond the routine and boring bureaucratic classifications, pre-packaged, off-the-shelf responses, and the easy and simplistic policy-making rationales.

The least one can say in confronting all these positions and actors is that the dialectics of the global and the local provide the framework for understanding the regional challenges for education and global citizenship and ways to address the challenges of global education.

The next chapters will offer an analysis of the responsibilities of the university in the quest for global citizenship education.

Notes

1. The first version of this chapter was presented as a keynote speech to the CSSE-SCEE Congress 2014 of the Humanities and Social Sciences, Brock University, St. Catharine's, Ontario, Canada, May 25, 2014.
2. Held, 1991, p. 9.
3. Luke and Luke, 2000, p. 287.
4. Urry, 1998.
5. Castells, 1996, 1997; Torres and Rhoads, 2006, p. 4; Touraine, 1968.
6. Alvin W. Gouldner, "Cosmopolitans and locals: Toward an Analysis of Latent Social Roles", *Administrative Science Quarterly*, volume 2, number 3 (December 1957), pp. 281–306—I; Alvin W. Gouldner, *Administrative Science Quarterly*, "Cosmopolitans and locals: Toward an Analysis of Latent Social Roles" II volume 2, number 4 (March 1958), pp. 444–480—II.
7. I, p. 290.
8. Ibid., p. 293. Yet.
9. II, p. 444.
10. Ibid., p. 446.
11. Ibid., pp. 447–448.
12. Ibid., p. 450.
13. Ibid., p. 497.
14. Friedman, 2005.
15. Bardhan, Bowles, and Wallerstein, 2006, p. 3.
16. www.oecd.org/els/soc/dividedwestandwhyinequalitykeepsrising.htm
17. Austen-Smith, Frieden, Golden, Moene, and Przeworki, 2008.
18. Atkinson, Piketty, and Sáez, 2011, p. 3.
19. Lauder, Brown, Dillabough, and Halsey, 2006, p. 45.
20. http://as.nyu.edu/docs/IO/2800/munck.pdf
21. Reich, 1988, 1992.
22. www.rebelion.org/docs/121968.pdf
23. Archibugi and Held, 1995, 13.
24. Falk, 1993, 2002.
25. Bowles and Gintis, 1986; Torres, 1998b.

5 Global Citizenship Education and the Role of Universities

Seven Iconoclastic Theses about Public Universities and Neoliberal Common Sense[1]

Introduction: The Importance of Neoliberalism: New Common Sense in Education

Neoliberalism has utterly failed as a viable model of economic development, yet the politics of culture associated with neoliberalism is still in force, becoming the new common sense shaping the role of government and education. This 'common sense' has become an ideology playing a major role in constructing hegemony as moral and intellectual leadership in contemporary societies. Neoliberal globalization, predicated on the dominance of the market over the state and on deregulatory models of governance, has deeply affected the university in the context of 'academic capitalism.' The resulting reforms, rationalized as advancing international competitiveness, have affected public universities in four primary areas: efficiency and accountability, accreditation and universalization, international competitiveness and privatization. There is also growing resistance to globalization as top-down-imposed reforms reflected in the public debates about schooling reform, curriculum and instruction, teacher training and school governance. Many question whether neoliberal reforms attempt to limit the effectiveness of universities as sites of contestation of the national and global order and thus undermine the broader goals of education. Neoliberal reforms have limited access and opportunity along class and racial lines, including limiting access to higher education through the imposition of higher tuition and reduced government support to institutions and individuals.

1. The University and Neoliberalism: What Is at Stake

My analysis, which surely will be considered at least polemical to some and completely unacceptable to others, tries to honor the long tradition of the university as a place to pursue the truth.

In my worst moments as a university professor I remember the example of the existentialist philosopher and playwright Miguel de Unamuno, Rector (Chancellor) of the University of Salamanca, the oldest university in Spain. On October 12, 1936, in the Paraninfo of the University of

Salamanca, Unamuno confronted the fascist hordes who won the Spanish Civil War, greeting the fascist general Milan-Astray, himself maimed in the war, with these words that should still resonate strongly in all university settings: "At times to be silent is to lie. You will win because you have enough brute force. But you will not convince. For to convince you need to persuade. And in order to persuade you would need what you lack: reason and right." Milan-Astray shouted in reply, "Death to intelligence! And long live death!" and drove the elderly Unamuno out of the university at gunpoint.[2] The Magnífico Rector of the University of Salamanca, Miguel de Unamuno, confined to house arrest, suffered a heart attack and died shortly after.

Unamuno's example is hardly common in our universities and institutions of higher education today. In addition to scholars, public universities are also inhabited by technocrats, 'wanna be' politicians, institutional bureaucrats, full-time faculty administrators who were at some point (or failed to be) scholars and have turned into university managers and a host of other professionals teaching part time or working as clinical professors. In addition to these roles, one should mention other key players in the university such as undergraduate and graduate students, part-time or full-time researchers who are not members of the teaching force and administrative staff. All these institutional actors may be pursuing different and sometime contradictory aims, agendas and practices compared to traditional university roles.

A word of caution is in order here because speaking of traditional roles in higher education may be misleading. There is no question that higher education, and particularly universities, have a plurality of traditional roles and functions in society, but these roles and functions are constantly reshaped by the transformation of the global, national and social contexts in which the university operates. Hence, the current debate about the impact of neo-liberal globalization on education cannot be ignored, particularly when my concern in this article is the transformation and challenges of the public university in the context of global capitalism.

Clearly my analysis is influenced by my work as a professor in a large public university system in the US, but I am convinced that the theses I advance below can be applied to most of the public university systems in core capitalist societies.

The next section will focus on the traditional roles and functions attributed to universities. These traditional roles and functions are also deeply affected by the history and legacies of specific social movements that have impacted the university as an institution; by the position of the university as an autonomous institution that is nonetheless linked to its home country's position within the world system; and by the models of governance and the role the nation-state plays.[3] I have argued elsewhere that:

> . . . particularly during the twentieth century, educational systems and practices were maintained, prepared, organized and certified by the

State. In fact, public education is a State function not only in terms of legal order or of financial support. The specific requirements for certification, the requirements and basic qualifications of teachers, the definition of textbooks, and obligatory courses in the basic curriculum are controlled by official agencies and defined by specific State policies.[4]

2.   Traditional University Roles and Functions

The specific mission of the university is to produce new knowledge in the cultural, economic and social spheres, but also to preserve the knowledge historically accumulated by civilizations, societies, communities and individuals. Institutions of higher education differ from elementary and secondary education as well as adult education and lifelong training in several ways, among them not only the different age groups they serve but also in their ability to produce original knowledge and to preserve a civilization's knowledge.

There are other key contributions of institutions of higher education such as the training and education of the labor force for participation in globalized and competitive labor markets and, in the traditional Napoleonic university model, the training of state civil servants. Pure, applied and technological research—much of which is done in universities—makes up one of the pillars that sustain the dynamism of what is now known as 'the knowledge economy.'[5]

Communications is another key element of universities. Universities also have key responsibilities regarding technologies of information, particularly when we are living in a 'virtual society' and when distance education models are creating new modes of lifelong learning.

Innovation is the central element of the university—that is, the possibility of creating new knowledge through interdisciplinary, multidisciplinary or transdisciplinary efforts. Universities are also warehouses of knowledge, preserving and making available historically produced knowledge—hence the role of museums, libraries and depositories where universities preserve and make available knowledge and artifacts of culture to a larger public.[6]

The role of universities in extension or continuing education cannot be ignored. Extension faculties were created as an educational opportunity provided by colleges and universities to people who are not enrolled as regular students. Particularly in the US, these faculties were prominent in the creation of the land grant colleges and universities. In fact, it is this role that facilitates all over the world the integration of universities with communities in pursuing similar goals. Perhaps it is instructive to remember that, in 1961, the first director of the newly created Faculty of Extension of the University of Recife (Servicio de Extensão Cultural/SEC), currently Universidade Federal de Pernambuco, was Paulo Freire.[7]

Universities, then, have historically had a responsibility in diffusing knowledge throughout the larger society. Some would argue that universities, as part of the 'public sphere' à la Jürgen Habermas should contribute to 'open science' and open codes of communication.[8]

In closing this section I should emphasize that critical theorists cannot be satisfied with this descriptive set of roles and traditional functions conventionally attributed to higher education and particularly to universities. We assume at the outset that it is impossible to fully dissociate the normative from the analytical in the construction of scientific thought, hence the importance of the notion of a good society guiding the intellectual, theoretical, meta-theoretical and empirical explorations of 'the real.' Similarly, we assume that it is impossible to deny the eminently political role of education, or what Paulo Freire has termed the "politicity of education."[9] Finally, it is impossible to avoid the historicity of thought and the policy prescriptions that emanate from a particular mode of theorizing. After all, not all social constructions are equally powerful in their logical configuration, methodological rigor or solid empirical proof, hence the need for serious analytical and scientific work.

I have argued for the need to reimagine critical theory as one of the most vigorous models of theorizing competing for recognition in the social field of the political sociology of education.[10] This reimagining of critical theory should also contribute to reimagining the roles and functions of universities in global capitalism. Yet, just to whet the appetite of the reader for what critical theory's political premise may imply for the university and the professoriate, I will argue that, in opposition to the commodification of knowledge and the mercantilization of the university, there is a fundamental role for university professors to become public intellectuals and, by implication, public universities must facilitate the creation of public knowledge and social justice education as a definition of their raison d'être. Perhaps it is in affirming the notion of parrhesia that we come full circle in this concept of the political role of the university in the search for the truth. As it is classically argued in the discipline of rhetoric, parrhesia is a figure of speech described as speaking candidly or asking forgiveness for so speaking.

The term is borrowed from the Greek, meaning literally "to speak everything" and, by extension, "to speak freely." It implies not only freedom of speech, but also the obligation to speak the truth for the common good, even at personal risk. It is a classic practice addressing the relationships between the subject and the truth that Foucault studied very closely in his late work.[11]

3.   Common Sense and Regimes of Truth: A Brief Excursus

There are three questions that need to be addressed here. First, what is 'common sense'? Second, was there a dominant common sense in the Western world that was modified by the advent of neoliberalism? Third, how can this new common sense can be defined in theoretical terms?

Generally speaking, people invoke common sense as sound practical judgment that is independent of specialized knowledge or training. Sometimes we refer to common sense as 'normal native intelligence.'

These definitions in turn give us two important concepts. One is that common sense becomes 'naturalized' in the lives of people as something normal that we do or ought to do just to get by and/or prosper. Common sense is a generalized truth about something; it is the normal way to do things, the normal way of becoming human beings.

Secondly, the idea of common sense is based on culturally shared understandings or values. That means that what is common sense for some people may not be common sense to others. Therefore, we ought to consider the notion of common sense as variable across cultures.

Common sense as a rhetorical device is different of course from common sense as a conceptual or practical tool for transformation, but there is significant overlap between the two. In other words, if one begins to argue that a given common sense was substituted by another common sense, we need to define what the previous common sense was all about and how the new neoliberal common sense came into being and displaced the previous one.

Before we proceed with the theses, let us clarify a potential conundrum: how we differentiate common sense from Foucault's concept of 'regimes of truth.' In my view the two concepts are different. For Foucault, a regime of truth is a historically specific strategy that produces discourses functioning as (or claiming to be) truthful in specific times and places. Without attempting a terminological debate or a heuristic analysis, let me suggest some differences between the concepts:

1. The effect of regimes of truth is similar to the convincing power of a hegemonic agenda. Meanwhile, common sense is elaborated as a discourse or set of discursive practices, but it has a much larger implementation agenda. Beyond ideology or hegemonic leadership, which is achieved through moral and intellectual persuasion, common sense entails the transformation of reality with specific directions, intentionality and values. It is in the last instance related to instrumental rationality and can be implemented by the use of sheer force.
2. Common sense has a degree of variability, which is contextual, but it has a hegemonic leadership built into the principles of a given common sense determining policy direction, intentionality and practices. While Foucault looked at regimes of truth in discursive practices, common sense is emerging, in my view, more as a mixture of discourse and 'self-evident' method for social transformation. In the realm of education, the tendency to adapt mechanisms from the world of business and engineering models of accountability, or creating a set of 'best practices,' is oriented to much more than defining a set of truisms that cannot be challenged in particular times and places. As Walter Mignolo suggests,

"Neoliberalism is not just an economic and financial question but a new civilizing design."[12]

3. Common sense is progressively cumulative and percolates in the social consciousness of peoples beyond what a simple set of premises or discourses can do. It becomes incorporated into the language, affects people's sense of identity, modifies their perceptions, alters the constant dialogue between perception and action and ends up constituting a course of action, almost an unchallenged set of principles that needs to be duplicated or replicated tout court.

4. While Foucault was concerned with the idea of truth or discursive truth, the idea of common sense is particularly concerned with the 'arbiters' of the discursive engagement, that is, the institutions that have propagated the neoliberal common sense.

5. Finally, according to Foucault's multiple definitions of power, the regime of truth has validity at several levels of power. That is, power is not a thing but a relation; it is not only repressive but productive; it is not only the property of the state but it is exercised throughout the social body and it operates at the micro level of social relationships. To be sure, the argument about common sense assumes a dialectic between agency and structure and one in which, while there are multiple powers at play, they are mostly subordinated to specific mechanisms of control, oppression, repression and manipulation of consciousness. Power, then, is defined on different levels than in Foucault's concept of regimes of truth and it plays different roles in the constitution of common sense.[13] Perhaps common sense is closer to the notion of power in everyday life and how it is underwritten by the dominant structures that articulate everything from rituals of inducement into the greater society (e.g., learning, identity formation and education more generally) to rituals of initiation (such as the foundations to build educational and occupational futures).

4.   Seven Iconoclastic Theses

With these theoretical considerations in mind, let me offer now a set of iconoclastic theses. They are iconoclastic because I would like to confront established dogmas or conventions and, most fundamentally, I want to challenge the growing presence of instrumental rationality and neoliberalism's common sense in the way we live, practice, work, teach, provide advice to our students, conduct research, work in committees and even profess our most cherished values in our professional work as academics. The time has come to recognize the need to speak the truth in the spirit of parrhesia as part and parcel of the politics of struggle in academia.

The first thesis that I would like to defend is that over the last three decades or so we have witnessed the growing presence of neoliberalism as the dominant ideology in public policy and governance.[14] Neoliberalism has created 'a new common sense' that has percolated into all public and private institutions and thus, despite their own autonomy, into institutions of higher education. The main argument of my analysis is that the emergence of neoliberalism in the late 1970s and early 1980s has dramatically altered the notion of common sense in education.

I believe that the previous predominant common sense in the US (and to a large extent in other parts of the Western world) was connected to the experience of the New Deal and educational liberal progressivism. It will be beyond the premises of this analysis to go into great detail of what liberal progressivism's common sense means, or how it came into being, but let me sketch some elements that are salient.

First, unlike traditional models of education, progressivism, particularly through the influence of John Dewey becomes student-centered and experiential rather than abstractly cognitive.[15] Second, it is concerned with the welfare of society and believes in the need to tame the more potentially destructive forces of capitalist societies towards improving overall equality and equity. Third, borrowing from the logic of the Enlightenment, education's aim is to enhance humanization, reason and conflict resolution. Fourth, education is a central and organic link of public policy in the construction of democracy and citizenship. Fifth, educational policies should increase upward social mobility and social cohesion. Finally, educational expenses, both individually and socially, should be considered not merely as an expenditure but as an investment. This premise, which began to take precedence in the 1950s and early 1960s, a time of educational expansion, opened the door for an economic view of educational goals.

A word of caution is in order here. This liberal-progressive common sense, though related to the revolutionary goals of the Enlightenment, is not exempt from serving as a tool for hegemonic domination, as the Enlightenment itself is deeply Eurocentric, anthropocentric and male-centric. It could easily be argued that a great deal of the narratives of the Enlightenment, particularly in the 19th century, were instrumental in defending colonialism as a progressive force, as a way to bring 'civilization' to barbarian societies. Marx himself considered the presence of England in India a civilizing revolutionary force to overthrow 'Oriental despotism.'[16]

With these theoretical considerations in order, my most general hypothesis, then, is that the notion of common sense becomes an ideology playing a major role in the process of constructing hegemony as moral and intellectual leadership in a given society.[17]

Liberalism has been displaced by neoliberalism, deeply affecting education and social policies. As Michael W. Apple argues:

> Liberalism itself is under concerted attack from the right, from the coalition of neo-conservatives, 'economic modernizers', and new right groups who have sought to build a new consensus around their own principles. Following a strategy best called 'authoritarian populism',

this coalition has combined a 'free market ethic' with populist politics. The results have been a partial dismantling of social democratic policies that largely benefited working people, people of color, and women (these groups are obviously not mutually exclusive), the building of a closer relationship between government and the capitalist economy, and attempts to curtail liberties that had been gained in the past.[18]

Neoliberal governments promote open markets, free trade, the reduction of the public sector, decreased state intervention in the economy and the deregulation of markets. These premises for the economic restructuring of advanced capitalism that have been under criticism, particularly after the crash of 2008, imply the reduction of public spending, reduction of programs considered wasteful, the sale of state enterprises and mechanisms of deregulation to prevent state intervention in the business world. Together with the aforementioned, it is proposed that the state should participate less in the provision of social services (including education, health care, pensions and retirement, public transportation and affordable housing) and that these services should be privatized.

The notion of the 'private' (and privatization) is glorified as part of a free market. It implies total confidence in the efficiency of competition because the activities of the public or state sectors are seen as inefficient, unproductive and socially wasteful. In contrast, the private sector is considered efficient, effective, productive and responsive. In contrast to the model of the welfare state in which the state exercises the mandate to uphold the social contract between labor and capital, the neoliberal state is decidedly pro-business, supporting the demands of the corporate world. Nevertheless, as Daniel Schugurensky rightly points out, this departure from state interventionism is differential, not total.[19] In this vein, "it is not possible to abandon, for symbolic as well as practical reasons, all of the state's social programs. It is necessary to diffuse conflictive and explosive areas in the realm of public policy."[20]

In Latin America during this time, academic affairs were increasingly regulated while the world of business was increasingly deregulated. As the experience of Latin America testifies, it was under neoliberal governments that autonomous public universities, considered bastions of free thinking and left politics, were squeezed by financial punishment and a new evaluation regime of increased regulation and accountability in universities, as well as by the intensification of academic work and productivity in line with the global model of privatization and Westernization. For instance, evaluation of articles published in English in international journals in English rather than in the vernacular languages and in journals that were indexed in the major indexes of science were privileged for resource allocation and academic advancement.

The second thesis that I outline here is that neoliberal globalization, the most powerful model of globalization predicated on the dominance of the market over the state, particularly through deregulatory models of governance, has deeply affected the university in the context of 'academic capitalism.' The publication of *Education and globalization: Critical analysis*[21] opened a line of inquiry into the possible implications of globalization in educational systems and policies. The globalization question was galvanized in the 1980s and 1990s, given the growing international discourse and contradictory national debates about globalization from economic, political and social perspectives. The globalization of the politics, culture and political economy of core capitalist societies as well as emerging and less developed economies has impacted the nature and operations of one of the most important avenues for social mobility and equity: the educational systems.

The globalization question is still on the table and the stakes are indeed high. Public policy during the past three US presidential administrations intensified the discourse of free trade and expansion of new markets. While this process hardly culminated in a widespread understanding of the phenomenon of globalization—after all, as Burbules, Torres and their contributors proposed, there are very different and contradictory definitions of globalization, its nature and its history—still, few research projects within the US and elsewhere have critically examined the ways in which educational systems have been guided or impacted by economic and social policies prompted by globalization.[22]

In a broad assessment of international patterns associated with globalization, it seems that public education has been called upon to develop a new labor force to meet the rapidly changing economic demands, presenting policy dilemmas on issues concerning the privatization and decentralization of schools.[23] This movement includes raising educational standards and placing stronger emphasis on testing and school accountability. Decisions based on economic changes have espoused new visions for school reform in universities as well. These reforms, associated with international competitiveness, are also known as "competition-based reforms."[24]

As past president of the Comparative and International Education Society, I can recall debates years ago about the importance of internationalizing US education. Scholars versed in comparative education complained about the poor understanding among their colleagues in our schools of education of the processes, systems, pedagogies and educational histories of other countries. In contrast, the political economy of the world system or the regulatory role of the state and international system emerged as new objects of analysis for comparativists. Most US-based education scholars seemed, in the view of many comparativists, parochially concerned with their own discipline and with research themes usually associated with specific local, state or national problems. While this degree of specialization and concern was commendable as a way to pursue rigorous research agendas, what was also remarkable was how they showed blatant disregard for international developments or international education.

I am convinced that this preoccupation of comparativists, anticipating to some extent the changes that have swept the globe in the last three decades, is now only partially valid. Many teachers, students, policy makers, legislators, community activists and parents—in short, people concerned with the educational democratic promise in the US—realize today that it is becoming more difficult to talk about the connection between education and national labor markets without considering the importance of global markets and, of course, the growing trends towards outsourcing production of goods and services. Few people would question that discussions about testing, accountability or curriculum—perennial issues for debates about local, state and federal jurisdictions in the US—are no longer national, provincial or state questions. These issues now have an international scope; they are part of an international research agenda of bilateral and international organizations like the World Bank, OECD and the IMF and have saturated educational discourses in most nations of the globe.[25]

Moreover, comparative education itself becomes a powerful tool in creating a global 'schooling grammar' and comparable international indicators:

> Comparative education functions as a lever that can destroy resistance at any level, both in scientific research and politics. It becomes a weapon in the political conflict over the organization of education. It mainly implements new information strategies for educational processes and provides information that weakens opponents' positions.[26]

Let us consider another example. When the World Trade Organization (WTO) discusses the liberalization of services worldwide, it would be wise for higher education in California, beleaguered by fiscal cuts and under serious financial constraints, to understand that if the WTO succeeds in making higher education part of the package of services, financial and otherwise, to be liberalized worldwide, this new policy not only will affect the rest of the globe, it will affect the US as well.

The debate on equity and equality in higher education and the time-honored preoccupation with raising the ability and presence of minorities in higher education, one of the great achievements of multicultural universities, will take a new turn. After all, many people would argue that under potential new WTO rulings, loans, grants and fellowships from state and federal governments, especially those earmarked for specific 'underserved' populations, might be considered unfair subsidies, comparable to farm subsidies in the US. Substantial funding from the state to higher education institutions could also be considered unfair subsidies to higher education and therefore subject to challenge in a WTO court. In this WTO scenario, the rules for privatization of elementary, secondary and higher education may be relaxed at national, state/provincial and municipal/county levels, thus allowing more entrepreneurs to open their own academies, schools and universities, offering services that would be less regulated by boards, professional organizations or state regulatory commissions.

Some would argue that liberalization of services would definitely help the core capitalist societies that have the strongest public and private systems of higher education. As the comparative advantage argument goes, they will continue exporting their services, now with renewed vigor, to emerging but also less developed economies. It is clear that in the last two decades universities in core capitalist societies have positioned themselves at the forefront of selling services internationally, through both overseas campuses and distance education. Many of them have not only captured the rich and burgeoning market for international students in the US, at least until September 11, 2001 and its student visa restriction aftermath, but they also expanded sales and services in societies far away from their campuses. Moreover, given sizable differential fees, international students are eagerly sought out by public universities in the US as a substantial source of revenue to deal with their financial woes.

There is no reason, however, to think that under a WTO ruling liberalizing educational services the situation will not be reversed, with many universities from emerging economies setting up their own campuses in the US, particularly geared towards specific populations connected somehow to their country of origin and, simultaneously, challenging the way financing of higher education takes place in the US. Is this a far-fetched scenario? It remains to be seen, but some trends in institutional debates and changes in the political economy of higher education in the US and elsewhere indicate that such changes are possible and if they take place, they will surely be lasting. The least one can say is that if and when they take place, they will disrupt the time-honored traditions of higher education.[27]

Not surprisingly, even the Fulbright Commission in the US is concerned about the question of globalization in higher education. A few years ago, the Fulbright New Century Scholars Program focused specifically on the study of changes in higher education brought about by globalization processes.[28] Will neoliberal globalization deeply affect the way each country trains its workforce? Will neoliberal globalization enhance the ability of countries and educational systems to comply with the growing demands of human rights? Will neoliberal globalization affect the way children and youth are socialized in the understanding and practice of the most deeply held cultural and social values, beliefs and common-sense knowledge of each society—a concern that would certainly impact the thinking of great educational sociologists of the past, like Emile Durkheim or Karl Mannheim, if they were still alive.[29]

The implications of the changes brought about by neoliberal globalization to universities, particularly the impact of the model of privatization, has been perceived by critical theorists. As Raymond Morrow incisively argues:

> The great benefactor of the desacralization of the university as a cultural institution has been the increasing penetration of market forces

into higher education and the reorganization of university governance around 'playing the game' of academic capitalism. . . . In this context the market becomes the Trojan horse for undermining academic autonomy by ostensibly nonideological and noncoercive means based on the interest of the 'consumers' of education and research.[30]

The third thesis that I would like to defend is that the institutional dynamics of higher education have been affected by changes at several levels. Perhaps the most important one in the last century, and one deeply connected with the process of globalization, is how universities have been transformed—in terms of access but also in terms of diversification—from elite institutions into democratic institutions and, most recently and particularly in core capitalist societies, into transnational institutions of knowledge production, change, distribution and consumption.[31]

Let us recap that the dominant neoliberal agenda for globalization in kindergarten through 12th grade education includes a drive toward privatization and decentralization of public forms of education, a movement toward educational standards, a strong emphasis on testing and a focus on accountability. Specific to higher education reform, neoliberal versions of globalization suggest reforms for universities in four primary areas: efficiency and accountability, accreditation and universalization, international competitiveness and privatization.

The reforms associated with international competitiveness could be described as 'competition-based reforms,' characterized by efforts to create measurable performance standards through extensive standardized testing (the new standards and accountability movement), introduction of new teaching and learning methods purported to create better performance at lower cost (e.g., universalization of textbooks), and improvements in the selection and training of teachers. Competition-based reforms in higher education tend to adopt a vocational orientation and reflect the point of view that colleges and universities exist largely to serve the economic well-being of a society. With regard to accreditation and universalization, major efforts are under way throughout the world to reform academic programs through accreditation processes and various strategies that produce increased homogeneity across national boundaries.[32]

I have argued in my work with Rhoads that the privatization of higher education in debt-ridden countries such as Mexico, Brazil and Argentina is typically advanced by the IMF and the World Bank as a precondition to further lending to these countries. A precondition of such lending involves the transfer of educational financing from higher education to lower levels of education, based on the premise that to subsidize higher education is to subsidize the rich, since the majority of students enrolled in higher education are from the middle classes and affluent families. Needless to say, these reforms are actively resisted in some of these countries by faculty, unions, parents, social movements and students. Indeed, globalization has had a major impact in education since international institutions have promoted finance-driven reforms, which eventually clash with the possibility of equity-driven reforms in many countries.[33]

There are, to be sure, different processes of implementation and adaptation of these financially driven, competition-based educational reforms in different countries. Differences depend on the history of each educational system, the type of government in power, the role of teachers unions and professional organizations and so on. Yet, while these reforms are implemented and adopted, there is also growing resistance to globalization. Resistance, controversies, contradictions and even activist confrontation with what is perceived as top-down-imposed reforms through globalization policies and priorities take place in diverse domains, including curriculum and instruction, teacher training and school governance[34] and this growing resistance is also reflected in the public debates about schooling reform.[35] Yet a central focus of these debates is the specific cultural values that need to be preserved in each nation-state in terms of citizenship building against the prevailing cultural globalization through mass media and the trends of competition-based educational reforms. Hence the question of educating the global citizen remains a central question hitherto not carefully explored and with little if any available historical and empirical evidence.

The fourth thesis that I would like to emphasize is that since privatization is the driving force of neoliberalism, 'academic capitalism' is a natural outcome of the process experimented with by universities and institutions of higher education in the last two or three decades. Analyzing the situation in the US, Sheila Slaughter and Gary Rhoades[36] argue that a pattern of increasing 'academic capitalism' is evident in US higher education. Such a pattern goes beyond the technology transfer activities Slaughter and Leslie[37] focus on in their book *Academic Capitalism* and extends to the fundamental educational functions of colleges and universities.

The emerging pattern, Slaughter and Rhoades argue, is rooted in increasing pressures and opportunities for college and universities to generate revenue through various partnerships with the private sector. Their suggestion follows work by Foucault[38] looking at the archeology of knowledge and conceptualizations of power and 'regimes of truth,' in that academic capitalism rests upon an academic-capitalist knowledge, learning and consumption regime. Thus, academic capitalism is a regime of power and they identify specifics by analyzing federal patent and copyright policies as well as federal policies and programs that support academic research.[39]

The fifth thesis suggests that by introducing managerialism as a new form of higher education institutional governance and the mercantile function of the university via the commodification of knowledge and subjects of higher education, universities have deepened and magnified their crises. Portuguese sociologist Boaventura de Sousa Santos sees the university facing three pressing crises: the crisis of hegemony, the crisis of legitimacy and the institutional crisis:

> The crisis of hegemony is the result of the growing intellectual deprivation of the university as it is increasingly called on to produce commercial

knowledge at the expense of other forms of knowledge. The crisis of legitimacy is the result of the increasing segmentation of the university system and the growing devaluation of university diplomas. The institutional crisis of the university is the result of the decreased support by the state and the erasure of the public benefit mission that universities, especially public ones, traditionally served. Concentrating on the institutional crisis served only to exacerbate the problems of hegemony and legitimacy. A key point of Santos' argument is that the nature of university knowledge has been transformed from scientific knowledge to what he terms 'pluriversity knowledge'. Pluriversity knowledge is application-oriented and extramurally driven.[40]

The sixth thesis argues that, given the fiscal crises of the state and the institutional crises of universities, any consideration of the relationships between higher education and global labor markets should first and foremost consider the implications for the university itself as a meaningful and sizable labor market. With the growing deterioration of salaries and intensification of working conditions in the university, even in core capitalist societies, there is a strong chance that in the very near future we will see an increase in the unionization of graduate students and new forms of social, political and economic representation of university professors, perhaps in the form of professorial unions—in Canada these unions have existed for some time and play meaningful roles in the debates about university governance.

One of the new phenomena in universities in the US is the drive towards graduate student unionization as a post-industrial social movement. Robert Rhoads and Gary Rhoades[41] examine the growing movement among graduate student employees in the US to pursue collective bargaining. As they point out, the unionization of graduate student employees has met with fairly stiff resistance from university administrators, who have argued that graduate students more or less serve as apprentices and that the work they perform is part of their academic experience: "As low-level wage earners in a corporate enterprise, graduate student organizers see collective bargaining as the logical extension of an organisation firmly entrenched in a business model of operation."[42]

The pressures for unionization of university professors are growing, considering the financial crises of universities and the growing managerialism that is affecting models of dual governance that prevail in many research universities. This model of 'dual governance' is built on a tradition of a systematic, open and, to a large extent, honest dialogue between the academic senate and administration regarding key teaching, research, administration and evaluation policies.

The relative autonomy of higher education, the importance of tenure as a keystone for the politics of teaching and inquiry in higher education and the tradition of self-governed universities may slow down or even counteract this movement towards unionization. However, pressures mounting on the university by the rise of neoliberal 'new public management' in the public sector, the consolidation of a managerial class in the university and the widespread use of business models and market principles, at least since the early 1980s, have undermined the autonomy of the professoriate. In addition, the pressure to find measureable outcomes of university 'products' and the growing pressure to create commodities through sales, services, inventions, patents, etc. by universities have affected the university and the way it is self-governed and operated. Thus, not surprisingly, many are arguing that if universities are becoming themselves capitalist enterprises, they should be subject to labor/management negotiations. In this context, the role of unions to defend the professoriate, administrative staff and even graduate students/workers becomes key.[43]

The seventh thesis discusses the overall implications of the process of neoliberal globalization for higher education. At a general level, one may argue that the impact of globalization on colleges and universities is both direct and indirect:

> An example of a direct effect is the way in which national economies are restructuring their systems of support for higher education as a consequence of shifting economic priorities and structural adjustment policies mandated from above. Examples of indirect effects include the manner by which the war against terrorism has come to limit academic freedom and the transnational flow of scholars and students and the way in which academic culture at some Latin American universities is shifting from a collectivist orientation to ideas associated with individualism. What is clear is that the various manifestations of globalization have the potential to produce different kinds of effects, although disentangling cause and effect can be quite problematic.[44]

I have argued elsewhere that these processes are coupled with attempts to infuse market logic into higher education, 'undermining its mission as an independent source of knowledge and inquiry.'[45] These efforts fit with the attempts to limit the effectiveness of universities as sites of contestation of the national and global order.[46]

It is difficult to completely disentangle the cause-and-effect relationship between the fiscal crises of the state and the new models of governance of neoliberalism, with its new common sense creating a hegemonic policy narrative in the world system. However:

> Increased entrepreneurialism in post-secondary education, especially in the most developed countries, has been led by efforts to expand revenue (or simply to replenish losses from decreasing state and federal support) through a variety of profit-seeking endeavors, including close collaboration with business in research, satellite campuses, and extension programs around the world. This has been coupled with recent

efforts to bring accountability regimes similar to No Child Left Behind to the university level, ensuring increased homogeneity and standardization and disempowering professors and counter-hegemonic ideas. In sum, neoliberal globalization has attempted to undermine the broader goals of education, pushing it to serve as the primary source of sorting and initial training for corporations. It has also attempted to undermine the ideological and political power of education, specifically disempowering teachers and teachers' unions. In many cases, neoliberal reforms have limited access and opportunity along class and racial lines, including limiting access to higher education through the imposition of higher tuition and reduced government support to institutions and individuals.[47]

Conclusion: Neoliberal Common Sense and the Politics of Struggle

Neoliberalism has utterly failed as a model of economic development. First evidenced with the Argentinean crisis of 2001, this financial and economic debacle culminated in the world crises of 2008 that brought the world capitalist system to its knees. Paradoxically, the capitalist state, so vilified by prominent neoliberal globalizers, was called upon to intervene, rescuing a deregulated capitalist system from its own demise.

Yet the irony is that the politics of culture associated with neoliberalism is still in force and quite strong because it has been able to formulate this new common sense that has percolated deeply into the social consciousness of many sectors of the population, particularly the professional middle classes. Many think tanks and professional associations like the World Bank and OECD continue to preserve and expand this new common sense in education, despite its contradictions and dubious claims of success.

There are, to be sure, different processes of implementation and adaptation of these financially driven, competition-based educational reforms in different countries and I have argued that these differences depend on the history of each educational system, the type of government in power, the role of teachers unions and professional organizations and the nature and dynamics of institutions of higher education.[48] Yet while these reforms are implemented and adopted, and while the neoliberal common sense prevails in many terrains, there is also growing resistance to globalization. A central focus of these debates are the specific cultural values that need to be preserved in each nation-state in terms of citizenship building against the prevailing cultural globalization through mass media and the trends of competition-based educational reforms.[49]

A key question specifically tied to higher education is whether education is a privilege or a right. This has become a major point of contention in Latin American countries where structural adjustments policies have situated participation in higher education as a privilege, while long-standing social contracts within these countries suggest otherwise. In the limited space of this chapter, it is impossible to discuss how this debate has shifted from the liberal to the neoliberal regimes and this therefore remains a subject for further research.

Despite the power of the neoliberal common sense and its politics of culture and hegemonic aspirations, there is a clash of oppositional agendas. One agenda argues that public universities should focus on serving the customer, emphasizing public managerialism. There is an alternative agenda that defends the role of public universities in educating the citizen rather than servicing consumers—even if now we can speak about a global citizen in the world system.[50] This alternative agenda reclaims the traditional role of universities serving the common good and postulates the need to finance universities through public funding, seeking alternatives to the neoliberal common sense. There is also, intermingled with the previous debate, a policy agenda that focuses on privatization and advancing competition-based social structures and another focused on social intervention and on advancing a spirit of collectivism.[51]

A new round of confrontation will revolve around the middle-range theory of 'world-class universities' and its multiple semantics, including the question of 'best practices,' benchmarking, rankings, international and comparative quality indicators in higher education and the implications for public policy. On the other hand, there is the ongoing struggle to preserve access to education for underrepresented populations in the face of draconian cuts in public funding to universities. These confrontations will open yet another chapter in this contradictory and controversial process of appropriating and implementing the neoliberal common sense in the life of universities, but also in ways of resisting and contradicting its orientation, strategies and tactics, developing alternatives to the neoliberal common sense.

Notes

1. Slightly modified article from *International Studies in Sociology of Education*, volume 21, number 3 (2011), pp. 177–197 republished with authorization. I have presented and discussed these ideas in various settings and have benefited from exchanges with friends and colleagues, to whom I am grateful. I delivered a keynote to the Conference on the Internationalisation of Higher Education: A Foresight Exercise for 2020 and Beyond, organized by the Spanish presidency of the European Union, at the Universidad Complutense de Madrid, Madrid, Spain, April 19–20, 2010; a keynote to the Seminario Internacional de Políticas Educativas, Universidad de Barcelona, May 17–19, 2010; a paper at the World Congress of Comparative Education, Istanbul, Turkey, June 13–19, 2010; a keynote to the Comparative and International Education Society-Western Chapter, California State University-Long Beach, October 14, 2010; a keynote to the International Sociology of Education Conference, London, November 5–7, 2010; and a keynote to the III Seminário Internacional de Educação, Teorías, Políticas e Pesquisas Educacionais Contemporâneas, Programa de Pos-Graduação em Educação (PPGE) UNINOVE, São Paulo, November 23, 2010.
2. http:// www.rjgeib.com/heroes/unamuno/unamuno.html

3. Dale, 2003; Dale and Robertson, 2007.
4. Torres, 1998b, p. 14; *Review of Educational Research.*
5. UNESCO, 2005.
6. Enders, File, Huisman, and Westerheijden, 2005; Rhoads and Torres, 2006; UNESCO, 2005.
7. www.ufpe.br/proext/index. php?option=com_content&view=article&id=116: revista-estudos-universitari-os&catid=17&Itemid=122
8. Habermas, 1973, 1991.
9. Torres, 2014.
10. Rexhepi and Torres, 2011.
11. Foucault, 2010.
12. Mignolo, 2000, p. 279.
13. Morrow and Torres, 1995.
14. Dale, 2003; Dale and Robertson, 2007.
15. Dewey, 1916.
16. "England, it is true, in causing a social revolution in Hindostan, was actuated only by the vilest interests, and was stupid in her manner of enforcing them. But that is not the question. The question is, can mankind fulfill its destiny without a fundamental revolution in the social state of Asia? If not, whatever may have been the crimes of England she was the unconscious tool of history in bringing about that revolution." Karl Marx, "The British Rule in India", www.marxists. org/archive/marx/works/1853/06/25.htm.
17. Gramsci, 1971; Schirru, 2010.
18. Apple, 2004, p. xxiv.
19. Schugurensky, 1994.
20. Torres and Van Heertum, 2009, 150–151.
21. Burbules and Torres, 2000.
22. Luke and Luke, 2000; Stiglitz, 2002.
23. Arnove and Torres, 2007.
24. Carnoy, 1999; Torres, 2009a, 2009b.
25. Burbules and Torres, 2000; Teodoro, 2003, 2008.
26. Bottani, 2001, p. 75.
27. Boron, 2008; Rhoads and Torres, 2006.
28. Altbach, 2007.
29. I emphasize neoliberal globalization because my analysis shows that there are multiple globalizations intersecting and interacting in the world system, but the dominant, top-down model has been neoliberal globalization. Torres, 2009a, 2009b.
30. Morrow, 2006, pp. xxvi–xxvii.
31. Teodoro, 2008, 2010.
32. Carnoy, 1999, 2001; Carnoy and Torres, 1992.
33. Rhoads and Torres, 2006.
34. Burke and Jackson, 2007.
35. Apple, 2004.
36. Slaughter and Rhoades, 2004.
37. Slaughter and Leslie, 1997.
38. Foucault, 1972, 1980.
39. Slaughter and Rhoades, 2004.
40. Rhoads and Torres, 2006, p. 28.
41. Rhoads and Rhoades, 2006.
42. Rhoads and Torres, 2006, pp. 34–35.
43. I have discussed the complexity of teachers unions' policy dilemmas, with a specific emphasis on elementary and secondary education, in my book *Education and Neoliberal Globalization* (Torres, 2009c, pp. 55–61). While the situation in

higher education may be different, clearly the tension between professionalization/ trade unionization will remain, playing a fundamental role in the configuration of these phenomena in the future.

44. Rhoads and Torres, 2006, 10.
45. Torres and Van Heertum, 2009, p. 155.
46. Boron, 2008.
47. Torres and Van Heertum, 2009, p. 156.
48. Torres, 2009a, 2009b.
49. Torres, 1998b, 2002, 2009a.
50. Soysal, 1994.
51. Rhoads and Torres, 2006.

6 Global Citizenship and Global Universities

The Age of Global Interdependence and Cosmopolitanism[1]

Introduction

Economic inequality is no longer a buzzword about capitalist economics, it is a palpable reality. The crisis of 2008 has made even more evident the importance of the growing inequality that has affected market democracies, and particularly affecting the middle class. As I said elsewhere, a casualty of these crises in the global economy has been jobs, the loss of which has in turn increased inequality and poverty. Facing a jobless society, the university has many challenges, from being able to offer a service without pricing itself out of the market or being partially responsible from what some see as the new bubble of crisis in capitalism, students' massive debts, to showing that the coursework in which students engage will have a positive pay-off in the markets and make students more marketable and productive, hence increasing the levels of accountability of universities.

This chapter focuses on the role of global universities and globalizations in an age of global interdependence and cosmopolitanism. Competing agendas that result from actions and reactions to multiple globalizations are considered in relation to global citizenship education. These agendas are crucial in understanding dilemmas of the local and the global in relation to education. Key emerging agendas are highlighted including those of the hyperglobalizers, skeptics and transformationists as described in Chapter 4. Three themes are central for this conversation, namely: a) how multiple globalizations are impacting global life and academics, b) how networks have become privileged sites for global education, and c) the implications of globalization and networks for global citizenship and global universities.

Key Concepts

Global citizenship education interacts with *globalization* and *neoliberalism*, key concepts which designate global movements that have come to define our era of global interdependence. *Global capitalism*, which reflects the interaction of *globalization* and *neoliberalism*, now defines the top-down model of global hegemonic dominance, which rests on the power of elites, multinational corporations, bilateral and multilateral organisms, and the global and regional power of nations, who in turn exercise control over people, commodities, territories, capital and resources of all kinds, the environment included.[2] The viability of the neoliberal model of economic development has been questioned, yet the politics of culture associated with neoliberalism are still in force and have become the new common sense shaping the role of government and not least, education.[3] This 'common sense' has become an ideology playing a major role in constructing a hegemonic moral and intellectual leadership in contemporary societies.

This chapter discusses some of the challenges faced by universities in the context of globalization, and by extension the development and sustenance of global citizenship education for social transformation. I argue that there are different kinds of public and private universities. Specifically, that some are more connected with models of *democratic cosmopolitanism*, while others are more connected with models of *localism*. Both respond differently to the challenges associated with globalization, and to the delineation of boundaries between national and global citizenship.

Three themes are central to this analysis, namely: a) how multiple globalizations are impacting global life and academics, b) how networks have become privileged sites for global education collaboration, and c) the implications of globalization and networks for global citizenship and global universities. A key question undergirding the analysis is: What should the goals of global citizenship education be in a decade marked by the UN Education First Initiative, which seeks to further global citizenship and the responsibilities of universities and governments?

A Plurality of *Globalizations*

Globalization is a central concept for the analysis in this chapter; it is complex and multifaceted. For example, globalization has been defined as "the intensification of worldwide social relations which link distant localities in such a way that local happenings are shaped by events occurring many miles away and vice versa."[4] Another view sees globalization as "a feature of late capitalism, or the condition of postmodernity, and, more importantly, . . . the emergence of a world system driven in large part by a global capitalist economy."[5] Others see globalization as the transformation of time and space in which complex interactions and exchange once impossible become everyday activities.[6] And still others see globalization as an assault on traditional notions of society and nation-state, whereby the very nature of citizenship and social change are dramatically altered.[7] The meaning of *globalization* thus takes on different forms and we really should talk about globalization's processes in the plural.[8]

Several forms of *globalization* can be conceived as follows. First, there is *"globalization from above."* This is framed by an ideology of neoliberalism and calls for an opening of borders, the creation of multiple regional markets, the proliferation of fast-paced economic and financial exchanges, and the presence of governing systems other than nation-states—particularly in the form of international trade agreements enforced by the World Trade Organization.

A second form of globalization represents the antithesis of the first. This form can be described as *"globalization from below"* or *anti-globalization*. It manifests itself in individuals, institutions and social movements that are actively opposed to what is perceived as corporate globalization. For these individuals and groups, their motto is "no globalization without representation."

Another distinct form pertains more to rights than to markets—the *globalization of human rights*. With the growing ideology of human rights taking hold in the international system and in international law, many traditional practices endemic to the fabric of particular societies or cultures (from religious to esoteric practices) are now being called into question, challenged, forbidden or even outlawed. The advancement of cosmopolitan democracies and plural democratic multicultural global citizenship is the theme of this version of globalization.[9]

Globalization can also be characterized as a trademark of our contemporary world: *hybridity*. There are multiple forms of hybridity crossing the globe. For example, hip-hop cultures that were born in the Bronx now have Japanese, Indian and Chinese practitioners and cultural modalities. What all of them have in common is that they are showing some form of opposition to the establishments and are new ways for youth cultures to express themselves. Another prominent form of hybridity is related to inter-marriages that create new categories not easily classified within traditional taxonomies of race and/or ethnicity in demographic surveys.

A fifth manifestation of globalization can be characterized by the intersection of two processes defined by the concepts of the 'information society' and the 'knowledge society.' The idea of the information society rests on the ability of digital cultures to beam information to all corners of the globe almost instantaneously, affecting the equation of time and space like never before—and is intimately linked with the idea of a network society made possible by developments in digital cultures and technologies.[10] This face of globalization is impacting global cultural and material production in ways that seem like science fiction. Its twin, the emergence of the knowledge society, itself an outcomes of robotization and digital cultures, dramatically impacts the way we conceive the factors of production, which were traditionally considered land, capital, labor and technology. Now we have to add a fifth factor of production, knowledge.

A by-product of the former yet distinct form is well articulated by Castells, who defined the threshold of the 21st century as the "network society."[11] Never before have social networks been as widely discussed as they are today—a day in which living in the so-called "network society" seems to be a prevailing motto. For instance, among the various concepts Giddens creates to explain contemporary social phenomena in his book *Beyond Left and Right*[12], it is particularly worthwhile to note "social reflexivity."

According to Giddens, this reflexivity refers to knowledge disseminated outside the realm of experts, or what Giddens calls "expert systems," through information and communication networks that have been established through the development of new computational technologies and the Internet. That is, due to these new forms of telecommunication, new forms of information and expertise have been gaining prominence on the Internet, going beyond the borders of the world of experts (that is, scientists and researchers or journalists). The presence of these networks alter a number of traditional dimensions of human life like the distinction between private and public domains of social action. There is also the particular importance in the politics of bloggers who, seated in their living rooms, persistently inundate the globe with messages of many kinds. Questions about academic authority and moral character become central elements in discussing the credibility of messages, methods, research, data, analyses and narratives that pullulate in the Internet. Interactions between the global network society and global citizenship education are considered further later in the chapter.

A seventh manifestation of globalization extends beyond markets, and to some extent is against human rights. It is *globalization of the international war against terrorism*. This new form of globalization has been prompted in large part by the events of September 11, 2001—which were interpreted as the globalization of the terrorist threat—and the reaction of the United States to the event. This form of globalization is represented by the anti-terrorist response, which has been militaristic in nature, resulting in two coalition wars led by the US against Muslim regimes in Afghanistan and Iraq, under the auspices of the "Global War on Terror." Islamophobia is also a theme of this globalization. Terrorism and the terrorist threat were made synonymous with Islam and Muslims, and became a global norm. Yet, the overall theme of this process was not only its military flavor, but also the emphasis on security and control of borders, people, capital and commodities—that is, the reverse of open markets and high-paced commodity exchanges. Security as a precondition of freedom is a key theme of this form of globalization.

Finally, an eighth form of globalization relating again to terrorism can be conceived, namely the globalization of terrorism, which is well represented by the Al Qaida network, with terrorist actions of many kinds. Examples of these actions include Boko Haram's kidnapping of 300 girls from a Christian school in Nigeria, forcing them to convert to Islam and having them forcefully married to fighters. Another example is the growing consolidation of ISIS in the Middle East, providing a platform, a kind of sacred fire for youth who are disaffected with modernity and Western practices. Thousands of youths have moved to Iraq and Syria to fight for what they believe is their sacred cause of social change, leading to the establishment of a new caliphate in the Levant and Middle East. The motto of terrorism is probably best defined in the following terms: Only chaos will bring about freedom.

It is worthwhile to emphasize the implications of some of these forms of globalization for education. Without any doubt, the dominant form of neoliberal globalization has effected "competition-based reforms," transforming educational policy in K-12 and higher education. These reforms are characterized by efforts to create measurable performance standards through extensive standardized testing (the new standards and accountability movement), introduction of new teaching and learning methods leading to the expectation of better performance at low cost (e.g., universalization of textbooks), and improvements in the selection and training of teachers. Competition-based reforms in higher education tend to adopt a vocational orientation and reflect the point of view that colleges and universities exist largely to serve the economic well-being of a society. Privatization is a major reform effort linked to neoliberal globalization and perhaps the most dominant.[13]

The growing importance of comparative educational analysis is playing a larger role in the globalization of education worldwide. A telling example is the OECD Program for International Student Assessment, highly influential in many countries and regions of the world beyond the country members of OECD. This program constitutes a landmark decontextualized definition of quality of education, and is an example of how a focus on education based on cognitive scores runs counter to the available empirical evidence of how to define quality of education.

There is no question that multiple faces of globalization and globalization agendas described above are playing a major role in defining the role and purposes of education today, and more so when one confronts the dialectics of the global and the local.[14]

Global Citizenship Education

If models of global citizenship education are built to provide collaboration and global cooperation: What resources are to be deployed? What agendas will predominate? Will governments, NGOs or social movements choose to support the last cast of characters, the transformationists? Or, will they support the hyper-globalizers or the skeptics? Many people want to be in the middle and not at the extremes. If the decision is to support the transformationists: Which of the varieties should be key stakeholders? The local New Democrats or the cosmopolitan ones, including the new orientation towards global citizenship? Could global citizenship education work around all these agendas without contradictions? Empirical research should seek to sort out these categories and questions.

Regional Challenges to Global Citizenship Education

This section highlights, albeit at a highly generalized level, some of the issues and challenges that are relevant to the way global citizenship education in higher education may be perceived, adopted and implemented regionally.

Asia, an immensely diverse and complex region, is confronting the fragility and/or absence of democracy in many contexts. Notably, "shadow education" plays a unique role as an offshoot of highly competitive public educational systems (often including the need to master English and compete for study in the West). These practices result in contradictory cultural effects for traditional families. Moreover, in terms of educational policies, new dilemmas emerge when trying to create elite global research institutions that are purely technical. For example, this can result in problematic experiments with branch-plants of Western universities. All of this accounts for difficulties of pan-Asian citizenship versus the idea of global citizenship, which may be seen by many as a by-product of Westernization.

Latin America confronts the tension between private and public education within democratization that undermines elite motivations for quality public education, the need for mass inclusion at the base, yet encourages enough differentiation for elite research institutions (e.g., Brazil versus Venezuela). An outcome is the possibility of a regional citizenship such as Mercosur or ALBA as part of steps toward global citizenship.

Sub-Saharan Africa confronts the catastrophic brain drain problem outside of South Africa, the increasing impact of China, which is now the single largest investor (mostly in resources), and 1 million Chinese who now live in enclaves throughout the region. Sub-Saharan Africa is also confronting the dilemmas of "decolonizing" educational systems that were impoverished even in their Eurocentric colonial form and the challenge of creating a relatively autonomous higher education system with a capacity for knowledge production that is neither neocolonial nor a capitulation to the potential mystification of appeals to Afro-centric indigenous knowledge. However, Sub-Saharan Africa is also confronting a most serious challenge of how to construct global citizenship when tribal differences continue to undermine plural nation-states.

North Africa and the Middle West is confronting the challenge of how to construct a global Islam that can accommodate sufficient pluralism for democratic transitions and tolerance of difference. Clearly there is a need to confront the failures of the Arab Spring in the context of education beyond religious differences, and also confront the enduring tribal and ethnic ones. It is also important to highlight the danger (also evident in Asia) of attempting to de-link science and technology from their "Enlightenment" origins, and the potentially distinctive role of high-quality, private, secular educational institutions (e.g., Turkey) in a region that despite its rich cultural heritage otherwise lacks constructive educational models and global perspectives. Finally, the tension in some countries between expatriates and 'locals' make for a profound schism in the social fabric of society and another citizenship deficit.

Europe and North America face the key problems of citizenship created by undocumented immigrants, the increasing impoverishment of mass forms of post-secondary education, with the US and most European countries subjected to draconian fiscal reform and massive tuition increases in parts of Europe, led by England. Additionally, large segments of youth cohorts are losing hope for the security of a middle-class way of life and corresponding retirement given the declining value of investment in higher education, student debt, lack of qualified jobs and stratification of degrees. These are clearly processes that erode solidarity and global citizenship formation. The recent episodes around distressful racial relations, police violence and unfinished citizenship exemplified in the Ferguson, Missouri affair should not be ignored.

Facing these regional realities, there is a challenge presented by the former Secretary-General of the United Nations, Mr. Ban Ki-moon in his launching the 2012 initiative entitled The Global Education First Initiative. Launched on September 26, 2012, the Global Education First Initiative is a five-year initiative which constitutes a global advocacy platform at the highest level, claiming, in the former Secretary-General's own words, that "when we put Education First, we can reduce poverty and hunger, end wasted potential— and look forward to stronger and better societies for all."[15] This is the first time that a UN Secretary-General has launched such an ambitious project on education in the UN system. Is former Secretary-General Ban Ki-moon one of the most visible leaders of the cosmopolitan New Democrats and therefore a transformationist?

Because education is among its core focus, UNESCO is playing a major role in the design and implementation of the initiative. There are three pillars in this initiative: putting every child into school; improving the quality of learning; and fostering global citizenship. While the first and second pillar are essential to the work of most schools of education and institutions connected with the fields of educational teaching, research and practice, the third pillar, fostering a global citizen education, is particularly relevant.

But can we do this global citizenship or global cooperation model in the context of a network society, which emerges as one of the key features of the new models of globalization?

Is Global Citizenship the Logical Outcome of a Network Society

The challenges of global citizenship education should consider the limits but also the possibilities of a networking society. According to Castells[16] this network can function for good or ill. In the case of the latter, the question of networks of drug trafficking, organized crime or arms trafficking cannot be ignored. Castells went so far as to develop a construct called "informational capitalism," which considers information technology and telecommunications as new productive forces that impose new laws on operations of production.

As discussed in Morrow and Torres,[17] the new global economy is more fluid and flexible, with multiple lines of power and decision-making mechanisms, analogous to a spider's web, as opposed to the static pyramidal organization of power that characterized the traditional capitalist system. We know that access to information on its own cannot produce a social network for its users. Thus, it is necessary that, beyond access, there is the possibility of appropriation of information by users in the network.

Let us consider the positionality of social networks. First, it is important to remember the traditional classification of such into primary and secondary networks. *Primary networks*, according to this classification, accrue from spontaneous, involuntary and thus informal linkages. Prominent among these are familial networks, networks within neighborhoods and so forth. *Secondary networks* result from desires for communication and action that are agreed upon voluntarily by participating members, coming together consciously as formal entities.

Above and beyond this, it is important to remember that the social relationships that constitute such networks do not have common boundaries. Thus we see that a social network is a combination of connections of people and groups, both voluntary and involuntary, whose boundaries of action are not the same, but which present themselves as a structure that, in certain contexts, works to achieve common objectives. A social network is a type of response to social fragmentation, imposing itself on one hand as an alternative, on the other as a mediating force between the state and society, or between the public and private spheres.

In all social networks, norms of complementarity and reciprocity are formed. Though not always explicit, such norms are implied through the members' shared contextual interests. Just as in communication (i.e., there will be no communication beyond the speaker, the receiver, the common code, the channels and the secret message, as if the message content was known by all). In the interaction of social networks different complementing competencies and diverse interests are reified by the action of the other.

Here are some questions if one were to take advantage of the network society to advance the goals of global citizenship education. Creation and sustainability of networks require resources. How could global citizenship education create a steady flow of resources to support and sustain not only the established networks that exist in each region, but also the new networks that are emerging, such as those responding to the pleas of youths and youth movements? How does the construction of these networks and their support through global citizenship education help to dis-establish structural hierarchies rather than subsidize elites and reinforce hierarchies? How do these networks become seeds for active transformative global spheres? Universities constitute one of the answers in the construction of global spheres and global citizenship education, to be discussed further in the next section.

Universities and Public Spheres: Global and Local Imaginaries

Some would argue that universities, as part of the "public sphere" should contribute to "open science" and open codes of communication. Brian Pusser et al put it well:

> The public sphere was the interlocking set of institutions, networks and activities sustained in independent civil society, beyond the nation-state and transactions in the market while intersecting with them at many points. It was found in dining establishments, in salons and clubs, in theatres and writers' festivals, and universities—all the places where people met and talked—and in the plethora of civil organizations that focus on changing common opinion or behaviors. The public sphere was sometimes critical of the state, and sometimes provided crucial ideas and support for state projects. Above all it was a forum for critical intelligence and creative discussion about the issues of the day and, alongside family, community, market and nation-state it was one of the mediums in which social solidarity was formed.[18]

With this perspective of the potentiality of universities as public spheres, let me turn now to the connection between universities and global citizenship education. In doing so I will purposefully create a typology that resembles the one between cosmopolitans and locals presented in Chapter 4. I will be speaking about global universities and national universities, respectively. This typology is both descriptive and purposeful. It is descriptive because I focus on the differential agendas at play in the context of the dialectic of the global and the local. It is purposeful because it may provide a theoretical marker for empirical studies.

University rankings are made as strategic positioning devices that have become normalized in the life of institutions. Traditionally the field of higher education has been analyzed assuming that there are somewhat common standards, roles and functions of higher education in the contemporary world. Today this narrative seems brittle, conflating the analytical with the normative. Because rankings are a model of strategic thinking, there is a natural tendency to blur the multiple distinctions that exist in reality, hence encapsulating large, formal and complex institutions within discrete uniform categories. As a result, the variability among and across departments and schools is not fully captured and understood. It is at this departmental level that excellence thrives in institutions of higher education. In the end, a great deal of research and policy simply pays lip service to the extraordinary diversity of these institutions worldwide, ignoring the differential ways in which they respond to the challenges of the global and the local as well as its intersections, and ignoring the way these institutions survive while defining themselves in the process of social transformation that most institutions are going through.

Finally, my typology is provocative at a different level. I want to emphasize the tensions between the emerging context of fewer 'global universities' and the daily practice of a multitude of national universities, which cannot be understood in the same analytical and political way that we do global universities. A university position in the world system leaves a deep imprint in its ability to capture surplus wealth from the global system beyond its geographical/national borders. Its location and 'brand' enhances its ability to capture or siphon off brains (human resources) both at the level of international undergraduate and graduate students and distinguished faculty. In turn, those endowments and practices enhance their ability to obtain sizable research funds from federal, state and municipal governments in the richest societies. Their particularly successful histories and practices are rewarded in the production of knowledge and in being the home of Nobel Prize–winning scientists and writers. In short, their global agenda marks the life of global universities, which are transnational by definition, purpose, intent, practice and impact.

On the other end of the spectrum, national universities comprise a cornucopia of institutions working at different levels (national, regional, local) defined exactly in the opposite way that I have defined global universities.

Global Universities, National Universities and Global Citizenship Education

Universities are at a crossroads of justifying their existence and significance for knowledge and civilizations, perhaps like never before. There is no question that higher education, and particularly universities, have a plurality of functions and roles in society as described in Chapter 3 where I have also discussed the implications of neoliberal globalization in education and universities. My argument is that the impact of neoliberal globalization on universities raises several important questions: Do shifts toward a market-oriented ideology within the wider society suggest similar and inevitable shifts within universities? Do such shifts bring about the inevitable commodification of professional activities, family life and the environment, or the life of the professoriate? If such responses are unavoidable, does this necessitate a move in the direction of a free-market ideology on a global scale and hence a need for comparative data to assess who is who in higher education? To what extent can the emergence of a single, global monoculture in higher education be expected once we have established a firm ranking of quality universities on a world scale? While not all these questions can be addressed in a conceptual chapter like this one, I would like to provide a set of tentative answers that may guide empirical research on the subject.

Why Global Universities?

There is no question that the world has been globalized to the point that one of the principal apologists of globalization, journalist Thomas Friedman, has characterized the world as flat. This flatness is the product of transnational business executives who have made the world, according to Friedman, a level playing field of commerce, with all competitors having the same equal possibility of success if they adapt to the vagaries of free trade, the inevitability of fast change, the landscape of the digital culture, and the cutthroat lives in the street—though this time at a global level and not only in your own neighborhood.[19]

What are the goals of a global university for the 21st century? Facing the challenges of globalization, some universities become global research universities. They try to educate students but also develop new knowledge to take into account a changing world, a world full of hybridity, competing values, different histories and geographies, dynamics, social structures and population levels. Yet they operate in a world that is fully interlinked and interpenetrated, hence exposed to the world's epidemics, intensification of trade and circulation of people, shifting climates, consumer tastes, social imaginaries conveyed via mass media and the like. All of this is happening while global research universities are built around scientific models that are conducted in English and with metrics of evaluation tributaries of the Anglo-Saxon positivistic world—though standard scientific narratives particularly in the social sciences and humanities are contested and new narratives are emerging. Thus, the traditional roles and functions of universities are under pressure. There are five key dimensions that need to be incorporated into any analysis of the role and functions of global universities. These include global learning, global research, global reputation building, global engagement and global service. Some global research universities attempt to become scientific and cultural hubs in specific regions of the world fully supported by regional and national governments. These roles and responsibilities contrast with the roles and responsibilities that are supposed to be carried out in the nationally oriented universities.

Global learning speaks to the ways in which universities focus their theoretical and political orientation, trying to offer knowledge, skills and dexterities to specific individuals, many of them connected with elites or aspiring to be elites, and joining the ranks of the democratic cosmopolitans or the hyper-globalizers. Professors, researchers and particularly graduate students in these universities see themselves as working with the depository of knowledge that has been created by humanity and trying to enhance via models of creativity and ingenuity the new frontiers of capital accumulation. Even examples of now-iconic figures like Mark Zuckerberg, Steve Jobs and Bill Gates and others who have developed digital culture products that changed the way we live, interact, communicate and produce commodities, were ultimately university drop-outs—but they were organically connected or at least linked to universities that facilitate these innovation. Most of these universities are ranked today as global research universities.

The pursuit of *global research* is intimately connected to and defines the nature of global research universities. Moreover, because research ranks so highly in the context of global universities, becoming a research university is the trademark of the global university. This reverberates in the quality of its researchers and professors and its contributions to knowledge, technology and productivity worldwide. Global research is a centerpiece of *global reputation building*, which is intimately related to rankings and they have all but proliferated in the last three decades. Consider for instance *The Times Higher Education World University Rankings*, the *Washington Monthly College Guide*, *QS World University Rankings* and the most read in the United States, *US News & World Report*. The majority of rankings look at teaching (and how many international students are attracted to campus), international outlook, industry income resulting from innovations in the universities, the type of research and collaborations through publications by scholars situated in diverse national borders, the citations that their research attracts, research funding and an overall score. Finally, global universities aim to provide *global services* and in doing so seek avenues for *global engagement*. The type of service they aim to contribute goes beyond the national boundaries of the nations in which they are located, occasionally aided by contributions from major donors who are not even nationals but alumni and want to produce symbolic gestures with their philanthropy so they are remembered and recognized in their alma maters. Many of the great global universities in the world, particularly the private ones, have sizable endowments. The type of global engagement that global universities pursue relates to institutions of the world system, multinational corporations or national and/or international activities of their own nation-states. The recent rush to create university hubs in the Asia-Pacific area and the struggle to acquire international prestige in the region is another indicator of this global engagement.

National learning models seem to qualify at the other extreme of the continuum, or what I have called for lack of a better term the *national universities*. They tend to be located in cities, nations and or regions that are not prominent in the global system. They tend to be more teaching-oriented than research-oriented. They lack the physical and technological infrastructure that the global universities have. They may even be much younger than traditional global university, though not always is the case if one thinks of the University of Santo Domingo or the University of Córdoba, Argentina. Yet Cambridge and Oxford come to mind here as well established centuries-old universities. Many national universities are not comprehensive universities.

National learning universities rely on part-time professors and have a small number of full-time professors, with only some of them conducting research. They cannot pay the faculty salaries at the levels that global universities can pay and therefore are continuously subject to brain drain, with their best professors being 'poached' by global universities. They do not have the same level of qualification in their faculty. Many of them do not have their PhDs and are practitioners rather than full-time faculty. They may be liberal professionals who occasionally teach, or work as part-time professors.

National learning universities aim to help the communities in which they are situated and draw from this premise their principal political legitimacy. With few exceptions, they do not tend to have a national presence, let alone a global presence, though with the disparity in departments and schools, some may have departments that are world powerhouses of knowledge in specific disciplines, therefore more prominent than some of their global counterparts, or may house scholars who are very prominent in their own disciplines and therefore known internationally. The strength of national learning universities rests on their location and community connections. Family and community relationships explain why not everybody would like to migrate furthering their own academic careers. Their work on projects for national development, family commitments and personal experiences, to name just a few factors, matter a great deal to some scholars. Thus it is not easy for global universities to capture, through brain drain, each and every scholar they want to attract, especially internationally.

The degree of collaboration between industries and national learning universities tends to be very limited, though there are experiences that diverge from the norm. In national universities, the connection between university and industry is occasionally affected by the presence of radical groups opposed to this collaboration and/or student movements, social movements and political parties within the national political system that challenge relationships between the university and the business world, claiming that they undermine university autonomy. Yet they may also challenge, in the name of university autonomy, any fluid relationship with the governments of their own nations. They do not get well situated in the international rankings—because rankings usually pay attention only to the top 100 institutions—but may aspire to play some meaningful role in regional agreements (e.g., Mercosur, NAFTA, ASEAN, ALBA), more so than in the global system.

There are a number of questions that one may pose in attempting to understand the global role of universities. Should universities propose models of global citizenship education not only based on geopolitical considerations, diplomatic orientations, scientific or technical considerations, but on humanitarian reasons? If one were to focus on the question of human empowerment worldwide, one must focus on the role of global citizenship education to address the societal dilemmas that education is confronting.

The Quest for Human Empowerment

I have argued that economic inequality—the gap between the rich and the poor—is no longer a buzzword about capitalist economics. It is a palpable reality backed by research studies and reported in many books and newspaper articles and can be observed in urban environments throughout the world. The financial crisis that rocked the globe in 2008 has made strikingly evident the growing disparity between rich and poor and has adversely affected world democracies.

As an educator, I wonder when we will take crises of capitalism seriously and look to see how education can ameliorate social inequities, a divisive and insidious malady that consistently undermines all possibility for true social cohesion. The equity divide, however, is not just financial but cuts across educational and cognitive domains.

We are enmeshed in a number of societal dilemmas that are difficult to address. But let me say from the outset, and this is particularly important for concepts of global citizenship, that education is not a direct answer to economic inequality. Yet, the policies and practices of education can and should contribute to solving such problems if existing economic and social policies which aim to diminish or eliminate inequalities in society fail to do their job. Education is not a lever of development, but without education there cannot be any real economic growth.

But what is the state of education today? One central problem is that the prevailing schooling model that we inherited from the industrial society is exhausted, and with few notable exceptions, no new national or worldwide model has yet emerged to replace it. A second problem, magnified by the current economic crisis, is that we continue to extend educational opportunity and access to the underserved, which demands more and more resources be drawn from wealthy individuals, families and societies. Unfortunately, the growing inequality and lack of solidarity of the world elites who are unwilling to pay their share of expenses via taxes compound the financial educational problem.

Yet the world's system of production and consumption is unable to produce sufficient job opportunities for what has now become a highly qualified population of workers. For instance, the unemployment of youth in Europe is twice as high as the rate for the overall population, and in some countries like Spain it is even higher. Many of the last generations of college graduates in the US have either not found the jobs they aspired to or they have found part-time or full-time jobs below their level of education.

Early school learning, reading, writing and arithmetic continue to be serious challenges for children and youth who come from non-schooled cultures such as those of some African nations and other developing countries. This is also true for those who find an alienating curriculum in schools, especially when high-stakes testing is in place, as it is in the US. Teachers are under attack in many countries. Their status has diminished, they are badly paid, and they are blamed for the low academic performance of students and schools. Teachers' training, while recognized as a major factor in the improvement of educational systems, lack integration of theory and practice. Few of the research findings in educational research about teachers are ever disseminated let alone implemented, and teaching and learning methodologies continue to be implemented as top-down models in schools, very often lacking basic institutional foundations, particularly in the developing world.

Findings and recommendations of educational research work only when they reach the right person at the right time and through the right platform. Otherwise, tons of pages (and tons of megabytes) are shelved in real and virtual archives with the hope of impacting practice some day. Educational reform and transnational regulation has emerged as the last conundrum. There is talk that education is in crisis, which has led many governments to attempt a series of cyclical and episodic reforms. Teachers, many parents and public opinion alike feel a serious mistrust with political action—and politicians in general—and doubt any real or credible process of change can happen in schools.

Education has been overlooked as a tool for transformation of economic and social inequities for far too long, though there is clearly in the European Union a concern about active citizenship in the context of lifelong learning. Likewise, we may have lost sight of the importance of education for furthering global citizenship.

I wonder if I will see in my own lifetime a revolutionary movement of education as the practice of freedom elsewhere, a movement in which the technocratic tools are subordinate to a democratic political rationale and strategy of an education for human empowerment and liberation. This goal should be at the top of the overreaching goals of global cooperation programs and global citizenship education. My humble hope is that the research and policy-making ideas of progressive forces about global citizenship may help to change this regrettable state of affairs.

Notes

1. A previous version of this chapter was published in *European Journal of Education*, volume 50, number 3 (September 2015), pp. 262–280, reproduction with permission.
2. Rhoads and Torres, 2006; Torres, 2009a, 2009b, 2011b, 2013c.
3. Torres, 2011b, 2013c.
4. Held, 1991, p. 9.
5. Luke and Luke, 2000, p. 287.
6. Urry, 1998.
7. Castells, 1996, 1997; Touraine, 1968.
8. Torres, 2009a, 2009b.
9. Rhoads and Szelényi, 2011.
10. UNESCO, 2005.
11. Castells, 1996.
12. Giddens, 1994.
13. Torres, 2013b.
14. Arnove, Torres and Franz, 2013.
15. www.unesco.org/new/en/education/global-education-first-initiative-gefi/
16. Castells, 1996.
17. Morrow and Torres, 2013.
18. Brian Pusser, Ken Kempner, Simon Marginson, & Imanol Ordorika, 2011,, p. 2.
19. UCLA, 2014.

7 Multiculturalism in the World System

Towards a Social Justice Model of Multicultural Education

with Massimiliano Tarozzi

Introduction

Multiculturalism burst into many places in the world with the winds of globalization. Fueled by immigration, cultural hybridity and normative regimes from multilateral and bilateral organizations, multiculturalism is a new challenge particularly for Asian economies, their politics of culture and their higher education institutions. Moreover, although heavily implemented from the start of the last century in the United States and in Europe to some extent, multiculturalism and multicultural education signify a premise in constructing models of cosmopolitan democracies and what has been known as 'global citizenship education.' Drawing from the more mature experiences of the European Union (EU) and the United States in this field, this chapter traces the theoretical contours of and debates within multiculturalism. We focus on the learning experience across borders, which is well represented in international comparative education studies. It probes the occurrence of any crisis in the field of multiculturalism in the United States and EU. Lessons learned from a comparison of the US and EU experiences may be instructive to the Asian economies and cultures that are dealing with multiculturalism as a new force in the world system.

Crisis in the Field of Multiculturalism: The Case of the European Union and the United States

According to several US newspapers, European multiculturalism is dead, citing the failure of public policies on multiculturalism in Northern Europe. That is, these policies have unsuccessfully integrated immigrants, and their goal of respecting or even praising cultures has not contributed to social integration. As the argument goes, multiculturalism would create separate communities and eventually promote the emergence of internal enemies within the nation. American neoconservatives look to Europe with renewed hope and enthusiasm, rejoicing in political judgments set down by heads of state Angela Merkel, David Cameron and Nicolas Sarkozy. On October 17, 2010, German Chancellor Merkel had declared in a meeting of her conservative Christian Democratic Union party that multiculturalism had "utterly failed." Her remark was met with a standing ovation. One year later, Prime Minister Cameron described Britain's long-standing state-sponsored policy of multiculturalism as a "failure." France's former president Sarkozy espoused relatively the same sentiment, claiming that French public policies were heavily concentrated on the culture of those who arrived and insufficiently focused on the host culture.

These pronouncements are the result of a superficial debate that follows neoconservative and populist tendencies. Such tendencies have been prevalent in a Europe concerned with growing migration, fear of Islam and historical tolerance that has been annihilated by an exceptional economic crisis. Nevertheless, other and more sensible criticisms of multiculturalism and intercultural education have emerged beyond this superficial debate, which should be considered to advance a constructive response.

Post-multiculturalist scholars[1] or scholars who overcome the traditional approach of multiculturalism by recognizing its weaknesses while adhering to its fundamental aims, as well as public intellectuals, have criticized multiculturalism, arguing that political theory and policies, programmes and initiatives seem to consistently retreat from multiculturalism.[2] A most serious backlash to multiculturalism occurred in the EU.[3] If some of the most strident cases of anti-multicultural public policy (e.g., Arizona anti-immigrant law) were considered, then the same sentiment could be expressed about the United States.

In this chapter, we refer to multiculturalism as the dominant version of the struggle to incorporate diversity into the United States, and interculturalism as the dominant model for assessing diversity in EU schools. Overall, both sets of practices and traditions have parallels. The focus of both concepts is related but not identical. Multiculturalism emerged as a response to 20th century inter-group relations, addressing the challenge of racialization or integration, and is fully ingrained in the Civil Rights Movement of the 1960s, as well as the new civil rights movement of the 21st century.[4] By contrast, interculturalism chiefly addresses the question of the integration of immigrants and attempts to create intercultural mediation based on a flexible idea of culture and the pursuit of a new concept of citizenship.[5] However, both models tend to converge towards a similar situation. In the United States, exemplified in the debates about protection of the border and the recent conflicts about the draconian anti-immigration measures of Arizona and Alabama, the question of multiculturalism (and ethnic studies) has been conflated with the question of the invasion of undocumented immigrants, and therefore approximates the European situation. Very conservative sectors in the United States demand a differential integration, following the example of the majority of the European countries that do not automatically grant citizenship to the children of immigrants who are born in their territory.

Our question is not rhetorical: What type of multiculturalism is dead? The discourse about multiculturalism cannot be characterized as homogeneous and coherent. On the contrary, the ideas, policies and practices implemented under the umbrella of multiculturalism or interculturalism are too heterogeneous and diverse to be considered a monolithic model. Although multicultural education prevails in North America and more broadly in the Anglo-Saxon world and in some Northern European countries, intercultural education has spread within continental European countries as well as at the institutional level within the EU bodies' terminology.[6]

'Intercultural education' and 'multicultural education' are two umbrella terms subsuming a number of approaches.[7] European scholars posit that intercultural education encompasses multicultural education as well as antiracist education for minorities.[8] However, intercultural education has been made a monolithic model for political purposes by the establishment and politicians who are advancing agendas that may collide with some of the key proponents of multiculturalism. Creating strawman descriptions like 'multiculturalism' has important advantages. Firstly, pushing for a particular critique of a complex and elaborated model that can be easily conveyed by mass media (particularly television) in a few seconds and with sound bytes is a simple approach. Secondly, jointly with the simplification of the discourse that may please hegemonic media outlets, such appeals to nationalistic ideals create fortresses to defend a locality, a region, a tradition, an ethnicity or a nation from 'outside' influences and threats. This approach is particularly handy when dealing with the critique of immigration and persons who are '*sans papiers.*'

Our central thesis is as follows: A social justice–oriented inter/multicultural education is necessary for overcoming the contradictory implementation of current multicultural policies and practices. Otherwise, multiculturalism will remain a sliding signifier. Moreover, a social justice multicultural paradigm is the one that will nurture a global citizenship education.[9]

Multiculturalism as a Sliding Signifier: A Brief Theoretical Excursus

Multiculturalism comes in various forms. Some versions have faced a serious backlash, whereas others are still relevant categories that can be useful for the interpretation of contemporary societies, representing effective practices for addressing diversity in several public spheres.

Multiculturalism is grounded in different *political theories*, such as communitarianism,[10] critical pedagogy[11] critical theory,[12] critical race theory,[13] post-structuralist theory,[14] anti-racist theory[15] theories of subjugated knowledge[16] and post-development theory.[17] Less radical perspectives exist in the wake of liberalism, such as human capital theory, John Dewey's liberalism and even liberalism's reworking in a post-contractual viewpoint provided by John Rawls.[18]

Moreover, different *approaches* to inter/multicultural education exist. Any systematic analysis of the multiculturalism literature[19] will show that the major goals of multicultural education vary from developing ethnic and cultural literacy (i.e., expanding the degree of information about the history and contributions of ethnic groups that traditionally had been excluded from the curriculum) to personal development (i.e., developing pride in one's ethnic identity); from changing attitudes and clarification of values (i.e., challenging prejudice, stereotypes, ethnocentrism and racism) to promoting multicultural competence (i.e., learning how to interact with people who are different from ourselves, or how to understand cultural differences); from developing basic skill proficiency (i.e., improving the reading, writing and mathematical skills of people whose ethnic/racial/class background is different from the mainstream cultural capital that predominates in formal schools) to striving to simultaneously achieve educational equity and excellence (i.e., developing learning choices that work across different cultures and learning styles); to individual empowerment and social reform (i.e., cultivating students' attitudes, values, skills, habits and discipline to become social agents committed to reforming schools and society with the goal of eradicating social disparities, racism, gender and class oppression, and therefore improving equality of educational and occupational opportunities for all).

Multicultural education consists of the following five stages:[20]

- *Teaching the exceptional and the culturally different* (1960s). This approach aimed to help students considered at-risk to fit into the mainstream of US society by implementing strategies for remediating their deficiencies.
- *Intercultural Education Movement.* This undertaking was further developed into the human relations approach. It focused on the interpersonal relationship, aiming at reducing prejudices and conflicts among people.
- *Single-group studies.* Characterized by attention to a single cultural group (women, Asian Americans, Native Americans, African Americans), single-group studies stimulated social action by providing information about a group and created new academic fields and subjects (ethnic studies, women's studies, etc.).
- *Multicultural education.* Multicultural education emerged in the early 1970s. It is both a specific approach and the general term describing "education policies and practices that recognize, accept, and affirm human differences and similarities related to gender, race, disability, class, and (increasingly) sexual orientation."[21] The term links a wide range of issues, including race, culture, language, social class, gender and disability.
- *Multicultural education that is multicultural and social reconstructionist.* This approach emerged in the late 1970s and 1980s as a further development of the previous ones. It extended multicultural education from a simple classroom activity to the realm of social action. In the fifth edition of their work Sleeter and Grant[22] adopted the term "multicultural social justice education" as an approach focused on equity and power relations.

The very meaning of social justice education is confusing and lacking in precision, and as a political pedagogical concept, deeply contested.[23] Adding to these complexities, the same definition of multiculturalism as part of the 'politics of recognition' accounts for various uses. Multiculturalism is a social movement, a social and curriculum theory as well as an institutionalized set of administrative and pedagogical practices that deal with the question of diversity in schooling and higher education. The fact that multiculturalism as a state policy has been laid out on top of other layers of public policy, and what some may view as a retreat from state policies towards multiculturalism (exemplified by the statements made by politicians quoted at the beginning of this chapter) does not necessarily mean that the backlash against multiculturalism has spurred less multiculturalist programs, as suggested by research on the indexes of multiculturalism analyzing OECD countries by Keith Banting and Will Kymlicka. Banting and Kymlicka argue that, "Most countries that adopted multicultural approaches in the later part of the twentieth century have maintained their programs in the first decade of the new century; and a significant number of countries have added new ones. In much of Europe, multicultural policies are not in general retreat. As a result, the turn to civic integration is often being layered on top of existing multicultural programs leading to a blended approach to diversity."[24]

This chapter reflects on the compatibility of multiculturalism policies and civic integration, arguing that more liberal forms of civic integration can be combined with multiculturalism, but that more illiberal or coercive forms are incompatible with a multicultural approach.[25] Consequently, we need to clearly identify *which form* of multiculturalism is dead.

Two Versions of Multiculturalism: Normative versus Constructive

We propose a fundamental distinction between a *normative* and a *constructive* multiculturalism. The latter is combined with social justice education, which is intended as a radical approach, widespread in North America and in Anglo-Saxon countries in continental Europe. Although social justice education is not univocally defined, it has become almost a *mantra* among teachers, scholars, school authorities and social movements, particularly in the United States. However, social justice education is an inadequately and ambiguously developed concept, despite various attempts to conceptualize it and to ground its preconditions in various social theories relating to educational policy.

Educational theory can provide a solid answer to the conundrums of diversity in capitalist societies only by linking the concepts of multiculturalism and social justice. To support our argument, we need to start from a fundamental divide between two forms of multiculturalism, namely, normative multiculturalism and constructive multiculturalism.

Normative multiculturalism, or strong multiculturalism, emerged in the 1970s and further developed in the 1980s. It is rooted in a rigid conception of cultures as objective, immutable and reified. It assumes that cultures can be univocally defined and that members have identical forms of belonging within them. Conservatives have used this brand of multiculturalism to highlight a civilization clash or to emphasize the need to protect national cultures from the dangerous hybridization induced by incoming migrant cultures. However, normative multiculturalism has also been used by progressives to liberate oppressed and discriminated groups.[26] In the public sphere, this multiculturalism entails concessions, grants and privileges to safeguard minority cultures in various sectors (health, religion, welfare, political representation, etc.) and to protect traditional languages, confessional schools or religious habits and customs. In sum, normative multiculturalism is an institutional perspective that is rooted in a political project based on a culturalized interpretation of the public sphere, requiring a rigid conception of culture.

By contrast, *constructive multiculturalism* is rooted in a mobile conception of cultures, which are never conclusively defined but are visible in both the private and public spheres and across interpersonal relationships. According to this vision, cultures are dynamic processes that are constantly influenced by contexts, circumstances and relationships and constantly changing. Cultures are neither static nor deterministic and therefore are never an indisputable destiny for individuals and groups.[27] Nor will a given culture be identified as a homogeneous identity without important fractures, tensions and contradictions among those who claim to belong to or are signified as part of such culture. This type of multiculturalism does not aim to reorganize society on the basis of the recognition of cultural groups' rights; instead, it seeks to establish fair rules of living together on the basis of cultural exchanges that require a rethinking of the notion of citizenship as predicated in this book.

Despite the struggles among subordinate groups that endeavor to position themselves in the context of the social struggle of civil minimums, and despite the rhetoricians who have made academic careers speaking about various forms of multiculturalism as if they were the forefathers of a new revolutionary movement, normative multiculturalism can be considered dead, if it was ever alive. Hence, the capacity of normative multiculturalism to influence public policies, institutions and practices outside the academic debate may be subject to variable interpretations.

However, cultural diversity cannot be eliminated as one of the substantive methods of defining our individual and collective identities. Moreover, the different models of globalization that we have experienced, particularly in the past three decades, have amplified in a gigantic soundboard-like fashion the discussions and the contradictions of diversity in capitalist societies. Although the motto 'unity in diversity' continues to be a reasonable approach that has animated a number of intelligent analyses of the conundrum of being different and simultaneously attempting to live together productively and peacefully,[28] two questions remain.

Firstly, how should we arrive at such scenario of a reasonable articulation of interests, or of a reasonable accommodation of different religious, political, economic, social and cultural practices, or at least a peaceful model of articulation of public policy, without criminalizing dissent or manufacturing consent as a method of preserving the governability of every day less governable democracies in the context of world capitalism? Secondly, what is the role of education in this scenario, both as a public policy and as school practice? Without answering these questions, the struggle for multiculturalism is a ruse, a window dressing to preserve the legitimacy of systems and legacies.

The influence of constructive multiculturalism is particularly evident in education, in which one of the conundrums of normative multiculturalism appears—that is, the theoretical conflict between culture and equality. Constructive multiculturalism should overcome the idea that respecting diverse minority groups denotes justifying social inequality. Particularly in Europe, the multicultural (normative) rhetoric has obscured the universal notion of equality stemming from the Enlightenment[29] and therefore for some scholars has weakened the struggle affirming social justice.[30]

The classical Enlightenment notion of equality, which is one of the pillars of modern liberal democracies, entails the formal equality of all citizens before the law and equal rights (i.e., the same opportunities regardless of diversities of gender, race, faith, sexual orientation or political perspective). This notion of equality, which is the basis for the idea of *fair education equality*[31] and allows democracies to fight against growing economic and social inequalities of the present globalized world, has been often overshadowed by multicultural rhetoric.[32]

By contrast, a multiculturalism focusing only on individual rather than collective rights renders the impossibility to confront some fundamental societal tensions, including discrimination, oppression and the hegemony of the majority. Through constructive perspective, culture still makes sense in socially constructed collective identities, in marking boundaries of difference between groups and in establishing power hierarchies, opportunities of inclusion or exclusion, as well as common norms and regulations based on these boundaries.

According to constructive multiculturalism, culture is not the only dimension that constitutes collective and individual identities. Moreover, cultures are not monolithic entities, but have rich internal variety and difference, tensions and contradictions. Therefore, establishing any type of intercultural dialogue entails the selection of those aspects of a culture "that represent the widest circle of reciprocity within that culture, the version that goes furthest in the recognition of the other."[33]

This premise may spur a model that seeks a 'reasonable accommodation' as provided by Bouchard and Taylor's analysis for harmonization practices in Quebec.[34] Bouchard and Taylor assume that several factors are involved, from a crisis of perceptions (and hence the role of mass media), to anxiety over identity, to the presence of secularism and its influence in the diversity of Quebec. This model of accommodating diversity, grounded in the legal-juridical tradition of Quebec, and in the political tradition of citizenship rights and obligations, is one of the most substantive models designed in a North American society. Although such model was a subject of ample debate in Quebec and even across Canada, simply the idea of finding models of accommodating different views in ways that could be used to the advantage of citizenship building, while simultaneously respecting the traditions and histories of those views and voices, is a mild yet remarkable example of social engineering.

In addition, constructive multiculturalism can recover the quest for equity and justice when combined with a culture-bound social justice perspective. Multiculturalism has overemphasized cultures as unique or major hallmarks of collective identities. By contrast, social justice and/or human rights approaches emphasize a concept of equality as an individual right.

Multiculturalism and interculturalism have been criticized for conflating the analyses of the social conditions and class assessment by paying excessive attention to the cultural dimension.[35] Focusing on cultural diversity is sometimes viewed as superficial, rendering social inequalities untouched and fragmenting the opposition of the oppressed by preventing them from fighting together for common social goals; in other words, "a politics of multiculturalism undermines a politics of redistribution."[36]

Multiculturalism, and even more so interculturalism, endorses a limited concept of equality.[37] By "limited," we mean relevant only to the recognition of cultural equality, ignoring the notion of equality as distributive justice. *Cultural equality* is not the same as *equal opportunities for cultures*, and overly stressing the former can result in disregarding the latter. Therefore, even within a multicultural education approach, issues of underachievement, drop-outs, racism, violence and crime, to name a few, must be addressed. At the same time, social justice education cannot ignore cultural diversity and consider individuals in a neutral, homogeneous manner by ignoring the cultural aspects of identity.

Change occurs very slowly in market democracies. When the dynamics of these changes claim to address the rights of diversity and the equal dignity of all groups, recognizing equal dignity for all cultural groups is inadequate. The promotion of equity within a social justice framework is therefore necessary.

Social justice education does not merely celebrate cultural diversity, but also examines and criticizes the role of society's structures in creating discrimination and institutional oppression experienced by certain groups, *a priori* limiting equal education opportunities.[38]

Constructive multiculturalism can claim equity and social justice. However, intercultural dialogue should be considered to make constructive multiculturalism work. Emphasizing the idea that we are not working in a zero-sum society, in which one group gains and the other invariably loses, is essential as well.

Change needs to be extracted through pressure, activism, defiance, critique, commotion, conflict and contradiction. The successes of the Arab Spring, Occupy Wall Street and the European Indignados are to some extent testimonies of the truism that nothing changes unless a revolutionary model exists. The aforementioned examples demonstrate that insurgent models can shake the very foundations of modern capitalist societies, revealing them as a house of cards.

The impasse between a European intercultural model unable to propose coherent policies, and a normative multicultural model stuck in the rigid notions of monolithic and segregated cultural groups, can be overcome by combining cultural diversity with a political tension between empowerment and disempowerment. In other words, cultural diversity can be considered a meaningful key for interpreting contemporary society and school reform only by linking diversity to power relations on a global scale and ascertaining how these policies exercise such power. Posing the question of cultural diversity and social equality along this continuum from empowerment and disempowerment may help identify the conditions to support intercultural dialogue based on equality.

The Enlightenment believed that we would become modern when we could eliminate cultural particularisms and pass from *Gemeinschaft* (community) to *Gesellschaft* (society).[39] However, (late) modernity has produced differences and revitalized a romantic idea of culture, roots and community instead. In the last two decades of the 20th century, the notion of culture has flourished and become an interpretive key for post-modernity. However, this same notion of culture, so ambiguous and polysemous, is also taken for granted and widely used in naïve ways.

The cultural-based identity of a group indubitably exists, but it depends on several factors, some of which are not always circumscribable. Cultural identity primarily depends on power relations established within a certain context. Therefore, ethnicity can be legitimately defined in various ways, by including or excluding elements such as gender, age, class, education, productive status/role, membership in specific organizations, etc. Anthropologists suggest considering ethnic identity as no more than a 'regulative fiction' which may stimulate anthropological discourse, but is insubstantially founded.[40] Thus, ethnic identities are always complex, plural, mixed, mobile and continuously recreated by people confronting their daily environment.

Unfortunately, both intercultural and multicultural education have ethnicized culture as a form of reductionism. In both discourses, but particularly within multicultural education, culture has been overemphasized. These approaches claim to protect the uniqueness of a culture by simplifying its features, and by default, stereotyping and prototyping its members, and by logical implication, stereotyping and prototyping members of other cultures.

Constructive multiculturalism reflects a basic epistemological principle of Paulo Freire's conscientization model: We have to learn to live with

tensions and contradictions but continue to work and walk towards a utopian future. By considering the tensions around the processes of empowerment and disempowerment, even across nations, we may reach an inter/
multicultural social justice education paradigm, rooted in the flexible and
negotiated identities well illustrated by new migrants moving within the
present globalized scenario. In this manner, a constructive inter/multicultur-
alism can evolve into an inter/multicultural social justice education.

What Multiculturalism Can Learn from Interculturalism, and Vice Versa

We lack the space to adequately compare multicultural education, which
prevails in North America, with the intercultural model mainstreaming
in Europe.[41] However, we would like to offer some insights gleaned from
this comparison of two different approaches. Deep historical, cultural
and theoretical differences exist between these approaches, primarily in
how they treat cultural differences and their ensuing social and educational responses.[42]

Although the intercultural model is highly problematic, the multicultural
model has been widely criticized as well. The multicultural model has had
the undeniable merit of moving the category of diversity from the margins
to the mainstream in the social and political interpretation of contemporary
society. However, it has offered a univocal response to manifold changes. At
the same time, it has raised basic questions, to which it has been unable to
provide adequate and convincing responses.

We argue that some strong points of the US approach can respond effec-
tively to the European weak points, and vice versa. From our perspective,
the United States can teach Europe at least two lessons; in turn, the United
States can learn two lessons from the European experience.

First Lesson: The United States Reminds Europe That Education Is Always Political

In the United States, multicultural education has had from the very beginning an eminently political character. Therefore, professionals and laypeo-
ple are widely aware that schooling has to do with political decisions that
are never neutral.[43] In this sense, multicultural education cannot be understood in a social and political vacuum. Indeed, no educational philosophy is
worthwhile unless it focuses on raising the achievement of all and providing
students with an opportunity to become full citizens.

Diversity in the United States is a matter of fact. In this country, the diversity of race, gender, culture, disability and sexual preference makes sense as
a claim to fill the gap of inequalities. Moreover, education can play a major
role in promoting equality of rights and opportunities, starting from equal
academic achievement. Public education is considered the 'great equalizer'

because it is supposed to remove the barriers of class and provide all students with equal access to a similar education.[44]

By contrast, in Europe, intercultural education is a predominantly technical approach (European Council 2008). This approach is a strategy of schooling, a teaching method or at most an educative horizon that is always related more to practice than to political action. It is a perspective that operates only on the surface of phenomena and leaves untouched the profound structure of social dynamics that cultural confrontation implies. Therein lies one of its chief limitations. Intercultural education faces social and political issues that neither begin nor end in the classroom.

Second Lesson: The EU Regards Immigration as Substantive to the Intercultural Arena

In the EU, intercultural education has been a response to the recent issue of immigration and not a model for the integration of linguistic or cultural minorities. Immigration is considered a key issue both at the Europe-wide level and by every national state, which requires appropriate responses from the education. The total population of immigrants throughout the world is about 232 million (UN Department of Economic and Social Affairs 2013). The status of this population represents better than others the contradictions and conundrums related to diversity and its recognition. The migrant is the most realistically emblematic condition of the planetary economy and culture nowadays. However, the United States apparently lacks a deep understanding of immigration because it continues to tackle it as a local problem.

In Europe and in the United States, recent immigration is a burning global issue. By 2005, more than 35 million immigrants were living in the United States, representing 12.5% of the total population; by 2040, one-third of all children are expected to grow up in an immigrant household.[45]

This phenomenon is an outcome of the global economy. It is not an autonomous process unrelated to other international processes. Thus, immigration is similarly attributed to the economic involvement of rich countries in the global economy and not only to the poor socio-economic conditions of the developing countries.[46] In this sense, measures to repel immigrants at the border and to block or deport illegal immigrants are completely useless.

The EU is not a good example of coherent and unitary policies for immigration either. Nevertheless, in educational terms, intercultural education is based on the acceptance of newcomers. This set of priorities has limitations but it has also stirred a huge debate and school innovations on various themes, such as the insertion of students during the school year, bilingualism and the teaching of a second language.

The native language of an individual is certainly a civil rights issue, but it assumes new meanings within the European framework, in which multilingualism is a widely promoted asset for the same demographic situation.

Within multilingual Europe, a widespread assumption is that in a global society, monolingualism is a dangerous anachronism and bilingualism, as a form to guarantee the same rights to the non-English speakers, is only a limited response.

Third Lesson: In the United States, Multicultural Education Means Social Justice Education

In the United States, diversity and diversity recognition make sense only within a social justice framework. Multicultural education is a means of dealing with social justice issues. This factor underlies the argument that multicultural education is social justice education.[47]

Recognizing the equal dignity of cultures is insufficient. Equality must be recognized within the framework of social justice. According to the European sociologist Michel Wieviorka, no difference exists without inferiorization and dominion; conversely, domination is a concept that cannot be employed with individuals, but only with collective categories.[48] Therefore, multicultural education aspires not only to accept and respect cultures, but also to empower students. Moreover, multicultural education cannot be defined without specifically focusing on academic achievement for all.

In Europe, diversity and school achievement have been perceived synchronously only recently (and only after the 2006 PISA test). The adoption of a limited concept of equality is one of the major shortcomings of the intercultural education practice. The European approach should pay more attention to social justice and to the socio-economic factors that influence school achievement. Paradoxically, the United States, which is growing increasingly unequal, can teach Europe that diversity and justice are not necessarily incompatible, but that these concepts can and should be combined in a workable paradigm.

Fourth Lesson: In the EU, Cultural Hybridization Is at the Center of the Debate

The prevailing education approach in Europe intentionally emphasizes the prefix "inter" to outline the special attention paid to the relationship, the exchange, the dialogue among cultures, as well as their mixing. By contrast, US multiculturalism has stiffened the cultures. As provocatively denounced by Pierre Bourdieu, the debate on diversity has been monopolized by a North American approach[49] and hence disregards the phenomena of hybridization, mixture and creolization typical of the European debate.

Metissage, which allows not only the reproduction but also the production of the difference, cannot find any political or juridical expression.[50] However, multiculturalism does. It offers political responses to recognition demands. Nevertheless, in doing so, multiculturalism may end up petrifying differences. The evaluation of the hybrid dimensions of individuals as members of a group without losing subjectivity or the membership to a collective difference is a challenge for education and public policy.

Epilogue

From the previous analysis of the parallel outcomes of the US and EU traditions, and the new winds of change in Asia considering questions of diversity and equity, we realize that a historical impasse has occurred. On the one hand, if we emphasize dialogue, hybridity and a weak notion of culture, then we fail to underline the quest for equity and justice endorsed by US multiculturalism. On the other hand, if we highlight the political dimension at the bottom of the cultural claims, then we support a social separation among groups and an unacceptable cultural essentialism, as the European approach has illustrated.

This antinomy has induced a new conservatism, which, traditionally hostile towards enhancing cultural pluralism, has now taken advantage of the anti-immigrant and anti-multicultural political climate. This backlash against multiculturalism is expected to occur in Asia once multiculturalism is fully implemented in the educational systems. The easiest responses of populist governments and some intellectuals that are organic to them are to reject the idea of cultural difference and to clamor for common values, trans-cultural universalism and national identity, which can protect the Western world from all types of enemies, including terrorists, the poor and unassimilable immigrants.

We think differently. We believe that diversity remains a key concept for understanding the contemporary world; it is constantly mobile and complex and should be combined with the equality of rights. We deem that education can play a major role in understanding diversity.

In this chapter, we addressed a distinction between constructive and normative multiculturalism. Although the latter is dead in the education field, the former, based on a weak idea of dynamic and relational culture, remains an effective approach for addressing diversity in public policies and practices. In particular, the approach helps us understand the complex migration processes impacting contemporary democracies. Constructive multiculturalism that combines a flexible, mobile and different idea of cultural identity with a claim for equity and social justice against discrimination and oppression can set the premises for building education policies and practices that are oriented towards an equitable and fair intercultural dialogue.

Through our comparative and international analysis, we seek to provide a sense of hope even in the context of the worst economic and environmental crises of our generation; even when education is being discounted as a solution to these emerging and multifarious crises; and even when some people believe that the organized governance models that have succeeded to maintain the tension between democracy and capitalism at a manageable level do not work any longer.[51]

Despite the odds, Eduardo Galeano's words quoting his friend Fernando Birri invite us to utopia, a fitting ending for this chapter:[52]

> Utopia lies at the horizon. When I draw nearer by two steps, it retreats two steps. If I proceed ten steps forward, it swiftly slips ten steps ahead. No matter how far I go, I can never reach it. What, then, is the purpose of utopia? It is to cause us to advance.

Notes

1. Banting and Kymlicka, 2010; Kymlicka, 2010.
2. Vertovec and Wessendorf, 2010.
3. Peters and Besley, 2014.
4. Bell, 1995; Landson-Billings and Tate, 1995.
5. Abdallah-Pretceille, 1999; Alleman-Ghionda, 2009; Gundara and Jacobs, 2000.
6. Maxwell, Waddington, McDonough, Cormier, and Schwimmer, 2012.
7. Hill, 2007.
8. Alleman-Ghionda, 2009.
9. We developed and documented this thesis in Tarozzi and Torres, 2017.
10. Etzioni, 1995; Sandel, 1982; Taylor, 1992,
11. McLaren, 1997.
12. Torres, 1998b, 2009a.
13. Ladson-Billings, 2004.
14. Sleeter and Grant, 1999.
15. Leicester, 1992.
16. Semali and Kincheloe, 1999.
17. Morrow, 2008.
18. Rawls, 1993, 2001.
19. Banks, 2009; Banks and McGee, 1995; Nieto, 1996; Sleeter, 1996; Sleeter and Grant, 1999.
20. Sleeter and Grant, 1999.
21. Ibid., p. 150.
22. Sleeter and Grant, 1999.
23. Gewirtz, 1998; North, 2006; Torres, 1998.
24. Banting and Kimlicka, 2013, p. 577, the quotation is from the abstract.
25. Ibid.
26. Benhabib, 2002.
27. Nieto, 1996.
28. Freire, 1998.
29. Barry, 2001.
30. Fraser, 1997; Tarozzi, 2015; Touraine, 1997.
31. Rawls, 2001.
32. Sen, 1992.
33. de Sousa Santos, 2002, p. 55.
34. Bouchard and Taylor, 1999.
35. Barry, 2001; Fraser, 1997; Gorski, 2006.
36. Barry, 2001, p. 8.
37. Tarozzi, 2005.
38. McDonald and Zeicher, 2009; Torres and Noguera, 2009.
39. Tönnies and Loomis, (1872) 1957.
40. Galissot, Kilani, and Rivera, 2000.

41. The arguments are further elaborated in Tarozzi and Torres, *Global Citizenship Education and the Crises of Multiculturalism.* London: Bloomsbury, 2017.
42. Grant and Portera, 2011; INRP, Institut National de Recherche Pédagogique, 2007; Santos Regò and Nieto, 2000.
43. Nieto, 1996.
44. Dewey, 1916.
45. Suarez-Orozco, Suarez-Orozco, and Todorova, 2008.
46. Sassen, 1998.
47. Nieto, 1996.
48. Wieviorka, 2001.
49. Bourdieu and Vacquant, 1999.
50. Amselle, 1998; Gruzinski, 1999.
51. Fukuyama, 2012.
52. Galeano, 1993, p. 230.

8 Global Citizenship Education and Global Peace *Vive la liberté!*[1]

Vive la liberté should be our battle cry. *Vive la liberté* should be the only possible reaction of educators and people of goodwill confronted with astonishment and sadness facing episodes of violence, brutal intolerance, social alienation, ethnic nationalism and violent religious fundamentalism of any stripe. *Vive la liberté* is our battle cry, and we should say this loud and clear to all people of goodwill who listen and are ready to act.

Recently as President of the World Council of Comparative Education Societies (WCCES), I added my voice on my behalf and in the name of WCCES to the clamor of people in solidarity with France and Nigeria, sites of two recent violent reminders that we still need in our human civilization more social justice, more peace and more dialogue across world views of many colors, languages and creeds. *Vive la liberté* is not only hope that we learned from the Enlightenment but our commitment to solidarity in peace. *Vive la liberté* should be the clamor of the Mexican people bitterly angered by the fluid working connections and relationships between narco-traffickers, police and civic leaders in Iguala, Guerrero Mexico, that cost the lives of dozens of student-teachers from a rural *école normal* in the region.

I write this chapter for the Second Forum of Global Citizenship Education, and in the year of celebration of the 70th anniversary of UNESCO in solidarity with the people and governments of Mexico, France and Nigeria and so many other places in which anonymous people have fallen because of structural violence, prejudice, irrationality and violent religious fanaticism.

These brutal violent events remind me that France, the land that gave us Voltaire and Rousseau with their deep commitments to education; Mexico who gave us Octavio Paz, Alfonso García Robles and Elena Poniatowska; and Nigeria, the country that gave us Chinua Achebe and Wole Soyinka, and as an African country is also the land of Ubuntu—which is a celebration of the collective ethos of the people and the nation—may show that all our best educational efforts in public and private education perhaps have failed. If so, we shall try again.

The question to educators, communities and governments is how can we create the conditions for Ubuntu and the Enlightenment and other egalitarian traditions to come alive again. We have no other choice. And if all other educational efforts have failed to convince men and women of goodwill of the need for rationality in preserving peace, nature, human lives and freedom, we shall start again. To preserve rationality and freedom, we must build a global citizenship education worldwide because we have no choice. We shall start again.

In closing this preface, I would like to remind us of the lessons provided by one of the most important *pensadores* of the 20th century, Herbert Marcuse. One of his lessons, in the middle of the cultural wars of the 1960s in the United States and the turmoil particularly in universities during the Vietnam War era, is that we have to make a distinction between liberating and repressing, or humane and inhumane teaching practices. As he indicated in 1965 to us, "this distinction is not a matter of value-preference but of rational criteria."[2]

Moreover, Marcuse, drawing from Freud, reminded us, "'Alienation' is the constant and essential element of identity, the objective side of the subject—and not as it is made to appear today, a disease, a psychological condition."[3]

With due notice to Marcuse's prophetic words, I still would argue that *Vive la liberté!* should be the motto of all people of the world struggling to build in solidarity a global citizenship education on the foundations of the Enlightenment as freedom and Ubuntu as educational ethics.

1. Global Citizenship Education and Global Peace

A claim of this chapter is that global citizenship education contributes to global peace. But how can we define global peace? The Global Peace Index ranks 162 countries covering 99.6 percent of the world's population. The Index gauges global peace using three themes: the level of safety and security in society, the extent of domestic or international conflict, and the degree of militarization. It ranks countries according to 22 indicators of peace.[4] Some of the key findings of the Global Peace Index are that:

i) Peace is correlated to indicators such as income, schooling and the level of regional integration;
ii) Peaceful countries often shared high levels of transparency of government and low corruption;
iii) Small, stable countries that are part of regional blocks are most likely to get a higher ranking.[5]

What are the main problems affecting global peace? Domination, aggression, exploitation, discrimination and oppression of people, families, communities, nations and the planet are crucial elements to undermining progress, peace and happiness on Earth.

Paulo Freire, recognizing that relations of domination are central to public and private life, argued that domination, aggression and violence are an intrinsic part of human and social life.[6] Any political education nourishing the construction of a public sphere should recognize that overcoming oppression, domination and exploitation is a central goal of any project of global democratic citizenship building.[7]

There are multiple manifestations of structural violence which add to individual, collective and government actions undermining peace. I would like to emphasize briefly some of the cardinal sins in the global system undermining peace and prosperity. These cluster of problems include but cannot be restricted to: 1) unabating poverty; 2) growing inequality; 3) neoliberal globalization, which has weakened the systems of organized solidarity of the democratic nation-state; 4) banking education with authoritarian and inadequate curriculum in elementary, secondary and higher education; and 5) destruction of the planet's ecosystem. What follows is a brief description of each cluster problems, which will deserve a specific in-depth description and analysis that cannot be provided herein.

Inequality

In his monumental study, *Capital in the Twenty-First Century*, Thomas Piketty, professor at the École des Hautes Etudes, argues, "Today, in the second decade of the twenty-first century, inequalities of wealth that had supposedly disappeared are close to regaining or even surpassing their historical highs. The new global economy has brought with it both immense hopes (such as the eradication of poverty) and equally immense inequalities (some individuals are now as wealthy as entire countries)."[8]

Poverty

Unabating poverty remains a stubborn fact deeply affecting the daily life of billions of people. Measurements of poverty abound, showing unequivocally that poverty and social exclusion are persistent, more so in rural areas than in urban areas—though the marginal labor force in urban areas, having migrated from the rural areas, remain mostly in an occupational limbo and temporary jobs. While the 2014 World Bank Global Monitoring Report[9] claims that there are gains, the line of demarcation of extreme poverty (people living under the poverty line of 1.25 US dollars per day) constitutes one-seventh of the world population!

Neoliberal Globalization

Neoliberalism has utterly failed as a viable model of economic development, yet the politics of culture associated with neoliberalism are still in force, becoming the new common sense shaping the role of government and education. Privatization policies are preferred policy instruments, even if the outcome of some of its instruments, as in the implementation of vouchers, are not clear in their benefits against traditional models of financing schooling.

This 'common sense' has become an ideology playing a major role in constructing hegemony as moral and intellectual leadership in contemporary societies. Two elements radically affect the formulation of public policy: privatization and the reduction of public spending. These two policies are highly compatible, and in fact, privatization can be considered an important strategy for achieving reductions in public spending.

The privatization policies require additional explanation. These policies are crucial elements of the reforms oriented toward promoting markets and, as such, they are important policy tools of neoliberalism. On the one hand, the pressure of fiscal spending is reduced by the privatization of public sector enterprises. On the other, privatization is also a powerful instrument for depoliticizing the regulatory practices of the state in the area of public policy formation. That is, privatization plays a pivotal role in the neoconservative and neoliberal models.[10]

Neoliberal globalization, predicated on the dominance of the market over the state and on deregulatory models of governance, has deeply affected the university in the context of 'academic capitalism.' The resulting reforms, rationalized as advancing international competitiveness, have affected public universities in four primary areas: efficiency and accountability, accreditation and universalization, international competitiveness and privatization. There is also growing resistance to globalization as top-down-imposed reforms reflected in the public debates about schooling reform, curriculum and instruction, teacher training and school governance. One of the most dominant outcomes of neoliberal policies and their attempt to undermine the regulatory policies of nation-states is the dilution of organized solidarity, and particularly the safety network implemented in the models (with national and regional variations) of the welfare state.

Neoliberal globalization is not wholly hegemonic, pervasive, all-encompassing or uncontested at the local and global levels. Likewise, while I insist that, in terms of policy orientations, the age we are now living is the age of neoliberalism, it does not, as any hegemonic model, go uncontested, nor has it demonstrated itself to be technically and, more importantly, politically, capable of ruling with an 'iron fist' that cannot be challenged or defeated.[11]

Banking Education

Traditional models of education built on the power of teachers in the classrooms through a teacher-centered pedagogy, and the overwhelming power of educational bureaucracies, had been challenged and criticized by Paulo Freire and a host of educational reformers as banking education. Paulo Freire collaborated with UNESCO for a long time, including working from 1987 to 1995 as a jury member of UNESCO's International Literacy Prizes, receiving the 1996 UNESCO Prize for Peace Education.

The metaphor of banking education, based on the idea that students are empty vessels that need to be filled with knowledge, is a strong metaphor that calls for changes at several levels. One of the key changes is to recognize that the students that come to our classrooms are of all ages, bring with them knowledge and experience, and can make serious contributions to teaching and learning. Freire posits this in the analogy of the teacher as a student (which is an obvious fact since we continue to learn until our last breath) and the student as a teacher (since they bring questions, analysis or live experiences that enrich, challenge, defy and even improve upon the instructional design). Authoritarian educational models, as argued by Freire and a number of pedagogues of liberation, undermine student autonomy and creativity, and reproduce rules and regulations that perpetuate domination, exploitation and oppression. The alternative that has been suggested is problem-posing education, which confronts students with questions, and very often their own questions, in learning and instructions, rather than "off-the-shelf" preconceived answers based on instrumental rationality.

For banking education, the teacher is the subject of the pedagogical adventure and the student is the object. Freire's contribution to understanding education as the act of freedom is an invitation to see the interminable dialectics in the struggle to free ourselves and to free others from constraints to freedom. In and of itself, the struggle for liberation is another form of intervention that can be considered part of the ethics of intervention. Certainly, education as the act of freedom implies a different perspective on local, socially constructed and generationally transmitted knowledge. It also implies a perspective that challenges normal science and non-participatory planning, constructing a theoretical and methodological perspective that is always suspicious of any scientific relationship as concealing relationships of domination. At the same time, while freedom is still to be conquered, freedom can be conquered because unequal, exploitative relationships are built by human beings and can be changed by human beings.[12]

Predatory Cultures and Destruction of the Planet

Predatory cultural and technical practices have deeply affected ecosystems. The planet is our only home, and we should prevent its ecological destruction. After a UN decade of education for sustainable development, the need for policy orientations linking planetary citizenship, global citizenship education, sustainable development and global peace is clear.[13]

These are some of the cardinal sins of the global system that must be confronted by the implementation of global citizenship education as an educational counterpart of global policy reform in areas of economics, politics, morality and ethics.[14]

A claim in this chapter is that any definition and theory of global citizenship as a model of intervention to promote global peace and sustainable development should address what has become the trademark of globalization: cultural diversity. Therefore, global citizenship should rely on a definition of *global democratic multicultural citizenship*. In addition, to be effective and acceptable worldwide, conceptualizing and implementing global citizenship with education, it is imperative that global citizenship adds value to national citizenship! Yet the expansion of a universalistic claim of world solidarity rests on the concept of cosmopolitan citizenship nested in a model of cosmopolitan democracies.[15]

Global citizenship cannot be seen as an alternative to or a substitution for national citizenship. On the contrary, it is a substantive policy tool to reinforce the robustness of representative and participatory democracies worldwide. Global citizenship education ultimately seeks to guarantee the social democratic pact on the rights of persons, and not only the rights of property (Bowles and Gintis, 1986; Torres, 1998b). Yet there is more. We have learned after a decade of education for sustainable development that we need also to guarantee the rights of the planet. Global citizenship will offer new contributions to expand education for sustainable development worldwide.[16]

The gist of my argument is that global citizenship adds value to national citizenship. Moreover, because the cause of national citizenship could be considered unfinished business or still a work in progress, the value added by global citizenship may be another layer of support for a process of transforming citizenship making and citizenship education into models based on principles of liberty and equality for all, including what Benhabib calls the "rights of hospitality" in the Kantian sense.[17]

I see global citizenship as being marked by an understanding of global ties, relations and connections, and a commitment to the collective good. Robert Rhoads and Carlos Alberto Torres advanced the idea of "democratic multicultural citizenship" in which education helps students to develop the dispositions and abilities to work across social and cultural differences in a quest for solidarity. They argued that such skills are essential to citizenship in a multicultural, global environment.[18]

Robert A. Rhoads and Katalin Szelényi have developed this thesis into another level of complexity and understanding with foci on the responsibilities of universities. Rhoads and Szelényi's position is, and I fully concur, that we should "advance a view of citizenship in which the geographic reference point for one's sense of rights and responsibilities is broadened, and in some sense, complicated by a more expansive spatial vision and understanding of the world."[19]

They go on to argue that ". . . the engagement of individuals as citizens reflects understandings of rights and responsibilities across three basic dimensions of social life: the political (including civic aspects), the economic (including occupational aspects), and the social (including cultural aspects)."[20]

Others scholars speak of a denationalized definition of citizenship considering new conditions affecting citizenship in novel terms. With the onset of multiple processes of globalization, the positions of nation-states in the world and their institutional features have changed. Secondly, these transformations in the nation-state have a parallel effect in the emergence of new actors, including transnational social movements unwilling to respect the traditional levels of political representation within nation-states.[21]

3. Global Citizenship, Democracy and Multiculturalism in a Global World

The questions of citizenship, democracy and multiculturalism are at the heart of the discussion worldwide on educational reform, deeply affecting the academic discourse and practice of education.[22] Cloaked in different robes, questions about citizenship, the connections between education and democracy or the problem of multiculturalism affect most of the decisions that we face in dealing with the challenges of contemporary education.

Theories of citizenship and theories of democracy mark the advent of modern political science and reflect, in their complexities, the theoretical and practical challenges to democracy in contemporary societies. Both also underline the dilemmas of negotiating power in democratic societies.

Theories of citizenship relate to every problem of the relations between citizens and the state and among citizens themselves, while theories of democracy relate clearly to the connection between established—hidden and explicit—forms of social and political power, the intersection between systems of democratic representation and participation in systems of political administrative organization of public governance, and in political party systems. Ultimately, theories of democracy need to address the overall interaction between democracy and capitalism.

Finally, theories of multiculturalism, so prevalent in the education field in the last 20 years, have emerged as a particular response to the constitution of the pedagogical subject in schools or to the interaction between the pedagogical subject and the political subject in democratic societies. They appear important in understanding multiple identities in education and culture. In short, theories of multiculturalism are intimately connected to the politics of culture and education.

Thus theories of multiculturalism relate to the main analytical purpose of theories of citizenship. Both attempt to identify the sense and sources of identity and the competing forms of national, regional, ethnic or religious identity. Yet theories of multiculturalism have addressed the implications of class, race and gender for the constitution of identities and the role of the state in a way that, by and large, mainstream theories of citizenship have not. While the interconnections between identity and citizenship are not at all evident in the specialized bibliography, they have a practical grounding that also brings them closer to theories of democracy. This is so because, not only are theories of democracy preoccupied with participation, representation and checks and balances of power, but some brands also are concerned with ways to promote solidarity beyond particular interests of specific forms of identity.

Theories of citizenship, democracy and multiculturalism, in their specific spheres of influence and empirical loci, strive to identify a sense of identity (for the notion of a democratic citizen and a multicultural political subject) including all its contradictory sources. They also seek to vigorously define the limits and possibilities of forms of sociability that will promote the ability of individuals to tolerate and work together with people who are different from themselves. Likewise, these theories may enhance people's (or in a more restricted formulation, citizens') ability and desire to participate in the political process of promoting the public good and accountability. Finally, these theories will help individuals' willingness to exercise self-restraint and personal responsibility in their economic demands and in personal choices that affect the health and wealth of society and the environment as well as the process of community formation. This is so because, as Jürgen Habermas so aptly has argued, "The institutions of constitutional freedom are only worth as much as a population makes of them."[23]

The dilemmas of citizenship in a diverse democratic multicultural society can be outlined as follows: Theories of citizenship had been advanced, in the tradition of Western political theory, by white, heterosexual males who identified a homogeneous citizenship through a process of systematic exclusion rather than inclusion in the polity. That is, women, identifiable social groups (e.g., Jews, Gypsies), working-class people, members of specific ethnic and racial groups (i.e., people of color) and individuals lacking certain attributes or skills (i.e., literacy or numeracy abilities) were in principle excluded from the definition of citizens in numerous societies.

Theories of democracy, while effective in identifying the sources of democratic power, participation and representation in legitimate political democratic systems, had been unable to prevent the systemic exclusion of large segments of citizenry. Thus formal democracy drastically differs from substantive democracy. More worrisome still is the fact that theories of democracy had been unable to differentiate the roots of representative democracy (based on the notions of equal representation, equity and equality) from their immersion in the foundational principles that articulate capitalist societies. By definition, capitalism requires differential representation in power and politics, fostering inequity formation through hierarchies and competing interests and inequality through the workings of a profit-seeking system.

Theories of multiculturalism have been effective in discussing the politics of culture and identity and the different sources of solidarity across and within specific forms of identity. They have been insightful in showing the remarkable complexity of multiple identities. However, they have been unable or unwilling to embrace a theory of citizenship and a theory of democracy that is workable, in practical, procedural terms; ethically viable, in moral terms; and politically feasible in the context of capitalist civil societies, more so considering the global interpenetrations of economies, cultures and politics.

We need a theory of global democratic multicultural citizenship that will take seriously the need to develop a theory of democracy that will help to ameliorate, if not eliminate altogether, the social differences, inequality and inequity pervasive in capitalist societies and a theory of democracy able to address the draconian tensions between democracy and capitalism, on the one hand, and among social, political and economic democratic forms, on the other.[24]

With these theoretical considerations in mind, it is imperative to define the terms of global citizenship. Our definition of global citizenship dovetails nicely with the central components of a global education for sustainable development. Our definition is based on the concept of global commons understood in parallel with the concept of common good.

4.   Global Citizenship, Global Commons and Common Good

Since ancient times, philosophers have discussed the concept of common good. This is not the place to provide heuristic analyses of this foundational concept in politics. Suffice it to say, following the ethicist Rawls, that "Government is assumed to aim at the common good, that is, at maintaining conditions and achieving objectives that are similarly to everyone's advantage."[25] This position clearly antagonizes the idea of the invisible hand of the market "that turns self-interest into common good."[26]

Though a key concept in the Aristotelian-Thomist tradition and entrenched in Catholic theology and social doctrine, there are a number of criticisms of the concept of common good. From a relativist position, it is argued that a concept of common good is inconsistent with a pluralist society. Second, there is the free rider problem in which some individuals benefiting from the common good without putting in their own share of effort in building this common good. A third criticism emerges from the utilitarian philosophy of individualism, rejecting what is seen as dominant communitarianism. Unequal sharing of the burden is a fourth critique, since developing and sustaining a common good requires different efforts by different groups.[27]

Despite these reservations, I would argue that the philosophy of human rights establishes a basic platform of values for the common good and the notion of the 'good society.' Individualism versus collectivism or communitarianism is a perpetual tension in organized societies, but this tension does not deny the importance of a concept of common good as the notion of a good society to guide citizenship building. Similarly, there are always differential appropriations and use of resources, but I will argue that developing a concept of common good that could inspire global citizenship will diminish rather than enhance free riders. The unequal sharing of burdens is already a problem with growing inequality. A global concept of the common good will confront this problem head-on, and help us think of a model of society we want to achieve and how to reach that goal.

Once a concept of the common good or global commons is defined, we need to define the concept of global citizenship. It is important to move beyond historical or legal considerations. To move beyond the notion of citizenship as a kind of personal status, a combination of rights and duties that those who are legal members of the nation-state hold or should hold.

I posit a theory of what a good citizen is or should be relatively independent of the formal premises of the legal question of what it is to be a citizen. This is so because of the dual theoretical concerns of citizenship: citizenship as identity and as a set of civic virtues. Yet civic virtues need a civil minimum that can be found only in a historical-structural context where these civil minimums overlap with basic material conditions. One may also ask what are those civil minimums and civic virtues in a globalized world?

Global citizenship need not focus on the status and role associated with citizenship (obtained either through *ius sanguinis* or *ius solis*) but on civic minimums that should work at a global level, and civic virtues that are needed to accomplish this model of global citizenship education.[28] Questions of stateless people, aboriginal communities and refugees challenge the nature of citizenship in our globalized societies.[29]

Two key elements of citizenship should be defined at the outset: first, civic minimums, because full participation in citizenship as argued by T. H. Marshall rests ultimately on material bases.[30] Hence, growing poverty excludes large segments of individuals from active citizenship—an economic citizenship that cannot be accomplished without bare essentials, including the right to a job, education, medical care, housing and retraining over the course of life. From a Marshallian perspective, the notion of democracy as a civil and political right cannot be excluded from the notion of democracy as a socio-economic right.[31]

A second important concept is civic virtue. Amy Gutman[32] has persuasively argued that "education for citizenship should focus on the justification of rights rather than responsibilities, and, at the same time, that schools should foster general virtues (courage, law-abidingness, loyalty), social virtues (autonomy, open-mindedness) economic virtues (work ethic, capacity to delay self-gratification) and political virtues (capacity to analyze, capacity to criticize)."[33]

With these general virtues, I would argue for the need for civic virtues nurtured by a democratic multicultural ethic, that is to say, "an antiracist, antisexist, and anti-classist philosophy based on tolerance, an epistemology of curiosity à la Freire, a rejection of cynicism and nihilist postures, a secular spiritually of love, and skillful engagement in dialogue as a method but also as a process of cognition constitute central virtues of a democratic multicultural citizenship, a bridge between foundational canons and cultures."[34]

I argue that global citizenship should add value to national citizenship and to the global commons. But what is this global commons? And how can global citizenship add value?

Global commons is defined by three basic propositions. The first one is that our planet is our only home, and we have to protect it through a global citizenship sustainable development education, moving from diagnosis and denunciation into action and policy implementation. Recently the government of Ecuador has enshrined in its constitution the rights of nature, which follows an important learning of a whole decade of education for sustainable development: climate justice. The long march for global planetary citizenship has begun.

Secondly, global commons is predicated on the idea that global peace is an intangible cultural good of humanity with immaterial value. Global peace is a treasure of humanity.

Thirdly, global commons is predicated on the need to find ways that people who are all equal manage to live together democratically in a world growing evermore diverse, seeking to fulfill their individual and cultural interests and achieving their inalienable rights to life, liberty and the pursuit of happiness. The great question about peace is how to cultivate the spirit of solidarity across the lines of difference.[35]

Global citizenship may help global peace, planet and people through its contribution to civic engagement, in its classical dimensions of knowledge, skills and values. There is a cosmopolitan imperative as suggested in many publications by Ulrich Beck,[36] an imperative of economic equality, welfare and cultural diversity that may produce an individual who may admire others more for their differences than for their similarities.

I believe in the importance of spirituality in the life of people and would like to echo the call of Rabbi Awraham Soetendorp for the creation of a movement of *global spirituality*. Soetendorp's early life experience with a Catholic family who risked their lives safeguarding him as a baby while his parents were sent to the gas chambers significantly shaped his commitments to multi-faith camaraderie. Since an early age, Soetendorp has worked to keep the memory of the Holocaust alive and to preserve the legacy of Anne Frank. His call is for the creation of a Council of World Consciousness as one of the engines of the global commons and one way in which our human civilization, creeds and faiths can accomplish a rich and informed dialogue in solidarity. I am sure we can work on this project as part of the conversation on global citizenship education. Thus planet, peace and people constitute the global commons.

This holistic definition of global citizenship can only be implemented if we focus on a global system of governance that plays the role of a global equalizer to smooth over the deficiencies emerging from nation-state conflicts affecting the rest of the system. Italian philosopher Norberto Bobbio, addressing a Kantian paradox, asks the appropriate question: "Can a state be fully democratic in a world that is not (as yet) democratic?" Posing a Kantian dilemma in considering the relationships between domestic and international systems, Bobbio points to a vicious circle: "States can become democratic only in a fully democratic international society, but a fully democratized international society presupposes that all the states that compose it are democratic. The completion of one process is hindered by the non-completion of the other."[37]

The Marshallian model argued that the nature of the welfare state guarantees social integration and cohesiveness of the polity and the exercise of rights and responsibilities of the citizen. Should we consider that this global system of governance might rest on a globalized form of the welfare state as a guarantee of global citizenship? If so, how can it be constructed? How can we deal with the challenge of scale, assuming that global citizenship works at several levels, from the documented individual to the undocumented immigrant, from the global city to the country side and to the nation-state, from the community to the individual, from application of the law in the nation-state to concrete practices of politics in disenfranchised communities.

Asking if global citizenship education may help global peace is an important question. It is also very relevant because traditionally, citizenship education has been associated with 'civic education,' that is, the teaching of constitutional democracy as a way to facilitate conflict resolution and conviviality. Three categories are associated with civics education: *civic knowledge*, which in the context of constitutional democracy entails the knowledge of basic concepts informing the practice of democracy such as public elections, majority rule, citizenship rights and obligations, constitutional separation of power, and the placement of democracy in a market economy that is used as the basic premises of civil society. The second category associated with citizenship building is *civic skills*, which usually mean the intellectual and participatory skills that facilitate citizenship's judgment and actions. The last category is *civic virtues*, usually defined around liberal principles such as self-discipline, compassion, civility, tolerance and respect. I have said in one of my books that "the present cannot be the measure of happiness, because happiness is simply a collection of images that vanish with distance and become distorted with proximity."[38]

The central question for us is the creation of a global democratic multicultural citizenship that facilitates an education for democracy. How to build better schools, intellectually richer schools, particularly for those who are the bottom of society? How to build a global democratic multicultural citizenship curriculum where everybody learns from the rich diversity of society and where the trends toward balkanization and separatism in modern societies can be prevented and even reversed. We can do a better job in preparing teachers who are capable of working in school settings that become the center of collective experience and solidarity.

Democracy is a messy system, but it has survived because there is a sphere for debates and a set of rules that people follow even if they do not benefit from them. Let us build global citizenship education, even if it seems beyond our control and an impossible dream. Only the search for what seems utopian will make the possible a reality in our lives.

The struggle for citizenship has been marked by revolutions and war, but also peaceful marches of non-violence side by side with bloodshed. Let us take advantage of the legitimacy of UNESCO's 'soft' power and launch the silent revolution for global citizenship education.

Notes

1. Paper prepared for the *Second UNESCO Forum on Global Citizenship Education: Building Peaceful and Sustainable Societies—Preparing for post-2015*, UNESCO Headquarters in Paris, France, 28 to 30 January 2015c. I thank Mr. Jason Dorio for his comments to a previous version.
2. Marcuse, in Feenberg and Leiss, 2007, p. 45.
3. Ibid., p. 53.
4. www.visionofhumanity.org/#/page/our-gpi-findings
5. www.prnewswire.com/news-releases/first-global-peace-index-ranks-121-countries-58694072.html
6. P. Freire, *Pedagogy of the Oppressed*. Trans. M.B. Ramos. New York: Continuum, p. 186.
7. Gadotti, 2004; Torres, 1998b: 246, 2014.
8. Piketty, 2014, p. 471.
9. World Bank Global Monitoring Report, 2014.
10. Torres, 2009b, pp. 30–31.
11. Ibid., p. 29.
12. Ibid., pp. 41–42.
13. Given the nature of this chapter, I cannot provide the data and analysis to document these cluster problems beyond a brief indication of themes, theories, topics and data.
14. For a theoretical analysis see Carlos Alberto Torres, "Neoliberalism, Globalization Agendas and Banking Educational Policy: Is Popular Education an Answer?", Paper prepared for the Max Weber Foundation Meeting in New Delhi, February 13–16, 2015b.
15. Habermas, 2004.
16. Ministers and heads of delegation attending the *UN Climate Change Conference 2014* — COP20, — (1–12 December 2014, Lima, Peru) have adopted *The Lima Ministerial Declaration on Education and Awareness-Raising*. This Declaration calls on governments to include climate change into school curricula and climate awareness into national development and climate change plans.
17. Benhabib, 2011, p. viii.
18. Rhoads and Torres, 2006.
19. Rhoads and Szelényi, 2011, p. 160.
20. Ibid., p. 17.
21. Sassen, 2002, p. 4.
22. Democracy is a slider signifier. It means different things to different people. There are minimal procedural conditions of democracy, advocated by constitutional models of democracy. A social democratic approach prefers aggregative forms of democracy as proposed by Robert Darhl, based on equal rights and liberties. More contemporarily, there is a deliberative concept of democracy: "On a deliberative conception of democracy, political actors are viewed as capable of being motivated by a desire to promote the common good." Song, 2012, p. 44.
23. Jürgen Habermas, 1992, p. 7.
24. Torres, 1998b.
25. Rawls, 1971, p. 233.
26. d'Avray, 2010, p. 30.
27. Velasquez, Andre, Thomas Shanks, and Meyer, n.d.
28. Torres, 1992, p. 102.
29. Saskia Sassen, *Globalization and Its Discontents: Essays on the New Mobility of People and Money*. New York: The New Press, 1999.
30. Marshall, 1950.
31. The question of relationship among citizenship, the nation-state and the city seems to be part of some kind of Greek law of eternal return. Citizenship was

created in cities, hence the *citoyen*. Currently, however, there is a disparity between citizenship building in the nation-state and citizenship building in the context of the cities, particularly the global cities: "In the context of a strategic space such as the global city, the types of disadvantaged people described here are not simply marginal; they acquire presence in a broader political process that escapes the boundaries of the formal polity. This presence signals the possibility of a politics. What this politics will be will depend on the specific projects and practices of various communities. Insofar as the sense of membership of these communities is not subsumed under the national, it may well signal the possibility of a politics that, while transnational, is actually centered in concrete localities" Sassen, 2002, p. 22.

32. Gutman, 1987.
33. Torres, 1998b, p. 111.
34. Ibid., p. 258.
35. Gitllin, 1995.
36. Beck, 2006.
37. Cited in Carlos Alberto Torres, *Democracy, Education, and Multiculturalism: Dilemmas of Citizenship in a Global World*. Lanham, MD: Rowman and Littlefield, 1998, pp. 95–96.
38. Torres, 1998b, p. 258.

9 Adult Learning and Global Citizenship Education[1]

with Jason Dorio

Introduction

UNESCO is promoting Global Citizenship Education (GCE), not only creating a new global norm in education but also a new analytical perspective. The concept of global citizenship is ambiguous and complex; we need a theoretical clarification of what it means and what it could mean. The purpose of the chapter is therefore to briefly introduce a global multicultural democratic citizenship theory of GCE and highlight the implications of GCE for adult education.

UNESCO has encouraged national government agencies, transnational and non-governmental organizations, teachers and researchers to pursue various policies, programs and pedagogies to foster and further develop global citizenship education. The idea is to not only create a new global norm in education but also a new analytical perspective. However, with such an ambiguous and complex concept as global citizenship, there must be a theoretical clarification of GCE.

Beyond Lifelong Learning of Adult Education

For decades, lifelong learning has been deeply connected to adult education. Lifelong learning as a paradigm focuses primarily on individual development and personal growth, including improved health and well-being. It links learning explicitly to the expansion of labor skills necessary to prepare or enhance abilities of adults for employment and innovation within the ever-changing technological and digital demands of a knowledge society and to compete in a global economy. In addition, this concept can to a lesser extent also address

> the core of political socialization, participation and integration of civil societies and democratic governance, including the challenges of immigration, multiculturalism and affirmative action.[2]

This approach to adult education tends to value individual development of skills for the knowledge society. A participatory educational approach focusing on the individual as a decision maker interconnected with a wider local and global community concerning virtues of the environment and cultural diversity is greatly overlooked. A global citizenship education approach to adult education intersects individual development as a partici-patory process with sustainable development and peace education fostered by a model of global commons.

Global Citizenship and Global Commons

We see global citizenship as being marked by a combination of an under-standing of global ties, relations and connections, with various forms of participation driven by a commitment to a global collective good. Global commons is defined by three basic propositions:

- First is that our planet is our only home, and we have to protect it through a global citizenship sustainable development education, moving from diagnosis and accusation into action and policy implementation.
- Secondly, global commons is based on the idea that global peace is an intangible cultural good of humanity with immaterial value. As part of the same coin, global peace is inseparably tied to environmental pres-ervation; we need to pursue both simultaneously for human survival. Global peace is therefore a treasure of humanity.
- Thirdly, global commons need to find ways that people, who are all equal, manage to live together democratically in a world growing ever-more diverse, seeking to fulfill their individual and cultural interests and achieving their inalienable rights to life, liberty and the pursuit of happiness.

So, why should stakeholders of adult education care about Global Citizenship Education? According to UNESCO, Global Citizenship Education is seen as an intervention dealing with:

> A new class of global challenges which require some form of collec-tive response to find effective solutions. These include increasingly inte-grated and knowledge-driven economies; greater migration between countries and from rural to urban areas; growing inequalities; more awareness of the importance of sustainable development and including concerns about climate change and environmental degradation; a large and growing youth demographic; the acceleration of globalization; and rapid developments in technology. Each of these elements carries far-reaching implications, and taken together, these represent a period of transition of historical significance. Education systems need to respond to these emerging global challenges, which require a collective response with a strategic vision that is global in character, rather than limited to the individual country level.[3]

The need for global citizenship is a growing global norm, but teaching, learning and implementing it currently faces many obstacles. There are of course many practical constraints to global citizenship education, such as limitations in human and material resources, timetable constraints, logistical and demographic constraints, and sensitivity of subject matter.[4]

On a deeper level there are epistemological constraints that will either serve to narrowly define the mission of GCE, or operate to manipulate the role of GCE into a tool used for domination. Let us have a closer look at two such constraints, neoliberalism and neo-imperialism.

The Burden of History

Neoliberalism: Over the past three decades, neoliberal policies have promoted open markets, free trade, reduction in public sector spending, decreased state intervention in the economy, and deregulation of markets. It is based on the paradigm that the state should participate less in the provision of social services (e.g., education), leaving these services to the free market and privatization. Regardless of its political economic failures, neoliberalism remains solidly established in the politics of culture, as an intellectual philosophy and "common sense" so pervasive that the neoliberal paradigm guides educational development around the globe.[5]

The culture of neoliberalism has therefore been increasingly embedded within the policies, pedagogies and purposes of education, placing value on possessive individualism and relegating civic participation to consumerism and labor contributions. Thus, the common sense of education has been limited to the skills and knowledge that best serve market interests and practices. Given neoliberalism's embrace of possessive individualism, citizenship around the globe has been conflated to narrowly define common good as being solely based upon self-interest.

Neo-imperialism: Education has played a significant role in promoting colonial cultural domination throughout history.

When global citizenship education is now being adopted by powerful states and international regimes, it is easy to see why some would view GCE with suspicion and skepticism.

Therefore it is the role of both practitioners and students of adult education to guard against visions and models of GCE constructed as a neo-imperial tool.

An important first step is the rethinking of the management, curricula, pedagogies and roles of adult education institutions, especially those tied to the mission of neoliberalism and those funded by international donors. This can be addressed through creating awareness and challenging power dynamics and uneven power relations between students and teachers; between students and students; between educational institutions and society; between the state and society; as well as between states.

To deter neo-imperial impositions of GCE, we must embrace an "ecology of knowledge."[6] This includes the recognition and inclusion of multiple wisdoms, learning, philosophies, culture practices and economic relationships that strive for communal peace and environmental preservation.

The Ubuntu Way

We think that the significance of a post-colonial understanding of GCE is a concept of global citizenship that does not rely solely on the often untranslatable political traditions of the global North and Eurocentric concepts, practices and institutions, but encompasses the dynamics of social, economic and spiritual relationships, organizations and egalitarian formations whose roots are found within the Global South. Moreover, since GCE is based on human rights, it is imperative to decouple human rights from imperialist practices and interventions. We envision a GCE for adult education that is grounded and contextualized in localities but combines multiple knowledges and multi-civic virtues that transcend borders for actions that endeavor to defend humanity and global commons. For example, *Ubuntu* is an African collective ethos of the universal bond between people based upon the sharing and collectivity of all humanity, which can be the foundation for GCE programs not only in relevant communities but might have the possibility of resonating with others around the world.

The democratization of program creation is a valuable solution to the sustainability of adult education programs for GCE. Pre-packaged, top-down models, especially driven by the institutions of the North, at best run the risk of failure, and at worst, omit the voices, histories, wisdoms, cultures and inclusion of its participants. An organic development program, beginning first with a problem-posing approach focusing on the most pressing issues identified and faced by marginalized localities, is best suited to guard against predatory cultural practices which create and/or reproduce structures of environmental degradation, paternalism, classism, sexism, racism, ableism, etc.—all detrimental to GCE.

Contextualized ownership, decision making and innovation can then synergistically meld with national and international agencies to build a sustainable program for GCE. Thus, the onus is on the stakeholders of adult education to answer the question: How can localities provide insight to and add value to the concepts, theories, pedagogies, processes and policies of GCE for adult education?[7]

Towards a Global Democratic Multicultural Citizenship

Torres argues in this book, any definition and theory of global citizenship as a model of intervention to promote global peace and sustainable development should address what has become the trademark of globalization:

cultural diversity. Therefore, global citizenship should rely on a definition of *global democratic multicultural citizenship*. It is imperative that global citizenship adds value to national citizenship! Yet the expansion of a universalistic claim of world solidarity rests on the concept of cosmopolitan citizenship nested in a model of cosmopolitan democracies. To this point, Beck stresses:

> *globality*, *plurality* and *civility*, that is, the awareness of a global sphere of responsibility, the acknowledgement of the otherness of others and non-violence—as defining features of a 'de-territorialized' concept of cosmopolitanism.[8]

With respect to education, some forms of citizenship education can be criticized for contributing to producing, on the one hand, passive, apathetic, consumer-driven and/or possessive, individualistic citizens. On the other, civic education can produce overly patriotic and narrowly nationalistic citizens, leading to citizens who favor exclusionary, ethnonationalistic and xenophobic visions for society. Counter-neoliberal and post-colonial models of global citizenship can enhance an education that is contextualized within an ecology of knowledges striving for "an antiracist, antisexist, and anti-classist philosophy based on tolerance, an epistemology of curiosity à la Freire, a rejection of cynicism and nihilist postures, a secular spiritually of love, and skillful engagement in dialogue as a method but also as a process of cognition constituting central virtues of a democratic multicultural citizenship, a bridge between foundational canons and cultures."[9]

Our view of GCE aligns with what Santos describes as "the retrieval of new processes of production and valorization of valid [multiple layers of] knowledges, whether scientific or non- scientific, and of new relations among different types of knowledge on the basis of the practices of the classes and social groups that have suffered, in a systematic way, the oppression and discrimination caused by capitalism and colonialism."[10] Providing much needed spaces for epistemologies of the South, GCE must be derived from the gaze of post-colonial theories, to counter neoliberal cultural influences and economic policies that have contributed to an international moral and ethical crisis linked to the commodification of our sense of global community, materializing our commitment to the environment, and trampling our global commons.

It is our belief that this model of GCE for adult education can assist to forge new egalitarian economic relationships based upon the synergy of local and global knowledges that strive to foster consciousness-raising actions of sustainable peace and environmental preservation for the betterment of humanity.

Notes

1. Published as "The Do and Don'ts of Global Citizenship Education", republished with permission.
2. Torres, 2013a, p. 9.
3. UNESCO, *Concept Note UNESCO Forum on Global Citizenship Education: Preparing Learners for the Challenge of the 21st Century*. Bangkok, Thailand: UNESCO, 2–4 December 2013.
4. Education Above All, 2012, p. 48.
5. Torres, 2013b.
6. Santos, 2012.
7. Freire, 2007.
8. Beck, 2002, p. 36.
9. Torres, 1998b, p. 258.
10. Santos, 2012, p. 51.

10 Global Citizenship Education
A New Global Social Movement?

1. Citizenship and Social Movements

I have argued that in the context of debates about globalization and the role of nation-state no coherent and clear definition of global citizenship has been articulated. It is fair to say that there is no consensus among academics, intellectuals, international organizations and government officials of what the concept means.[1]

British scholar Lynn Davies, while wondering if global citizenship education is an abstraction or a framework for action, concludes that: "There is a reasonable consensus on the importance of global citizenship, and on the listings of knowledge, skills, values and behaviors which would characterize the area."[2]

Perhaps it will be useful to start with a simple idea that global citizenship may become reinforced as a concept or framework for action associated with globalization and particularly the network society intimately connected with the growing importance of digital cultures.

The network society is one of the key concepts defining our globalization age. The network society was very well presented in the trilogy of sociological books published by Manuel Castells at the sunset of the 20th century.[3] Following his mentor, French sociologist Alain Touraine,[4] Castells focused on the question of identity and social movements confronting globalization processes and challenging structures of existing institutions and cultural norms.[5]

The social theory of Touraine and Castells has made social movements central to understanding our theories of society, social change and citizenship. Social movements are different than non-governmental organizations, which are usually defined by their autonomy from government control. Touraine, from an actionalist perspective on social actors' behavior, instructed us that social movements refer to collective efforts to promote strategies to change power.

Touraine distinguished two main types of social movements. The first type is conflicting action, which can be best characterized as defensive collective behavior, including struggles to overcome the perils of unemployment, or the defense of minimums of health care and education. The second

type can be classified as including groups seeking to change the social relations of power in cultural actions, ethical values, science or production.
Among the many social movements, this type includes feminist, ecological,
peace or anti-nuclear movements. However, it has become clear that if we
understand politics as the struggle for power, both types cannot easily be
interpreted in political terms. More and more they represent cultural and
moral practices seeking to construct new social spaces and new collective
identities. They have become increasingly independent of traditional institutions of political representation like political parties or unions.

For some scholars the Middle East, uprising is the result of "wired citizenship," with prominent youth movements and activism drawing from the
digital possibilities that the network society entails.[6]

2.   Globalization and Anti-Globalization Movements[7]

What is known in the mass media as the anti-globalization movement had
its first known death in Genoa, Italy. On the sunny afternoon of July 20,
2001, in Piazza Alimonda, a young Italian demonstrator, Carlo Guliani, the
son of a labor union organizer from Rome, was killed by an Italian carabin-
ieri. Then, the police van ran over Guliani's body while trying to get away
from the scene. This instantaneous death was endlessly broadcast all over
the world by television and the Internet. Blood and violence marked the last
summit of the G8 leaders in the old port of Genoa, changing forever the way
that neoliberalism and globalization proponents broadcast their arguments
to the world through annual G8 summits.

The anti-globalization movements seemed to gather steam, with important voices of dissent beginning to appear. The cast of characters reveals
strange bedfellows, ranging from Pope John Paul II, who prior to the meeting called for Third World debt forgiveness and urged the leaders of the
richest nations to be more concerned with poverty in neoliberal times, to
distinguished French sociologist Pierre Bourdieu, professor of the Collège
de France, who enlightened educators in the early 1970s with his work
on education as social reproduction. Bourdieu, in a most pessimistic tone,
equated globalization and neoliberalism with the most infamous illness of
the 20th century, AIDS. Bourdieu, implacable in his position regarding the
G8 meeting in Genoa, states that "The violence of the masses has, at least,
some utility: It forces the main actors of neoliberalism, who like to appear
calm, serene, and rational, to show their own violence."[8]

Some movements refuse to seek leadership outside the movement (e.g.,
the movement of Sem Terra[9] in Brazil or Occupy Wall Street), but some like
Podemos tried to construct a new political party as an alternative to the
traditional Spanish political parties.[10]

The end of the Cold War saw the transformation of the world into a new
global economy fueled by rapid technological transformations, with faster
transactions of financial capital in increasingly unregulated international

capital markets. Labor has increased its mobility across borders, justifying a commonplace assessment by a journalist that "borders are political lines of convenience—lines that one crosses if history makes it necessary to do so."[11]

Genoa shows to the globalized world new intellectual and political realities. On the one hand, there is a multinational social movement of disparate allies, including factions of the Catholic Church and Protestant churches, Greenpeace, women's and indigenous rights groups, and every anarchist and socialist movement in the industrially advanced countries, confronting the heads of state of the eight most industrialized nations on Earth—though Russia is a last-minute invitee for political reasons, not as an industrial power comparable to the rest. These movements also vary in their opposition to globalization. Resistance movements involve those who from protectionist or nationalist perspectives oppose international world exchange and interdependency as well as those who oppose the growing inequalities that economic globalization is creating and demand global social justice and equality. On the other hand, those leaders who are confronted by anti-globalization movements seem to exercise less control over the world economy than they pretend to command. This has led some analysts to argue that we are witnessing the corporatization of the world, not simply its globalization.[12] Similarly, Octavio Ianni has argued that this is the difference between globalization, an ineluctable historical process, and globalism, a process articulated by neoliberalism and the rule of global corporations.[13]

The European Union is an example showing that national borders are blurred by economic realities, postmodern mass media cultures are confronted by local communities and traditional cultures, and new movements toward cosmopolitan democracies based on the program of human rights are being confronted by renewed ethnic and nationalistic struggles. Moreover, business analysts like Kenichi Ohmae denounce the nation-state as sclerotic, arguing that the centers of wealth creation are regional states.[14] From his neoliberal position, Ohmae adds to his devastating critique of the nation-state a critique of liberalism and democracy because they are being overrun by demands from the population for more public minimums while democratic political structures are unable to satisfy those demands. Ohmae's argument could be considered a right-wing version of James O'Connor's "fiscal crisis of the state" and the dilemmas of legitimacy of Jürgen Habermas.[15]

Needless to say, these questions are most relevant for education, because, particularly during the 20th century, education has increasingly become a function of the state. Educational systems and practices are sponsored, mandated, organized and certified by the state. Indeed, "public education is not only a state function in terms of legal order or financial support; the specific requirements for degrees, teacher's requirements and qualifications, mandated textbooks, and required courses for basic curriculum are controlled by state agencies and designed under specific public policies of the state."[16]

The results of the Brexit vote is evidence of the impact of immigration and globalization upon countries, families and individuals. However, I shall add that a knee-jerk reaction to Brexit's alleged veneer of racism should be examined more closely. It would be naïve and certainly dangerous to ignore that Brexit may empower nativists and rabid nationalism, undermining human rights, security and conflict resolution in the world system; but we shall also recognize that globalization produces winners (usually white-collar workers) and losers (usually blue-collar workers) and that there is always a tension between the politics of identity and the politics of class, which cannot be fully overcome, nor be brushed aside as racist veneers.

Global citizenship education as defined in this book proposes an alternative to racist and xenophobic models of citizenship, as global commons invites dialogue across lines of difference, the promotion of a culture of peace and solidarity, and the universal protection of human rights, the environment, and life, liberty and the pursuit of happiness.

3.   From the Network Society to the Movement Society

As one of the foremost specialists in social movements, Sidney Tarrow has documented that we are living in a "movement society." What defines the nature of social movements is their contentious politics or their contentious collective action. This process is based on "first mounting collective challenges, second drawing on social networks, common purposes and cultural frameworks, and third, building solidarity through connective structures and collective identities to sustain collective action."[17]

These are certain premises of action of social movements. First is social protest, that is, collective challenge marked by interrupting, obstructing or rendering uncertain the activities of others.[18] Second is to obtain a common purpose, with overlapping interests and values as the basis of their common actions. A third crucial element is to tap into feelings of solidarity and identity. Fourth, a main challenge for social movements is to sustain their contentious politics over time. They could produce movements of resistance, but unless they maintain the challenge, their either evaporate or retreat into isolation. Finally, they work with the premise that there are political opportunities and changes in constraints that create the most important incentives for initiating new phases of contention.[19]

The resolution of grievances from social movements requires tangible outcomes, so the social movement knows and feel that they have won in their struggle, that they have achieved their goals. Yet, no social movement usually gains all that they want. However, some of these movements become transnational, like the World Social Forum, and constitute an alliance of actors from different orientations, perspectives and political affiliation that coincide on central aspects of social struggle. There is a rich and growing bibliography on the World Social Forum and its contributions to social, political and economic policies. It is pertinent to cite at length Milani and Laniado's conclusion about the World Social Forum:

> The World Social Forum is a relevant open-space movement precisely because it contrasts with the formalist self-referred political system of representative democracy and traditional international relations. The social and political orders (national and international) of modern societies have been observed as balanced structures that have supposedly contemplated a predictable and universal material progress and a class society based on interests and a general sense of citizenship. The new social movements and later the transnational movements question the democracy deficit and the ineffectiveness of international regulation of world politics which have resulted from this received model of society. Globalization forces the emergence of strong paradoxes of both contemporary democracy and the asymmetric international relations. It uncovers the enormous cleavage between an idealized progress promised by liberal Keynesian democracy (not to speak of socialist experiences) and the limited institutional capacity to guarantee liberty and to provide equality worldwide and within the principle of justice. Consequently, the transnational social movements have played an important role by exposing the disconnections between liberty, distribution and recognition
>
> (2006: 31).

In Latin America and elsewhere, new social movements have challenged the hegemony of neoliberal governance.[20] Since several national leaders in Latin America embraced the neoliberal model in the 1980s and early 1990s (for instance, Salinas de Gortari in Mexico, Carlos Saúl Menem in Argentina, or Fernando Henrique Cardoso in Brazil), and considering its effects on the subordinate social sectors in the region, particularly the increase in the region's inequality, neoliberalism has been deeply challenged by social movements, community organizations and critical intellectuals. They have resisted the premises and policies of neoliberal governments and managed to support the emergence and growth of social democratic models of governance.[21]

These 'new' social movements differ greatly from the 'old' social movements in the regions, however. First, they are territorially located and do not attempt to give regional or national answers to the social problems they confront. Second, they search for autonomy from governments and political parties. In this regard they consistently and continuously consult with the rank and file about their policies and actions. Third, instead of conceptually accepting the homogeneity of a national culture, they revalue the cultural identity of the social sectors that they represent. Fourth, they believe in their capacity to train their own organic intellectuals and educators—by implication, they do not trust schools and universities to help them organize.

Fifth, there is a new and active leadership role for women—for instance, the highly visible female indigenous and *campesino* leadership exemplified by the Zapatista comandantes. Sixth, there is a constant preoccupation with the organization of labor and the question of sustainable development in the process of production. Consequently they strive for new forms of hierarchy and equity pay in the process of work and for organizational forms of production that will not damage the environment. And last but not least, they promote new forms of instrumental action to carry out their demands. While the old social movements' favorite weapon was the labor strike, the new social movements occupy spaces, streets, plazas and squares (like the mothers of the Plaza de Mayo) and even cities (e.g., the Cordobazo in the early 1960s). Many thought that these movements constituted a post-neoliberal strategy to confront global crises.[22]

These new movements create a visible and prominent presence in urban environments, making their membership at odds with the majority of the urban middle classes. Finally, they have helped unleash a new era, one that analysts such as Marco Aurelio García, who was Lula's principal adviser on international relations, call "post-neoliberalism" as the strategy to overcome global crises.[23] A decade later from the post-neoliberal governments, the return of neoliberalism with a vengeance to the region shows that social movements and political progressive parties have a very uphill battle ahead of them.

Would it make sense to build GCE as a global social movement, and if so, what would be its identity and responsibilities?

4. How to Build GCE as a Global Social Movement

Building GCE as a social movement requires a diversity of approaches and practices as well as robust agendas for research, teaching, activism and policy.[24] This social movement should focus on transforming social relations of power into cultural actions for the defense of ethical values; should be based on a model of science education which seeks liberation, not simply regulation, of social actions; should be implemented with a political pedagogical model that facilitates critical thinking and the systematic introduction of a human rights regime in the school curriculum, in non-formal education and in informal education through critical mass media literacy; should be a social movement that incorporates new epistemological principles into the creation of new educational models and good practices for the good society, and that challenges the dominant instrumental rationality of our educational environment, particularly in how to teach controversial issues in classrooms.[25]

It is a movement that may challenge the existing educational systems, pushing for a new model that for the lack of a better term I will call *citizen's schools*, following the insights of Freire's model of *"escola cidada"*—that is, a school that incorporates the 'public' and the 'popular' (e.g., as an ethos or the *volksgeist* of the people) together. NGOs should pledge to work towards expanding their programs on global citizenship education, for instance, pushing to introduce formal courses in human rights from early childhood education and up.[26] Governments should create a fund to support the development of associated forms of global citizenship education, linking to education for sustainable development, impacting not only schooling but also non-formal education models and adult learning.

This new civic global movement will seek new alternative models of production in the preservation and defense of environmental practices based on a sustainable development education as presented in the UN sustainable development goals.[27]

For decades there has been a debate asking if technological progress will increase productivity, wealth and jobs. In the context of sustainable development goals, new evidence is worrisome. Speaking about the productivity paradox, Nico Stern discusses " . . . an issue widely debated among economists in response to the empirical observations in advanced economies that large investments in so-called Information and Communication Technologies (ICT) do not appear to have much of an impact on productivity and prominently summarized by Robert Solow" (1987) as "you can see the computer age everywhere but in the productivity statistics."[28]

Technological transformation is affecting labor markets: Robots that can learn, self-driving cars and replacement of labor by machines will increase the pressure for youth to find jobs, thus raising inequality.[29] As one economic editorialist of the *New York Times* put it, "Jeffrey D. Sachs of Columbia University has been working with a series of colleagues on *an economic model* of a world in which robotization both raises economic output and immiserates workers, pushing them out of their jobs."[30] The only alternative, and one that should be pursued by youth, is to demand a universal income, expanding the concept of social security, unemployment insurance and perhaps what is called social living wages.

It is a social movement that seeks to develop a planetary citizenship, hence defending the planet's environmental rights and the rights of nature, which should be enshrined in our democratic constitutions.

It is a movement to construct a durable and reasonable culture of peace across the planet. Such approach requires a viable model of participatory politics and participatory democracy[31] and will strive to create, enhance and protect models of conflict resolution embedded in a culture of peace and public diplomacy. It is a movement that will support the rights of people alongside the rights of property, seeking to legitimate the rights of people as civil and human rights and avoiding subsuming the rights of people to the rights of property, a practice so prevalent in capitalist systems, particularly if we are concerned about the pursuit of happiness in our lives.[32]

It is a social movement that strives to develop a global consciousness that includes the work of civil society and NGOs, governments, multilateral and bilateral institutions and communities. Corporations should be challenged to develop platforms for global consciousness on their websites and to pledge to act ethically, respect the rights of their employees, support movements such as green capitalism, fair trade, fair living wages and prevent cyber-crime and cyber-espionage, promoting cyber-security strategies.

It is a social movement striving to bring the question of diversity as a central component of school curriculum and instruction, and particularly in higher education. Not only we shall recreate the understanding of citizenship building in our elementary and secondary schools, incorporating the concept of global citizenship, but we shall work for the creation of a network of high schools and undergraduate university courses on global learning and global citizenship education, a course dealing with the complex dynamics of social diversity and the dialectics of the global and the local, courses that should inspire all university students and their practices for social transformation.

Is a social movement that strives to develop public diplomacy so nations negotiate their differences on equal footing and reach reasonable accommodations through conflict resolution rather than through war? Manifold examples of programs aiming to expand public diplomacy have existed since the Second World War, such as the Fulbright programs and the Fulbright-Hayes programs in the US[33] or the new idea of public diplomacy developed by the government of Korea, one of the most committed governments to nourish global citizenship education.[34]

Yet, above all it should contribute to developing new forms of insertion of youth into the global culture, considering that many youth are neither studying nor working in formal markets—what in Latin America are called the NINI youth ("ni estudian ni trabajan"; "neither study nor work").[35] The growing technocratic policy environments usually focus on competencies to be evaluated for functional life and work; fortunately there are other alternatives such as the "capability approach," which emphasizes individual capabilities to achieve a life they value and the ethical and moral choices embedded in that concept of life. The capability approach was developed in the early 1980s by Nobel Prize economist and philosopher Amartya Sen and has been implemented in the United Nations Development Program as an alternative to narrow econometrics to measure poverty or development. This could be done particularly through new models of leadership and youth movements. For instance, the World Bank Young Professional Programs could be remodeled to become more inclusive of global citizenship education and education for sustainable development[36] and the important projects of the UN Youth Leadership Program (UNOSDP)[37] and the UNESCO Youth Program[38] could be scaled up. Let us analyze these principles in detail.

4.1 Social Epistemology[39]

Global Citizenship Education, in order to become a social movement, may consider the following social epistemological principles as their epistemological bedrock:[40]

1. Global Citizenship Education, or GCE, should promote an ethics of caring, or what Saint Ignatius termed "*Cura personalis.*" The care for the individual person and human rights remains a central characteristic of GCE. A global ethics of caring is central to the implementation of Global Citizenship Education, embracing as well a key concept from feminist theory.
2. GCE is framed within a social justice education framework. Without bare essentials, we cannot fully accomplish citizenship. Bare essentials speak of economic citizenship, including the right to a job, education, health care, affordable housing and retraining over the course of life. Global citizenship cannot substitute for national citizenship but has to add value to local, national and regional citizenship(s).
3. GCE helps to produce a new narrative in education. The new GCE seeks an education beyond numbers and technocratic thinking, and beyond cognitive learning. It pursues holistic learning that encompasses ethics, aesthetics, spirituality, art and includes the goals of peace building in the spirit of the Jacques Delors' UNESCO Commission, *Learning: The Treasure Within*, particularly the principle of learning to live together, learning to live with others.[41]
4. GCE will seek to identify new models of conflict resolution and negotiation strategies for different regions of the world. For example, in contexts riven by conflict and post-conflict situations, GCE is seen in the rubric of peace education. GCE as civic education is a premise for democratic participation prevailing in those contexts that have experienced totalitarian regimes or dictatorships. Slightly different are areas where regional cooperation mechanisms have placed much emphasis on other critical elements of GCE, such as civics and citizenship, democracy and good governance, as well as peace and tolerance.[42]
5. Based on an ethics of caring and compassion, GCE seeks to understand, explain and solve the immigration crisis of today. The question of the human rights of immigrants remains elusive for the human rights regime.
6. The world is changing, cultures are intersecting, and borders are more permeable than ever. Global citizenship education will be able to respond to one of the most important impacts of globalization: the *growing cultures of hybridity that crisscross the world*. Hybridity is everywhere— in music and youth cultures, taste, dress and speech codes, culinary delights and aesthetic expressions—and it is also changing identities.
7. Global Citizenship Education is a way of learning with a strong emphasis on the collective dimensions of knowledge in a rapidly evolving

epoch where we are bombarded by "self-directed learning," "individualized modules" or "possessive competitive individualism"—these mostly connected to neoliberalism as outlined by Mayo.[43]

8. Global Citizenship Education will help to connect the global and the local dimensions, synchronizing national educational policies to the global policies advocated by the United Nations. The 69th Session of the United Nations Assembly set 17 Sustainable Development Goals and 169 targets demonstrating the scale and ambition of a new universal post-2015 development agenda. For global citizenship education, goal 4.7 is most relevant: "By 2030, ensure that all learners acquire the knowledge and skills needed to promote sustainable development, including, among others, through education for sustainable development and sustainable lifestyles, human rights, gender equality, promotion of a culture of peace and non-violence, global citizenship and appreciation of cultural diversity and of culture's contribution to sustainable development."[44]

The most complete formulation of public education responsibilities is the *Universal Declaration of Human Rights* (1948), a document issued in the aftermath of World War II when the international community, shocked by the contemporary tragic events, convened to find ways to prevent such conflagrations from ever happening again. The *Universal Declaration* states in Article 26:

> Education shall be directed to the full development of the human personality and to the strengthening of respect for human rights and fundamental freedoms. It shall promote understanding, tolerance and friendship among all nations, racial or religious groups, and shall further the activities of the United Nations for the maintenance of peace.

In this spirit, GCE brings together the agendas of different fields of education including development education, human rights education, education for sustainability, education for peace and conflict prevention, intercultural and interfaith education and the global dimension of education for citizenship.

9. GCE will enhance the threshold of a new global consciousness based on human rights and universal values, but also incorporate diversity and a critical analysis of power relations and global inequalities. A key component of research should focus on teachers and teachers' education. Research methods such as the practice of participatory action research will cultivate strategies that work in promoting GCE.

10. GCE can address issues of the youth bulge by contributing to develop new 21st century skills for youth worldwide who are growing restless and facing a jobless future. And the future is already here. In the faces

and dreams but also in the anguish and hopelessness of those children and youth who wonder about their own future; wonder how they can participate in politics and society and help their communities; wonder how they can understand and solve local and global crises; wonder whether they will have a job; wonder if those jobs will produce inner satisfaction; and wonder if they will be able to pay their bills. A large number of youth today do not work, study or actively participate as citizens. Through GCE research, policy and practice, we should seek to understand, address and offer viable sustainable solutions for disenfranchised and marginalized youth.

11. GCE employs a new lifelong learning perspective in the transition from education to work. Challenging inequalities of many kinds, we face the need to incorporate more poor and underrepresented people as well as women and girls and racial, ethnic and religious marginalized minorities in different educational environments; this particularly entails reshaping the investment in higher education. For instance, we may consider implementing GCE as a diversity requirement course throughout undergraduate education in the US and worldwide, or perhaps even create a network of GCE courses as a diversity requirement in many universities of the world committed to quality of education and the interruption of inequality. This would be compatible with the strategy of internationalization being pursued by quality universities in the world system, particularly the universities I have defined as global universities.

12. In a world that is increasingly interdependent, GCE promotes a *sense of belonging and active responsibility* to the global community and the planet. It emphasizes a shared common humanity and destiny among people and a critical stewardship of our biosphere and natural environment.

4.2. Citizens' Schools[45]

Citizens' schools or *escola cidadã* was a concept developed during Freire's administration as Secretary of Education of the City of São Paulo and further expanded by the Paulo Freire Institutes.[46] The concept of *escola cidadã* in Latin America is very strongly linked to the movement of popular and communitarian education, which in the 1980s resulted in the movement for a public popular school as a model to be implemented in various regions of Brazil. The concept of popular education is the most important contribution of Latin American educators to universal pedagogical thought. Citizens' schools are a new type of school that does not simply impart knowledge, but creates and administers knowledge. It is an ecopolitical and pedagogical project; that is to say, it is an eminently ethical project, an innovative school, constructing meaning while it is intimately connected to the world. In an interview Freire gave to the TV Educadora do Rio de Janeiro on March 19, 1997, he defined *escola cidadã* as a social

and political-pedagogical space that becomes a center of rights and responsibilities, and therefore citizenship building takes place.[47] It is a public
and popular school system, one in which people from all walks of life but
particularly those who are discriminated and marginalized, find ways to
express themselves, to learn about themselves, the world and the cultural
domains. Freire's conscientization is a way to work towards new models
of social transformation of both social relationships and productive forces
in a given society.

Citizens' schools (*escola cidadã*) is a center of rights and responsibilities,
where citizenship is created. It cannot be a *citizen school* in itself and for
itself: It is a citizen school or *escola cidadã* insofar as it facilitates the building of citizenship among those citizens who use its space. An *escola cidadã* is
a school that is consistent with an experience of freedom and works through
a formative and liberating discourse. It is a school that is struggling for itself
and for all those who educate and are educated, so that they can be themselves. And because people cannot be themselves alone, an *escola cidadã* is
a school of the community, of camaraderie. It is a school where knowledge
and freedom are produced in common, all together. It is a school that can
never permit a kind of cavalier licentiousness; similarly, it can never allow
authoritarianism. It is a school that lives the tense and always fragile experience of democracy.

The curriculum of the *escola cidadã* is considered the space of socio-
cultural relationships. It is not only the space of knowledge but also the
space of debates about human and social relationships; the space of power,
of work and of caring; the space of respectfully living together. This is the
link with ethics, with the notion of sustainability,[48] with the question of
how education can contribute to prevent violence. The curriculum and the
eco-political and pedagogical project of the school are inseparable realities.
The curriculum reveals the political-pedagogical trajectory of the school,
its successes and failures. For the school to facilitate the achievement of the
possible dreams and desires of all their members—teachers, staff, students
and community—then the curriculum has to be intimately related to the
life project of each one of them. That is why the curriculum needs to be
constantly evaluated and reevaluated.[49] The project of an *escola cidadã* is
considered, in terms of process and context, an institutional and individual
life project.

Education for citizenship is at the same time an education for a sustainable society. *Escola cidadã* and eco-pedagogy sustain the principle that all of
us, from the time we are children, have the fundamental right to dream, to
make possible our projects, to invent. As Marx and Freire have argued, we
all have the right to decide our own destiny, including the children defended
by the distinguished Jewish-Polish educator Janusz Korczak, who refused to
be set free and stayed with his orphan students when they were sent from
the ghetto to Treblinka extermination camp, accepting to die in the Nazi
gas chambers jointly with his students. Yet, the issue is not to reduce the

school and pedagogy today to a *tabula rasa* and build on its ashes the ideal *escola cidadã* and eco-pedagogy. We are not talking about an alternative school and pedagogy in the sense that these would have to be constructed separately from today's existing schools and pedagogy.

Rather, this new pedagogical and political model is starting from the school we have and the pedagogy we actually practice, in order to dialectically build other possibilities without destroying what already exists. The future is not the annihilation of the past, but its improvement.[50]

4.3.   Planetary Citizenship

On the basis of the theoretical intuitions of Paulo Freire and his remarkable theoretical work, the Paulo Freire Institutes continue to reinvent his legacy.[51] Our current problems, including ecological problems, are provoked by our way of living; in many respects, school bears a great deal of responsibility for how we live. Our understanding of the world we live in and our way of life depends to a considerable extent on what the school does or does not teach, the values that are or are not transmitted, and the curriculum or the books that are taught or not taught. There is a growing bibliography on the connections between education and planetary citizenship, including case studies and new theoretical developments on the topic.[52]

We thus need to reorient education, starting with the principle of sustainability—that is, to redress education in its totality. This implies a revision of curricula and programs, educational systems, the role of the school and the teachers and school organization. The notion of eco-pedagogy as developed by the Paulo Freire Institutes implies a reorientation of curricula to make us understand that we need to consider the planet a unique community and the Earth our mother, an organism that is alive and in evolution. We also need to build a new consciousness of what is sustainable, appropriate and makes sense for our existence. We need to be gentle with the Earth as our home, our unique address, and to develop a sense of socio-cosmic justice, seeing the Earth as a victim of poverty and oppression.[53] We need to promote life, communicate among ourselves, share, problematize, create new relationships and live with enthusiasm. As Greg Misiaszek explained, following Moacir Gadotti:

> Planetary citizenship is based on a unifying vision of a planet and a worldwide society. It manifests itself in different expressions: 'our common humanity', 'unity in diversity', 'our common future' and 'our common homeland'. Planetary citizenship expresses a set of principles, values, attitudes and behaviours that brings a new perception of the Earth as a single community. Frequently associated with the concept of 'sustainable development', it is much broader than simply a relation with the economy.[54]

This debate is particularly relevant for higher education. The conclusion of this analysis is stated in an article we published with Greg Misiaszek and Lauren I. Jones:

> We argue that to develop a planetary citizenship in which the earth is a participatory democratic member; higher education must adopt a model of ecopedagogy. Ecopedagogy refers to alternatives to traditional models of environmental education that are often placed in a framework of economically based sustainable development theories. Ecopedagogy, by definition, focuses upon social justice in the teaching of environmental problems and the development of possible solutions beyond the scope of existing scientific, political, and economic frameworks. Rather than teaching, which focuses solely on the tangible reasons and most immediate sources of incentives for various forms of environmental degradation, a progressive, macro-perspective pedagogy is needed for multi-variant, planetary sustainability to determine the deeper sources of problems and solutions to them.[55]

4.4. A Culture of Peace[56]

To secure a culture of peace is one of the main reasons why we need Global Citizenship Education and why we need it now. In a previous chapter I discussed how we can define global peace, referring to the Global Peace Index.[57]

What are the main problems affecting global peace? Domination, aggression, exploitation, discrimination and oppression of people, families, communities, nations and the planet are crucial elements undermining progress, peace and happiness on Earth. Paulo Freire, recognizing that relations of domination are central to public and private life, argued that domination, aggression and violence are an intrinsic part of human and social life. Any political education nourishing the construction of a public sphere should recognize that overcoming oppression, domination and exploitation is a central goal of any project of global democratic citizenship building.[58]

There are multiple manifestations of structural violence that add to individual, collective and government actions undermining peace. There are multiple causes in the global system undermining peace and prosperity, and to put it into the conceptualization of Freire they may be considered structural violence.[59] This cluster of problems includes but cannot be restricted to: 1) unabating poverty; 2) growing inequality; 3) neoliberal globalization, which has weakened the systems of organized solidarity of the democratic nation-state; 4) banking education with authoritarian and inadequate curriculum in elementary, secondary and higher education; and 5) destruction of the planet's ecosystem.[60]

The importance of these problems cannot be minimized and needs further exploration and analysis as well as imaginative solutions, to which a global citizenship education social movement may contribute.

4.5.   Global Consciousness

Global citizenship could be based on a particular appraisal of the importance of spirituality (secular and/or religious) in the life of people and communities. In multiple debates it is argued for the creation of a movement of *global spirituality as global consciousness.*[61] Many have argued for the need of a *Council of World Consciousness* as one of the engines of the global commons, and one way in which our human civilization, creeds and faiths can accomplish a rich and informed dialogue in solidarity.[62] Global consciousness is not the same as international global-mindedness as the keystone for 21st century learning and predicated by the International Baccalaureate (IB).[63]

The question has been posed: If it exists, is global consciousness an aggregate of emotions and experiences that could be considered non-random? A group of Princeton researchers have developed the Global Consciousness Project based on the hypotheses that (and I quote from their website): "Coherent consciousness creates order in the world. Subtle interactions link us with each other and the Earth."

As described on their website, their argument is that:

> When human consciousness becomes coherent, the behavior of random systems may change. Random number generators (RNGs) based on quantum tunneling produce completely unpredictable sequences of zeroes and ones. But when a great event synchronizes the feelings of millions of people, our network of RNGs becomes subtly structured. We calculate one in a trillion odds that the effect is due to chance. The evidence suggests an emerging noosphere or the unifying field of consciousness described by sages in all cultures.[64]

On their website, they have argued that:

> The Global Consciousness Project is an international, multidisciplinary collaboration of scientists and engineers. We collect data continuously from a global network of physical random number generators located in up to 70 host sites around the world at any given time. The data are transmitted to a central archive which now contains more than 15 years of random data in parallel sequences of synchronized 200-bit trials generated every second.

Our purpose is to examine subtle correlations that may reflect the presence and activity of consciousness in the world. We hypothesize that there will be structure in what should be random data, associated with major global events that engage our minds and hearts. Subtle but real effects of consciousness are important scientifically, but their real power is more immediate. They encourage us to make essential, healthy changes in the great systems that dominate our world. Large-scale group consciousness has effects in the physical world. Knowing this, we can intentionally work toward a brighter, more conscious future. "The Global Consciousness Project, created originally in the Princeton Engineering Anomalies Research Lab at Princeton University, is directed by Roger Nelson from his home office in Princeton. The Institute of Noetic Sciences provides a logistical home for the GCP."[65]

For this methodology, events like the September 11, 2001 attack on the World Trade Center towers will either induce simultaneous emotions or attract simultaneous attention of a large number of individuals, hence showing that there is a connection between individual consciousness and systems that eventually become less random, forming more coherent forms of consciousness:

> We hypothesize that our instrument (the network of "eggs") will show anomalous deviations associated with Global Events when there is widespread participation or reaction to the event.[66]

They claim that the results of 500 simulations show that "The overall result is highly significant. The odds against chance are more than a trillion to one."[67]

While this discussion is absolutely fascinating, my goal is to think of a global civic movement that may promote global consciousness as an individual but also collective phenomena, as a social product and therefore one that could be educated, reaching a greater level of conviviality across cultures and crossing the lines of difference in celebration of diversity, which should be the ultimate goal of global consciousness.[68]

This section will take advantage of the contributions of phenomenology, existentialism and particularly the peculiar and rich synthesis provided by Freire. The goal is to speak about the nature of individual and collective consciousness, both as global social consciousness, and to speak about values that would be emphasized in an ethics of consciousness raising for global citizenship education.

To begin with, I would like to discuss the nature of consciousness and the nature of culture, themes that I have defined in detail in other works, with a particular emphasis on the historical possibilities of consciousness.[69]

To understand the dialectics between consciousness and culture, the anthropological concept of culture used by Freire is very important: *Culture* is the systematic acquisition of human experience, and knowing is equivalent to modifying. Freire identifies here with the personalist concept of culture following Mounier's analysis: "Culture is not one sector, but a comprehensive function of the personal life. For a being who finds himself, and forms himself by a process of development, everything is culture, the management of a factory or the formation of a body no less than the conduct of a conversation or the cultivation of the soil. That is to say there is not a culture, in distinction from which every other activity is uncultured (a 'cultured man') but there are as many kinds of culture as of activity."[70]

Psychological (individual) consciousness carries out a movement towards things, towards objective reality, with the purpose of knowing them, while things in turn, calling out to this psychological consciousness, challenges it.[71] This is because things are not presented in their immediacy but covered in a patina. For Freire, drawing from the rich phenomenological tradition, there are four historical possibilities of consciousness. The first movement or historical possibility of consciousness is *intentionality*. Consciousness is always about something, about some object; it is always sensed, projected towards the outside, towards the 'other.' The second historical possibility or movement is that consciousness transforms the 'thing in itself' into an object of knowledge. We will denominate this second possibility as *objectivity*. In this moment consciousness carries out an inventory of the objects surrounding it: It is descriptive. A third historical possibility which presupposes the other two is *criticality*. Here the consciousness scans the identified 'thing in itself,' in an effort to know its internal components. It is no longer only simple identification and recognition—the level of objectification—but rather tends towards discovering the laws of the development of the object. This moment, without any doubt, is qualitatively superior to the others.

Finally, transcendentality constitutes a fourth possibility. Concerning this, Freire says, "Transcendence in this context signifies the capacity of human consciousness to surpass the limitations of the objective configuration. Without this 'transcendental intentionality' consciousness of what exists beyond limitations would be impossible. For example I am aware of how the table at which I write limits me—only because I can transcend focus my attention upon is limits."[72] This transcendentality resembles in no way vertical transcendentality, which directs its explanatory effort outside of the material and concrete universe in search of an infinite beyond. This transcendentality, on the other hand, is eminently finite, an unfailing property and characteristic trait of the human being. This finiteness allows human beings to seek the tendential laws of the development of the phenomenon at the same time that the consciousness grasps the internal components of the object. That is, human beings grasp its laws of development, as phenomenon, just as much as they grasp its inherent contradictions and also capture the material immediacy and pure essentiality in its tendential forms. If we were to express it metaphorically, then we would say that the consciousness tends to capture the life of the object and its destiny.

To summarize: The first historical possibility, *intentionality*, marks genetically the effort of consciousness to express the moment of knowledge, going outside of itself (abstract); the second moment, or *objectivity*, converts the object into object-of-knowledge; the third moment or historical possibility, *criticality*, discovers the internal components of the object-of-knowledge and expresses it in concepts, to arrive at the fourth moment or historical possibility, *transcendentality*, which captures the internal movement of the object-of-knowledge in its fundamental components and in its contradictions in such a way as to facilitate the projection of a 'rational' action-praxis which does not affect the object as such (it does not mutate it), and whereas, in turn, it is an historically viable action.

The theoretical model of Freire describes different forms of consciousness as follows: semi-transitive consciousness, transitive naïve consciousness and transitive critical consciousness. Defining the characteristics of the semi-intransitive consciousness, Freire says, "There is a mode of consciousness which corresponds to the concrete reality of such dependent societies. It is a consciousness historically conditioned by the social structure. The principal characteristic of this consciousness, as dependent as the society to whose structure it conforms, is its 'quasi-adherence' to objective reality . . . [The] dominated consciousness does not have sufficient distance from reality to objectify it in order to know it in a critical way. We call this mode of consciousness 'semi-transitive' . . . ."[73]

The second level of possible consciousness has been denominated as *transitive naive* consciousness, which ". . . is characterized, among other aspects, by simplicity in the interpretation of problems; by the tendency to judge that the better time was the past time; by the underestimation of the common man; by a strong inclination towards gregarianism, characteristic of massification; by impermeability to research, to which corresponds a heightened taste for fabulous explanations; by fragility in argumentation; by a strong emotional fear; by the practice not exactly of dialogue but rather of polemics; by magical explanations."[74]

The last phase of consciousness is represented by the *transitive critical consciousness*, which, being the immediate opposite of the previous one, obtains a structural perception of problems resulting from its (committed) critical insertion in the process of transformation (social change). Freire uses Goldmann's concept here, by which consciousness would attain its antithesis, which is the *maximum consciousness possible.*[75] *Altogether Freire described four forms of consciousness:*

> *Critical consciousness* ". . . is the representation of things and facts as they appear in empirical existence, in their causal and circumstantial correlations," notable for "its integration with reality."[76]
>
> *Ingenuous (or naïve) consciousness* ". . . (on the other hand) believes itself superior to the facts, dominating them from outside and therefore thinks itself free to interpret them however it wishes." It is notable for "what it superimposes on reality."[77]
>
> *Magical consciousness* ". . . on the other hand, does not consider itself superior to the facts, dominating them from the outside, nor does it think itself free to interpret them however it wishes. People simply believe them, granting them a greater power which they fear because it dominates them from outside and they docilely submit to it. This leads to fanaticism."[78]

> *Fanatical consciousness*, ". . . whose pathology of ingenuousness leads to the irrational . . . " and its hallmarks are ". . . [to settle for] what is adequate, to accommodate, to adjust, and to adapt."[79]

Freire's typology is useful to emphasize the need to identify forms of consciousness that will be beneficial to cultural understanding of human rights as a quintessential landmark for a model of global solidarity and conviviality, hence the suggestion that we need to develop a global consciousness.

Yet we encounter a typical dilemma, a typical conundrum of the human rights regime: There is not a universal culture that applies to all individuals in the same way and with the same level and patterns of understanding and meaning-making. How can we then have a common humanity and a global consciousness? Accepting that understanding dialogue across cultures and making this dialogue the cradle of seeking collective understanding and enjoyment of the global commons is entering into unchartered territories, there we must enter, tiptoeing as if we were in field full of personal mines.

We need to do more empirical research on the interrelations between culture and consciousness. Yet there is a basic supposition that makes sense: Global problems require global solutions, and to achieve global solutions we need global consciousness as a form of intentionality to solve the problems.

The idea of global consciousness cannot only be a rhetorical device or a metaphor; it has to be a goal to achieve in creating sustainable development. Despite the deniers, global warming is a serious problem that requires global science and global consciousness to implement through political power but also through intellectual persuasion measures that require a basic global consciousness.

What is global consciousness? How it can be defined and measured? Perhaps these questions do not have a clear answer yet and should be the subject of empirical research and capacity-building teaching workshops. There are to be sure, a number of global citizens who seem to display a different consciousness. Examples are presented by Richard Falk's typology[80] of five categories of global citizens including: (1) the "global reformer" and supporter of supranational government; (2) the elite class of globetrotters engaged in global business activities; (3) individuals committed to global economic and ecological sustainability; (4) supporters of regional governance structures as in the example of the European Union; and (5) transnational activists involved in grassroots organizations fighting for human rights and democracy.

A fundamental trait of the intentionality of the consciousness should be civic engagement, well argued by John Rogers and described in UCLA *Ampersand* newsletter:

> Rogers underscores the importance of robust civic learning and engagement for low-income youth, and says that it is particularly critical in

low-income communities and immigrant communities where civic participation levels have not historically been as high as in other communities. His 2013 study titled, "Learning to Lead: The Impact of Youth Organizing on the Educational and Civic Trajectories of Low-Income Youth" (with Veronica Terriquez, USC), examines the many positive outcomes that occur when low-income and immigrant youth participate in youth organizing, addressing issues such as educational equity and school policy making. Their findings charted the effect of youth organizing on 18–25-year-olds who had participated in these activities.

"Youth organizing groups have focused most of their attention on educational reform," says Rogers. "One of the reasons that I've become interested in this is that efforts to make schools more equitable and responsive to the needs of the community traditionally have focused a lot of their attention on teachers or researchers, [who] have a limited role that they can play in transforming the politics. Youth and community organizing groups can play a really substantial role in changing the inequalities that exist.[81]

In addition to valuable work like that of my colleague John Rogers, one of the best Dewey experts, one may ask: How useful are these typologies to understanding global citizenship education and global consciousness and to solving practical problems?

Professor Liliane Windsor from the University of Illinois-Urbana Champaign School of Social Work has developed a scale of consciousness inspired by a Freirean understanding. They are in the pilot stages of the initial validation of a new scale designed to assess critical consciousness about health disparities. Specifically, they want to measure people's knowledge about social determinants of health and health disparities and they want to measure how their behavior may contribute to or address social determinants of health and health disparities.[82]

The States of Engaged Awareness include:

1. *Active Conformity*: Lack of understanding about social determinants of health with destructive action: Someone who is oblivious to social determinants of health and who actively engages to maintain the status quo. Scores high on destructive action and low on understanding.

2. *Conformity Coping*: Deep understanding about social determinants of health with destructive action: This is a person who gets the concept of social determinants of health very well but who continues to knowingly maintain the system and engage in destructive action (e.g., someone who knows they experience privilege and takes steps to maintain their privilege). Scores high on understanding and destructive action.

3. *Passive Conformity*: Lack of understanding about social determinants of health with no critical action: A person who does not get social

determinants of health and avoids actions that can disrupt the status quo. Scores low on understanding and high in inaction.

4. *Alienation*: Deep understanding about social determinants of health with no critical action: The person who gets social determinants of health but avoids actions that can disrupt the status quo. Scores high on understanding and inaction.

5. *Critical Unconsciousness*: Lack of understanding about social determinants of health with critical action: Oblivious to social determinants of health but haphazardly engages in critical action. Scores low on understanding and high on critical action.

6. *Critical Consciousness*: Deep understanding about social determinants of health with critical action: This is a person who understands social determinants of health and engages in action to change the world. Scores high on critical action and understanding.

Words in **bold** are dimensions and those not in bold are the typology we want to achieve.

Would it be possible to devise a scale to assess understanding, implementation and outcomes of global citizenship education and global consciousness that may help the common problems of humanity?

Now, if we can achieve global consciousness raising through a GCE global social movement, what should be the principles that might inspire the practices?

A global hegemonic culture or a global cultural canon should be questioned and challenged if one were to follow the social epistemological principles of this movement. Human rights have become a consensual principle of action which needs to be periodically revisited to decouple it from neo-imperial actions or hegemonic forces.

We need to move beyond cognitive learning into emotional affective learning that constitutes the real drama of human beings, and we should do so as fleshed human beings, as men and women with our distinct bodies, in our corporality.

Ethnocentrism of any kind should be carefully avoided by cultivating a sense of epistemological self-vigilance. This is not a call to postmodernist relativism but a call for reasonable multicultural accommodation of differences and the virtues of self-reflection and self-criticism.

Table 10.1

	High Understanding	*Low Understanding*
High Critical Action	Critical consciousness	Critical Unconsciousness
High Inaction	Alienation	Passive Conformity
High Destructive Action	Conformity Coping	Active Conformity

We shall start from a double assumption that is difficult to accept. First, there is human finiteness, which should invite us to refuse the tendency to honor absolute or sacral truths that cannot be inspected. The script of the *Big Short*, a movie that was a candidate for the Oscars in 2016, tells us in laughable ways about the tension between the sacred incommensurable and rational explorations for self-perceived truths:

Rabbi: Paul is a fine boy. But his brother . . . Mark . . . He is the best student of the Torah and the Talmud . . .
Mom: Then what's the problem, Rabbi?
Rabbi: It's the reason . . . He says he studies so hard because . . . he is looking for inconsistencies in the word of God.
Mom: So has he found any?

A most difficult assumption is to accept our own incompleteness as human beings, which also applies to our incompleteness as communities, as regions and as nations.

Bill Pinar tells a story about the iconic and famous US existentialist philosopher of education, Maxine Greene from Teachers College, Columbia University. She was asked to speak about "her present passions" and what were they when she faced her 80th year. Pinar writes: "How does she think of herself? She asked that question that morning, toward the end of the speech. 'Who am I?' she posed, half to us, half to herself, then paused before the answer: 'I am who I am not yet.'"[83]

Fellow philosopher Paulo Freire speaks of the world, and of us, individuals, as incomplete and unfinished work in progress:

> . . . to teach demands conviction that change is possible. . . . Knowledge that history as possibility and not as determination. The world is not done, the world has been constructed. As subjectivity which is curious, intelligent, interfering with the objective reality with which I relate to; my role in the world is not the one that observes what happens but to intervene as a subject of changes. I am not only the object of history but I am the subject of history. I understand the world of history, of culture, of politics not to adapt but to change.[84]

Searching for key principles that we can nurture in our search for a global consciousness, it seems that Goldmann's "maximum consciousness possible" should be our mantra.[85] But how to reach our levels of maximum possible consciousness and how to nurture this process remains very elusive.

Even at risk of signifying concepts that are different things for different people, I have come to conclude that some elements should be part of a hermeneutic dialogue about global citizenship education in the search for global consciousness.

The first civic value that comes to mind is empathy. Without the ability and the sensibility to feel what the other feels it is near impossible to be able to share the pain and the dream of someone else who is not part of our own group, of our own ethnicity, race, gender, class, abilities, sexual preference, region, nation, culture, tribe or civilization. Some people are born with a great disposition to empathy; some are not. In any event we need to nurture the capacity of people to affectively participate in the reality of others.

Without empathy, calls for solidarity become an empty shell. It is easy to be in solidarity with people we love, know intimately, appreciate or are part of a group we feel we belong to. But what about to be in solidarity with people we do not know, or about whom we do not really have a predisposition to care? This is the great dilemma of solidarity in any society and across civilizations and cultures. Therefore the importance of an ethic of solidarity towards the other—no matter how different or how opposing our viewpoints are.

In the tradition of Western societies, solidarity had been confined first and foremost to the family and eventually extrapolated to our religion and our churches, which in many cases constitute the best evidence of our existential network of emotional support. Ultimately, but with a greater degree of generalization, the question of solidarity has been projected in the idea of citizens of a nation-state. At this level, the democratic state become the lynchpin of how to construct solidarity across differences, and this very important social function which constructs as well as builds social cohesion cannot be left to the vagaries of the market or the private sector.

Thus philanthropy and charity as a form of solidarity, as important as they can be, cannot be left to individual wishes and ethics. It requires an organized structure. Solidarity as a form of living together should be inspired, organically coordinated, financed and implemented by the democratic nation-state, which is the ultimate source of organized solidarity, particularly in the form of the welfare state. That is what is meant when politicians refer to the 'safety net.'

Solidarity should be a public good. Marginson, following the Keynesian economist Samuelson, defines public goods as "nonrivalrous and nonexcludable. Goods are nonrivalrous when they can be consumed by any number of people without being depleted—for example, knowledge of a mathematical theorem. Goods are nonexcludable when the benefits cannot be confined to individual buyers, such as social tolerance or law and order. Few goods are both fully nonrivalrous and fully nonexcludable, but many have one or other quality in part or full. Goods with neither quality are classified as fully private goods."[86]

To fully achieve empathy and solidarity, we need to nurture dialogue as a method as much as a social epistemological position.

4.6. *Public Diplomacy*

The creation of a GCE social movement should influence the domains of public diplomacy, both at the level of an emerging field of study which is well represented in new programs created in many countries and universities—for instance, the Center for Public Diplomacy at the University of Southern California,[87] and government interactions as people's democracy. The concept was originally formulated by Edmund Guillion, a career diplomat, in 1965 with the aim of:

> . . . influence of public attitudes on the formation and execution of foreign policies. It encompasses dimensions of international relations beyond traditional diplomacy . . . [including] the cultivation by governments of public opinion in other countries; the interaction of private groups and interests in one country with those of another . . . (and) the transnational flow of information and ideas.[88]

Many governments have sections for public diplomacy in their foreign affairs offices. For instance, the United States government has an Under Secretary for Public Diplomacy and Public Affairs. See the following description on the website:

> The mission of American public diplomacy is to support the achievement of U.S. foreign policy goals and objectives, advance national interests, and enhance national security by informing and influencing foreign publics and by expanding and strengthening the relationship between the people and Government of the United States and citizens of the rest of the world.
> The Under Secretary for Public Diplomacy and Public Affairs . . . leads America's public diplomacy outreach, which includes communications with international audiences, cultural programming, academic grants, educational exchanges, international visitor programs, and U.S. Government efforts to confront ideological support for terrorism. The Under Secretary oversees the bureaus of Educational and Cultural Affairs, Public Affairs, and International Information Programs, as well as the Global Engagement Center, and participates in foreign policy development.[89]
> The goal of public diplomacy is to develop a people's to people's exchanges, trying to advance models of communication and eventually propaganda, that facilitate international exchanges, global dialogue, foreign policy development. Many Centers for Public Diplomacy have been formed in the past century, and the field as a research and teaching field has grown in academic institutions. As an expression of media relations it has been linked to the propaganda efforts of the United State to convince its citizens that the United States has to enter the war in Europe to defeat Fascism, and then was intimately linked to the Cold War efforts to prevent the spread of Communism. For instance U.S. Congressman, Henry Hyde (R-IL) in November 2001 argued, "The role that I would set for our public diplomacy [is] to enlist the populations of the world into a common cause and to convince them that the goals that they seek for themselves—freedom, security, and prosperity—are the same as the those the United States seeks.[90]

The statement by Hyde has a recognizable hegemonic stance. Most contemporarily, it has been associated with new roles that emerging countries with economic surplus and ready to flex their muscle in their regions are beginning to create, mechanisms in which public diplomacy plays a major part in this effort worldwide. A case in point is Korea, which considers public diplomacy as a tool of soft power.[91]

As a diplomatic strategy based on soft power, "The Republic of Korea (ROK) designated the year 2010 as the starting point to promote public diplomacy. We established the 'Korea Public Diplomacy Forum (KPDF),' a permanent civilian advisory group in the field of public diplomacy. Likewise, an ambassador for public diplomacy—to control and coordinate public diplomacy strategy—was appointed."[92]

Peter G. Peterson, chairman of the Peter G. Peterson Foundation, argued in 2001–2002 in the influential *Foreign Affairs* journal for the importance of public diplomacy for the War on Terrorism. He claims, "An essential starting point is to recognize that U.S. foreign policy is weakened by a failure to include public diplomacy systematically in the formulation and implementation of policy. The motivation for such inclusion is not simply to win popularity or to drive U.S. policy by forging foreign public approval. Rather, public diplomacy is important because foreign attitudes and understanding can affect the success or failure of initiatives. Examples of misunderstood or misguided policies include the rejections of the Kyoto Protocol on global warming, the treaty to ban anti-personnel land mines, the agreement to create the International Criminal Court, and the Genocide Convention."[93]

It seems that the concept of public democracy, or people-to-people exchanges, has evolved from being a subterfuge for official government propaganda to becoming a tool of soft power in the hands of people, socially conscious governments and administrations trying to create new forms of social, cultural and civic engagement, and of international organizations like UNESCO or the United Nations exercising an influence, albeit fragile and limited it might be.

A global youth social movement should take advantage of these developments and implement a robust and innovative model of public democracy as youth soft power, a model that is based in academic and political work in high schools and universities, themselves a marketplace of ideas, for creating new forms of consciousness promoting solidarity, conflict resolution and a culture of peace. The soft power of public diplomacies should be exercised by youth who are trained in specific leadership programs and may find ways to present their voices and programs in the context of nations and international relations. Multiple leadership programs exist,[94] but they lack coordination and comparable visions; moreover, their numbers are insufficient to help promote the plight of youth voices and under-represented, socially subordinated sectors.

5. GCE as a Global Youth Social Movement

Citizenship building is not exclusively but primarily about identity formation, a central topic in civic education, and a great challenge for youth in the 21st century. Traditional forms of socialization are in peril with the digital culture transformation in the globalization era, homogenizing but also fragmenting what sociologists have called "cultural capital" or the "cultural wealth" of communities.[95] Schools have been deeply affected by multiple changes, particularly and most recently by the multiple waves of immigration crossing borders.

Globalization has created multiple pockets of modern, highly educated populations, including postmodernist expressions in art, humanities and science, side by side with premodern, peripheral, marginal or indigenous populations and cultures. Heteronomous groups of immigrants in multiple waves, fueled by a diversity of determinants (i.e., war in their own territories, persecution, or simply poverty or lack of jobs), are forced to find new landscapes for their own lives, crossing borders constantly.

These cultures are marked by deep cultural and linguistic discontinuities with the dominant cultural capital prevailing in schools and societies, particularly when public schools were conceived by the state as central tools and tenets of a modernist discourse.

Thus it is not too risky to argue that schools and universities are facing a crisis of hegemony which requires finding new concepts to take stock of the new subjects, both teachers and pupils in the changing political landscape of contemporary social formations, in a world defined by Ulrich Beck as a risk society, as expression of the new modernity.[96]

Hegemony is a complex concept that has not lost its power to characterize current institutional formations. As I have said elsewhere: "Gramsci introduces the notion of hegemony as a more "extensive" notion to assess the "ideological" phenomena of capitalist societies. Insofar as hegemony is founded on coercion and consensus, it is an educative relationship. Similarly, despite the fact that hegemony is exerted by the ruling class, it is organized in capitalist society by a particular social category, the intellectuals. The notion of hegemony then, refers to the relationships between groups, especially social classes. A social class can be thought of as exercising hegemony over other "subaltern" classes. However, hegemonic domination does not rest exclusively on ideology but on material relationships in society that inspire the basic values portrayed as legitimate and successful. Hugues Portelli (1972) argues that Gramsci's notion of ideology as a world view, and hence a concept close to the notion of *weltanschauung*, is manifested in art, law, economic activity and any manifestation of intellectual and collective life. Portelli emphasizes that Gramsci suggests a three-fold approach: "(a) ideology as such, as content; (b) the ideological structure of society, such as the cultural organizations that create and transmit ideology; (c) the ideological material, that is the language that is structuring a conversation in terms of a determinate syntax or grammar but exercising only partial control over the content of the communicate exchanged."[97]

These hegemonic crises get even more complex when they intersect with institutional crises and crises of legitimation, as it seems is the case in universities today. Portuguese sociologist Boaventura de Sousa Santos sees the university facing three pressing crises: the crisis of hegemony, the crisis of legitimacy and the institutional crisis as I have discussed in Chapter 5, concluding in agreement with Boaventura de Sousa Santos that concentrating on the institutional crisis served only to exacerbate the problems of hegemony and legitimacy.[98]

Schools and universities are important sites where youth try to understand and construct their own identities, and connect, if even so slightly, with the culture of their ancestors and with the logical and legal strictures of the nation-state. So it is important to understand how these crises (of hegemony, institutional crisis and legitimation crisis) relate to the problem of national identity; what role the state attributes to the school system and teachers' professional work; how the public/private cleavage in education is changing in the context of neoliberalism; and how the new social problems drastically depart from the social problems school systems faced in the past. These questions become magnified with the new challenges of the 21st century.

These new social problems in the new globalization era include but are not limited to the educational needs and educational activities of children and youth who have been expelled from the systems—some of them are named 'street children' in the underdeveloped world, or youth who do not study or work; how the culture of drug trafficking is affecting educational establishments; and how private networks of communication and informatics are changing the status, reliability and accessibility of school knowledge. Add to this the lack of entry-level jobs and full-time jobs with security of employment and benefits for youth 15 years of age and older—there is a deficit of 1.8 billion jobs for the young generations worldwide. Jointly with the crises of schooling and universities, the lack of jobs makes for a very explosive cocktail in identity formation.[99] Add to this already complex list of activities, which are by no means comprehensive, the questions posed to UNESCO by many governments of how education can prevent violent extremism, and we have a most difficult task ahead of us.

Moreover, as newspaper articles remind us time and again, "The crash of 2008 showed how globalization creates losers as well as winners," said Mark Leonard, the director of the European Council on Foreign Relations. "In many countries, middle-class wages are stagnant and politics has become a battle over a shrinking pie. Populists have replaced contests between left and right with a struggle between cosmopolitan elites and angry nativists."[100]

In this context, a global social movement should first and foremost serve youth as a historical category, becoming a vehicle for youth's voices to be heard and initiatives implemented. New leadership models should help develop "competencies and capabilities of future global leaders to shape peaceful and sustainable societies, through transformative learning across knowledge, sectoral and geographic boundaries."[101]

But do we need a single global youth social and civic movement, or do we need an articulation of movements? There are many possible emphases and perhaps not a single response to this question. For instance, a first emphasis following the principle of intentionality of consciousness is that unless specific, universal yet discrete efforts are made to push the project of global citizenship education beyond the realm of the nation-state or the corridors of power of the world system exemplified by the UN's specialized agencies, it may not come to life as a social movement. A second emphasis is about intersections. There is no question that many of the activists struggling for social justice, sustainability or citizenship share an immense number of commonalities. Thus, the intersectionality of a transnational social movement is a crucial network which could be expanded even more, and could constitute the cradle of a global consciousness. These emphases suggest that there is not an either/or option, but we shall seek models of implementation that make it possible for global citizenship education as part of a youth global social movement to become a reality.

As a critical theorist I have learned several lessons in my research and teaching: Politics and education intersect continuously—there is an inherent and ongoing politicization of education. Power plays a major role in configuring schooling and social reproduction. Social change cannot be simply articulated as social engineering from the calm environment of the research laboratory, in the hectic environment of bilateral, multilateral or international organizations, or even within the corridors of a ministry of education building.

Social change needs to be forged in negotiations and compromise as well as through struggles within political systems. This is an intrinsic part of the struggle—in the streets of social movements and community organizations. It is an outgrowth of schools that challenge bureaucratic and authoritarian dictates and defy the growing corporatization of educational institutions, particularly in higher education. In this context it should be a social movement striving to implement a rational dialogue, a dialogue that is achieved even in the cozy and joyful environment of our gatherings with our family and friends. Dialogue and reason cannot take vacations if one pursues the dream of social justice education and peace.

6. Confronting Dilemmas and Barriers

I would like to raise in these concluding comments two important dilemmas that, if we want to advance the course of Global Citizenship Education, and if we want to create a social movement, may need to be addressed via theoretical and empirical research.

The first one has to do with people's interests and pragmatic implementation of GCE. From a theoretical perspective, it is already difficult to understand social justice education in its intersectionality in terms of class, race, gender, sexual preference or disability, to name few intersecting 'variables' in the struggle for social justice education. Yet it gets even more complicated with other models of intersectionality—that is, social justice education related to economic justice, social justice, racial justice and ecological justice.[102]

Thus assuming that social justice education is a framework for implementing citizenship building, there is ample evidence that a great deal of courses connected with citizenship building (or civics) are merely rhetorical formulae that make little impact, if any, in the lives of youth and children or in the constitution of the nation-state.

Though there is a shift in the rhetoric regarding the importance of global citizenship education, there is evidence in many places one could argue, that citizenship building is not even implemented at all or that citizenship building has failed.[103] Its goals and purposes are well beyond the interest of people and communities in many places. This is particularly relevant when one thinks of the traditional philosophical tension in Western philosophy between freedom and need.

Global citizenship education is a model promoting human rights, freedom and liberty. It is an emblematic concept of the struggle of how to live together while being different. But how can we convince people whose standard of living is less than two dollars a day, for instance, in the case of Egypt so well studied by Jason Dorio's dissertation,[104] that we shall focus and spend energies in developing global citizenship education when their fundamental question is survival?

I have argued in this book that it is imperative to solve and provide the civil minimums for people to be considered citizens and act properly. The tensions between exercising freedom while being unable to provide for one's family provides an immense conundrum, more so in the context of neoliberal politics which have made the living conditions of the poor even worse.

There is another conundrum: Shall we focus on the creation of a new global social movement, or seek the articulation of interests, practices and narratives of multiple transnational social movements that compete for recognition while trying to address various forms of citizenship building within and across nations?

For example, there is overlap between the goals of Occupy Wall Street, *Podemos*, the World Social Forum, Black Lives Matter, and the clamor for "bread, freedom and social justice" in Egypt, to cite a handful of relevant cases with an strong impromptu in civil society. A relatively similar case can be made for UN attempts to build youth social movements and represent youth voices in international meetings.

Next is the question of the ideological character of such a movement. Assuming that the arguments made in this chapter and in other publications and forums will inspire such movement, this movement will be definitely very progressive. This includes a defense of democracy and the democratic state while criticizing the bureaucratization of policy and particularly the growing dominance of elite financing in public policy and public life. It will seek to promote global commons, defending the principles of planetary citizenship, a culture of peace as a treasure of humanity and precondition for growth and development, and provide a model that allows people to pursue their inalienable rights to life, liberty and the pursuit of happiness. These are the meta-theoretical principles of such a worldwide movement.

Based on the human rights regime, this social movement will pursue democratic engagement, decoupling human rights from imperialistic practices, hence assuming a post-colonial perspective. Defending a cosmopolitan democracy—after all most of the social movements that may form part of an alliance to establish this global social movement are transnational in nature and in practice—they will seek to find the exact balance between those who feel that national identity is under attack—particularly because of the growing immigration across borders—and defend the history and legacies of their own nations, regions and communities, as well as their national identities as bedrock of citizenship, and those who argue that the best way to protect national identities is to promote cosmopolitan identities and global citizenship education.

This balance is achieved by finding a way to harmonize the local and the global in a growingly diverse way, which needs international solidarity to protect people, planet and peace. As I said before, a global youth social movement will challenge the hierarchical and unequal principles according to which neoliberalism is built, and should defend democracy and democratic practices in the context of a global consciousness with cosmopolitan multicultural ethics: "Democracy is a messy system, but it has survived because there is a sphere of debates and a set of rules that people follow even if they don't benefit from them. Schools and universities for democratic communities cannot be less committed to expanding the democratic discourse and to challenging the political economy of capitalism. Without serious explorations of the intersections between cultural diversity, affirmative action, and citizenship, the plural bases for democracy and the democratic discourse per se are at risk. Without a technically competent, ethically sound, spiritually engaging, and politically feasible theory and practice of democratic multicultural citizenship, the people will perish."[105]

Addressing these conundrums so they do not become a barrier should be the subject of theoretical and empirical research.

Notes

1. A good discussion about the ambiguities of the concept is in Gaudelli, 2016, pp. 9–13.
2. Lynn Davies, "Global Citizenship Education: Abstraction or Framework for Action?", *Educational Review*, volume 58, number 1 (2006), pp. 5–25, www.tandfonline.com/doi/full/10.1080/00131910500352523

3. Manuel Castells has written a trilogy of books that are important reading to any sociologist or concerned citizen. See Castells, *The Rise of the Network Society*. Oxford: Blackwell, 1996; *The Power of Identity*. Oxford: Blackwell, 1997; and *End of Millennium*. Oxford: Blackwell, 1998.
4. Touraine, 1988, The return of the actor.
5. Torres, 1998b, p. 127.
6. Herrera and Sakr, 2014.
7. This section has been borrowed from Carlos Alberto Torres Editorial: "Globalization and Comparative Education in the World System", *Comparative Education Review*, volume 45, number 4 (November 2001), pp. iii–x; take from pp. iii–v.
8. Pierre Bourdieu, "O Neoliberalismo é como a sida", interview by Romain Leick, *Diario de Noticias* (July 21, 2001), p. 18.
9. Sem Terra. www.mstbrazil.org/content/what-mst
10. https://podemos.info/
11. Ruben Martinez, "The Ties That Bind Latinos", *Los Angeles Times* (August 5, 2001), sec. M, p. 2.
12. R. Burbach, *Globalization and Postmodern Politics: From Zapatistas to High-Tech Robber Barons*. London: Pluto Press, 2001; N.C. Burbules and C.A. Torres, "Globalization and Education: An Introduction", in *Globalization and Education: Critical Perspectives*, ed. N.C. Burbules and C.A. Torres. New York: Routledge, 2000.
13. José Eustáquio Romão, *Globalización o Planetarizacion. Las Trampas del Discurso Hegemónico*. Saõ Paulo: Instituto Paulo Freire, 2001; Octavio Ianni, *A era do globalismo*. Rio de Janeiro: Civilização Brasileira, 1996 and *A sociedade global*, 2nd ed. Rio de Janeiro: Civilização Brasileira, 1993.
14. Kenichi Ohmae, *The Borderless World: Power and Strategy in the Interlinked World Economy*. New York: Harper Business, 1990; Kenichi Ohmae, *The End of the Nation-State: The Rise of Regional Economies*. New York: Free Press, 1995.
15. James O'Connor, *The Fiscal Crisis of the State*. New York: St. Martin's Press, 1973; Jurgen Habermas, *Legitimation Crisis*, ed. and trans. Jeremy J. Shapiro. Boston: Beacon, 1975.
16. Carlos Alberto Torres, "State and Education: Marxist Theories", in T. Husen and T.N. Postlethwaite (Eds.), *International Encyclopedia of Education: Research and Studies*. Oxford: Pergamon, 1985, p. 8: 4793; cited in Carlos Alberto Torres, *Democracy, Education and Multiculturalism: Dilemmas of Citizenship in a Global World*. Lanham, MD: Rowman & Littlefield, 1998, p. 14.
17. Sydney Tarrow, 1998, p. 4.
18. When *Time* magazine named "The Protester" the 2011 person of the year, they consecrated the social protester as the most important actor of the year, and in a way a new global citizen.
19. Tarrow, 1998, p. 7.
20. Gadotti, 2010; Milani and Laniado, 2006; Torres, 2009b.
21. These comments are drawn from Torres, "Dancing on the Deck of the Titanic", *International Review of Education*, volume 1 (1955)–volume 57 (2011), pp. 39–55.
22. Zibecchi, 2003; n/d.
23. Dialogo, Reportaje a Carlos Piñeiro Iñiguez, *Página 12* (Monday, July 12, 2010), p. 12. www.pagina12.com.ar/diario/dialogos/21–149326–2010–07–12.html
24. Maria da Glória Gohn, *Teorias dos Movimentos Sociais. Paradigmas Clássicoes e Contemporáneos*. 5th ed. São Paulo: Edições Loyola, 2006.

25. Recent field research in Israel showed several controversial issues demanding serious attention in teaching citizenship building. They include the Israeli-Palestinian conflict; the ethnic/racial issue, i.e., the racial/ethnic conflicts between different Jewish groups mainly Mizrahi and Ashkenazi; racial issues, i.e., racism against Ethiopian Jews; questions related to growing social inequality; and the growing militarization of the Israeli society with the sacredness of its army. Other issues deserve serious attention as well, including whether Israel is a Jewish or a democratic state, and the tension between Jewish and Arab citizens. (CAT, research notes, March 2016). No doubt there are different topics in different societies. A clear recollection of what these controversial issues are and how they can be taught in classrooms constitutes a lynchpin for the conversation on citizenship building in general and global citizenship education in particular.
26. ThinkEqual NGO.
27. https://sustainabledevelopment.un.org/?menu=1300
28. Nico Stern, *Education, Knowledgeability and the Labor Market*. Paper, Zepelin University, Lake Constance, Germany, May 2011, pp. 5–6.
29. *Tech Leaps, Job Losses and Rising Inequality*, www.nytimes.com/2014/04/16/business/economy/tech-leaps-job-losses-and-rising-inequality.html?version=m eter+at+null&module=meter-Links&pgtype=article&contentId=&mediaId= &referrer=http%3A%2F%2Fwww.nytimes.com%2F&priority=true&action =click&contentCollection=meter-links-click
30. *Jobs Threatened by Machines: A Once 'Stupid' Concern Gains Respect*, www.nytimes.com/2016/06/08/business/economy/threatened-by-machines-a-once-stupid-concern-gains-respect.html?hp&action=click&pgtype=Homepage& clickSource=story-heading&module=second-column-region&region=top-news&WT.nav=top-news
31. Katherine Daly, Daniel Schugurensky, and Krista Lopes (Eds.), *Learning Democracy by Doing: Alternative Practices in Citizenship Learning and Participatory Democracy*. Toronto: Ontario Transformative Learning Centre, Ontario Institute for Studies in Education, University of Toronto, 2009.
32. The proliferation of scientific journals concerned with the question of happiness should not surprise us. Similarly, there is the growing impetus of dialogue across diverse religions and philosophies on what is happiness and how it can be achieved in respectful solidarity across diverse *weltanschauungs*. Yet Zizek argues, following Jacques Lacan and Alain Badiou, that "In psychoanalysis, the betrayal of desire has a precise name: happiness." From this perspective, one may question what are the fundamental conditions of happiness and particularly whether knowledge would facilitate those conditions. See Slavoj Zizek, *Welcome to the Desert of the Real*. London and New York: Verso, 2012, p. 73.
33. https://eca.state.gov/fulbright
34. www.huffingtonpost.com/philip-seib/koreas-public-diplomacy-o_b_4326708.html; http://uscpublicdiplomacy.org/users/philip_seib; www.publicdiplomacy-council.org/regions/korea
35. http://blogs.worldbank.org/education/nini-youth-latin-america-out-school-out-work-and-misunderstood
36. www.worldbank.org/en/events/2015/08/26/youth-summit-2015; http://web.worldbank.org/WBSITE/EXTERNAL/EXTJOBSNEW/0,,contentMDK:23149 336~menuPK:8453554~pagePK:8453902~piPK:8453359~theSitePK:84533 53,00.html
37. www.un.org/wcm/content/site/sport/YLC
38. www.unesco.org/new/en/social-and-human-sciences/themes/youth/

39. "Until recently, epistemology—the study of knowledge and justified belief—was heavily individualistic in focus. The emphasis was on evaluating doxastic attitudes (beliefs and disbeliefs) of individuals in abstraction from their social environment. The result is a distorted picture of the human epistemic situation, which is largely shaped by social relationships and institutions. Social epistemology seeks to redress this imbalance by investigating the epistemic effects of social interactions and social systems." http://plato.stanford.edu/entries/epistemology-social/

40. Kenneth J. Gergen and Ezekiel J. Dixon-Román have written a wonderful article justifying the critique of social epistemology as empiricism and its applicability to the politics of assessment. Social epistemology shares with social constructivism a number of traits, first and foremost its concern with ideology, which has been so well presented in the phenomenological works of Paul Ricoeur and Paulo Freire, suspecting that all social relationships involve a moment of domination. Second, the linguistic turn in literary theory helps inspect claims of accuracy, objectivity and truth, crucial to the baggage of empiricism. Third and perhaps foremost, social constructionism applied to scientific concepts, or what I have defended in most of my work, that reality is a social construction and each explanation of reality constitutes a social construction built through narratives. As cultural workers, we need to inspect these narratives, the quality of their sources, methods, empirical data and theoretical as well as meta-theoretical foundations.

41. In this important document that marked an epoch, preparing the narratives to understand learning in the 21st century, four principles were identified as the four pillars of education: (1) learning to know; (2) learning to do; (3) learning to live together and learning to live with others; and (4) learning to be. http://unesdoc.unesco.org/images/0010/001095/109590eo.pdf

42. UNESCO, 2014, p. 18.

43. Mayo, 2015, p. 865.

44. Retrieved October 6, from www.un.org/ga/search/view_doc.asp?symbol=A/69/L.85&referer=/english/&Lang=E

45. This section draws from the article by Gadotti and Torres ("Development and Change") and further reprinted with modifications as Chapter 1 of Torres, 2014.

46. O'Cadiz, Wang and Torres; Torres, 2014, pp. 1–11p.

47. Paulo Freire Archives, [Sao Paulo], https://www.paulofreire.org/

48. In this study, Gadotti, 2008a quotes Leonardo Boff: "The category sustainability is central for the ecological cosmos vision and possibly constitutes one of the bases of a new civilization paradigm that searches to harmonize human beings, development and Earth, understood as Gaia." See www.acervo.paulofreire.org:8080/xmlui/bitstream/handle/7891/3080/FPF_PTPF_12_077.pdf

49. MIT has developed a wonderful website that contributes to teaching and instruction in high school curriculums with a specific focus on linking high school students with MIT students with the goal to solve a program connected with global understanding. In addition, they provide fellowships for teachers and MIT faculty to mentor, coach and inspire MIT students who are interested in K–12 urban education. As stated on their website, they "Receive professional development focused on teaching for global understanding and integrating problem-based curriculum design into their practice." See https://generationglobal.mit.edu

50. These arguments and the original work of Freire is defined in Torres, 2014.

51. We speak of Freire's intuition in terms of both its normative and analytical dimensions. Carl G. Jung (1968) identified a number of functions in consciousness, and also distinguished the ectopsyche and the endopsyche. When he spoke of the ectopsychic functions ("a system of relationships between

the contents of consciousness and facts and data coming in from the environment," p. 11), he described the functions of sensation, thinking, feeling and intuition. Intuition, then, although mystical in the view of many, is very practical. Jung argued, "Whenever you have to deal with strange conditions where you have no established values or established concepts, you will depend upon that faculty of intuition" (p. 14). Jung was referring to anticipatory dreams or telepathic phenomena, but also to intuition in day-to-day interactions with people, things and animals. Freire was able to let his intuition guide his theorizing, and we believe that much of what we learn in our lives is as connected to intuition as it may be connected to sensations, thinking or feeling.

52. See for instance Olga Moreno Fernández, "Education and Planetary Citizenship. Conceptions of the Students Participants in Educational Andalusian Programs", *Pedagogía Social. Revista Interuniversitaria*, volume 26 (2015), pp. 229–261, www.upo.es/revistas/index.php/pedagogia_social/ ISSN: 1139–1723. © SIPS. doi:10.7179/PSRI_2015.26.09; See also Greg Misiaszek, "Ecopedagogy and Citizenship in the Age of Globalization: Connections between Environmental and Global Citizenship Education to Save the Planet", *European Journal of Education*, volume 50, number 3 (2015), pp. 280–292, doi:10.1111/ejed.12138.
53. There are no simple solutions to complex problems like poverty. Some critics argue that the resolution of the poverty problem has generated a "poverty-solving industry" which contributes to augmenting the problem rather than solving it. The controversy cannot be simply ignored or swept under the carpet. See the award-winning documentary *PovertyINC*: Website: PovertyINC.org Twitter: #PovertyINC
54. See Misiaszek, 2015, p. 290 and M. Gadotti, "Adult Education as a Human Right: The Latin American Context and the Ecopedagogic Perspective", *International Review of Education*, volume 57 (2011), pp. 9–25. doi:10.1007/s11159-011-9205-0, especially p. 20.
55. Greg Misiaszek, Lauren Ila Jones, and Carlos Alberto Torres, "Selling Out Academia? Higher Education, Economic Crises, and Freire's Generative Themes", in B. Pusser, K. Kempner, S. Marginson, and I. Ordorika (Eds.), *The University and the Public Sphere. Knowledge Creation and State Building in the Era of Globalization.* New York: Routledge, 2011, p. 192.
56. This section comes from the introduction to my chapter in *The Oxford Research Encyclopedia of Education* entitled "Education for Global Citizenship" (in press).
57. www.visionofhumanity.org/#/page/our-gpi-findings
58. Carlos Alberto Torres, *Democracy, Education, and Multiculturalism: Dilemmas of Citizenship in a Global World.* Lanham, MD: Rowman and Littlefield, 1998, p. 246. See also Carlos Alberto Torres, *First Freire: Early Writings in Social Justice Education.* New York: Teachers College Press, 2014; Moacir Gadotti, *Os Mestres de Rousseau.* São Paulo: Cortez Editores, 2004.
59. For an analysis of Freire's contributions, see Torres, *First Freire.*
60. For a description and analysis, see Torres ORE, in press.
61. https://m.youtube.com/watch?v=-xfEcC2RXro
62. The Tony Blair Foundation has worked since 2002 to engage youth in dialogue across faiths. Their new program, Generations Global, emphasizes fundamental principles of dialogue. See their teaching modules, such as *Essentials of Dialogue*, see http://tonyblairfaithfoundation.org
63. www.pamojaeducation.com/global-mindedness-and-21st-century-learning/
64. http://global-mind.org
65. Ibid.

66. http://noosphere.princeton.edu/results.html
67. Ibid.
68. Needless to say, this conversation can be entertained at several levels, and one of the most recent contributions is linking consciousness with quantum physics, perhaps a concept to be further explored from a constructivist perspective for those committed to understanding if a global consciousness is possible. See for instance Alexander Wendt, *Quantum Mind and Social Science Unifying Physical and Social Ontology*. Cambridge: Cambridge University Press, 2015.
69. Torres, *First Freire.*
70. Emmanuel Mounier, Op. cit., p. 118. Emmanuel Mounier, *Personalism*, Trans. Philip Mairet. London: Routledge and Kegan Paul Ltd., 1952.
71. Torres, 2014, p. 32.
72. Paulo Freire, *Cultural Action for Freedom*. Harmondsworth, UK: Penguin Op. cit., p. 52.
73. Ibid., p. 62.
74. Paulo Freire, *La educación como práctica de la libertad*. Buenos Aires: Siglo XXI, 1973, p. 82. (my translation from Spanish).
75. Lucien Goldmann, *Las ciencias humanas y la filosofía*. Buenos Aires: Nueva Visión, quoted by Freire in "Sobre la acción cultural", ICIRA, Santiago, Chile, 1972, p. 84.
76. Ibid., p. 102.
77. Ibid.
78. Ibid.
79. Ibid.
80. Falk, 1993, 2002.
81. https://ampersand.gseis.ucla.edu/john-rogers-empowering-communities-to-improve-public-schooling/
82. Personal email to the author.
83. William Pinar, "Notes on the Intellectual. In Praise of Maxine Greene", p. 120, in William C. Ayers and Janet L. Miller (Eds.), *A Light in Dark Times: Maxine Greene and the Unfinished Conversation*. New York: Teachers College Press, Columbia University, 1998, pp. 108–121.
84. "2.8—Ensinar exige a convicção de que a mudança é possível. Um dos saberes primeiros, indispensáveis a quem, chegando a favelas ou a realidades marcadas pela traição a nosso direito de ser, pretende que sua presença se vá tornando convivência, que seu estar no contexto vá virando estar com ele, é o saber do future como problema e não como inexorabilidade. É o saber da História como possibilidade e não como determinação. O mundo não é. O mundo está sendo. Como subjetividade curiosa, inteligente, interferidora na objetividade com que dialeticamente me relaciono, meu papel no mundo não é só o de quem constata o que ocorre mas também o de quem intervém como sujeito de ocorrências. Não sou apenas objeto da História mas seu sujeito igualmente. No mundo da História, da cultura, da política, constato não para me adaptar mas para mudar" Paulo Freire, *Pedagogia da autonomia*. 1st ed. São Paulo: Paz e Terra, 1997, p. 85. The English text in this book is my translation.
85. Lucien Goldmann, *Las Ciencias Humanas y la Filosofía*. Buenos Aires, Argentina: Nueva Vision, 1972.
86. Simon Marginson, "The 'Public' Contribution of Universities in an Increasingly Global World", in B. Pusser, K. Kempner, S. Marginson, and Imanol Ordorika (Eds.), *Universities and the Public Sphere: Knowledge Creation and State Building in the Era of Globalization*. New York: Routledge, 2012, pp. 7–26.
87. http://uscpublicdiplomacy.org/users/philip_seib
88. www.publicdiplomacy.org/1.htm

89. The following bureaus and offices report to the Under Secretary: Bureau of Educational and Cultural Affairs (ECA); Bureau of International Information Programs (IIP); Bureau of Public Affairs (PA); Global Engagement Center (GEC); Office of Policy, Planning and Resources (R/PPR).
90. http://commdocs.house.gov/committees/intlrel/hfa76189.000/hfa76189_0. HTM
91. https://uscpublicdiplomacy.org/pdin_monitor_article/republic-korea's-public-diplomacy-policy-tool-soft-power. The term "soft power," which has gained much recognition and usually is attributed to the negotiating power of international or bilateral institutions like UNESCO was coined by Joseph Nye, University Distinguished Professor and former dean of Harvard's Kennedy School of Government. This concept in Nye's analysis highlights the role that private activities have on national interest. That includes the impact that business activities, popular cultures and many forms of sports, tourism or fashion have in affecting foreign policy and international relations.
92. Korean Consul of Political Affairs at the Korean Consulate General in Los Angeles, Tae-Wan Huh, https://uscpublicdiplomacy.org/pdin_monitor_article/republic-korea's-public-diplomacy-policy-tool-soft-power.
93. www.cfr.org/terrorism/public-diplomacy-war-terrorism/p4762
94. The Young Professional Programs at the World Bank is one of these programs. See http://web.worldbank.org/WBSITE/EXTERNAL/EXTJOBSNEW/0,,contentMDK:23149336~menuPK:8453554~pagePK:8453902~piPK:8453359~theSitePK:8453353,00.html; the United Nations UNOSDP Youth Leadership Programme is another such program, see www.un.org/wcm/content/site/sport/home/unplayers/unoffice/YLC
95. Cultural capital; Cultural wealth, Cecilia Rios-Aguilar and Judy Marquez Kiyama, "Funds of Knowledge: An Approach to Studying Latina(o) Students' Transition to College", *Journal of Latinos and Education*, volume 11, number 1 (2012), pp. 2–16. http://dx.doi.org/10.1080/15348431.2012.631430
96. www.shi.or.th/upload/risk0002.pdf
97. Torres, *Globalizations and Education*. New York: Teachers College Press-Columbia University, 2009, p. 54.
98. Torres and Rhoads, 2006, p. 28.
99. As I have discussed elsewhere, Jim Clifton, chairman of Gallup Corporation, argues that of the 7 billion in the world, 5 billion are over 15 years of age. Three billion said they currently worked or wanted to work, yet only 1.2 billion have full-time formal jobs. Hence there is a shortfall of 1.8 billon jobs worldwide. Clinton, *The Coming Jobs War*. New York: Gallup Press, 2011; Torres, *Comparative Education*, 4th ed., 2013, p. 472.
100. *New York Times*, 29 May 2016, p. 1.
101. Change Makers Programme for Young Leaders. Initiative of the UNESCO MGIEP.
102. One of my students, Susan Wiksten, has argued in many of her papers, following a theoretical model she is designing for her dissertation, that one has to identify three different sets of premises in looking at the question of social justice education. The first one is connected with the commitment of the institution, that is social justice as the purpose of the institution or the institutional mantra, that defines the identity of a particular program such as the Graduate School of Education and Information Studies at UCLA. The second premise is to consider social justice as a subject matter or specialization that should define the nature of a particular academic degree or specialization program. Finally she identifies social justice as inspiring and guiding the administrative and institutional procedures of a given institution—i.e. what kind of students the institution wants to attract, what faculty they hire, how

they handle controversial issues, etc. Raising the conversation at a level of public policy, social justice education is one of the many possible angles in the kaleidoscope of justice involved in issues which are by definition globally, national, regional, locally and within groups of people; yet this is simply a descriptive kaleidoscope in terms of foci, there is then the public policy area that includes economic justice, legal justice, racial justice, and political justice to name just some of the conundrums embedded in the context and narratives of justice. An interesting and well-argued review is Connie E North. "What Is All this Talk about 'Social Justice'? Mapping the Terrain of Education's Latest Catchphrase", *Teachers College Record*, volume 110, number 6 (2008), pp. 1182–1206.

103. Y. Lapayese, "Review: Toward a Critical Global Citizenship Education", *Comparative Education Review*, volume 47, number 4 (2003), pp. 493–501.
104. Jason Dorio, *The Struggle for "Bread, Freedom, and Social Justice": (Re) Imagining citizenship(s) and University Citizenship Education in Egypt*. A dissertation submitted in partial satisfaction of the requirements for the degree Doctor of Philosophy in Education.
105. Torres, 1998a, p. 259.

11 Implementing Global Citizenship Education
Challenges

The Challenge of Scale: Do We Need a World State to Have Global Citizenship?

Let us pause for a second and look at the first tension emerging from blending educational goals with a citizenship building goal at a global level: Is Global Citizenship Education an attempt to create a global or world state? If so, this concept might be related in some form or shape with a hegemonic model of leadership.

There has been a renewed interest at the turn of the century in the idea of a world state particularly with the work of Alexander Wendt, the Ralph D. Mershon Professor of International Security at the Ohio State University.

Wendt's arguments, following a selective critique of Kant and Hegel yet defending their teleological explanations, is that dramatic changes in technology (including war technology) are making the call for anarchy more prominent, and therefore the alternative, for world government is more relevant.

Speaking of Kant and Hegel's cosmopolitanism, Wendt indicated that neither anticipated the dramatic technological changes of the past century, which are in part caused by the security dilemma and thus endogenous to anarchy. As Daniel Deudney (1999, 2000) convincingly argues, "these changes have greatly increased the costs of war and also the scale on which it is possible to organize a state. With these material changes the struggle for recognition among states undermines their self-sufficiency and makes a world state inevitable. Via the struggle for recognition, in short, the logic of anarchy leads to its own demise."[1]

Wendt concludes ". . . that a global monopoly on the legitimate use of organized violence—a world state—is inevitable. At the micro-level world state formation is driven by the struggle of individuals and groups for recognition of their subjectivity. At the macro-level this struggle is channeled toward a world state by the logic of anarchy, which generates a tendency for military technology and war to become increasingly destructive. The process moves through five stages, each responding to the instabilities of the one before—a system of states, a society of states, world society, collective security and the world state. Human agency matters all along the way, but is increasingly constrained and enabled by the requirements of universal recognition."[2]

Judging by the growing presence of terrorism in the world, the growing immiseration of workers worldwide, particularly of blue-collar workers as a product of neoliberal globalization, and the lack of full-time jobs particularly for the youth, these are signs that could be read as an indication of growing levels of anarchy in the world system; hence Wendt's argument acquires new luster. Yet the question is whether it is at all possible to implement such model of world governance as global citizenship, and if so, how?

This is a whole chapter in the conversation that unbeknownst to most educators is looming in the background of this concept, its possibilities of implementation and how to achieve success without losing national autonomy. Thus, these questions of cosmopolitanism need to be addressed.

The Challenge of Cosmopolitanism

In the popular press, cosmopolitanism is used and occasionally abused as a marker that defines the terms of reference of politics and culture in our contemporary modernity. Conservative analysts call cosmopolitanism a myth.[3] A conservative *New York Times* columnist revisiting the coalitions behind the Brexit vote and Trump's followers concluded that

> The people who consider themselves "cosmopolitan" in today's West, by contrast, are part of *a meritocratic order* that transforms difference into similarity, by plucking the best and brightest from everywhere and homogenizing them into the peculiar species that we call "global citizens."

"This species is racially diverse (within limits) and eager to assimilate the fun-seeming bits of foreign cultures—food, a touch of exotic spirituality. But no less than Brexit-voting Cornish villagers, our global citizens think and act as members of a tribe."[4]

So, there it is! The concept of cosmopolitan democracies, true bedrock of the concept of global citizenships, despite its solid background in Kant's philosophy, is nothing more than a ruse, a model to create a new kind of global tribalism by reaffirming a new meritocratic order.

Yet, there are multiple existing cosmopolitanisms, and one cannot speak of cosmopolitanism as a new single and dominant canon. Noah Sobe argues that "studying actually existing cosmopolitanisms is a useful strategy for examining the ways that solidarities are formed, identities are developed, and principles of inclusion and exclusion are elaborated amidst local and global assemblages."[5]

Thus cosmopolitanism is an utmost concept to be explored in all its potential dimensions for global citizenship education, either as ethical cosmopolitanism, or as defined by Sobe, "vernacular cosmopolitanism" as an analytical tool:

> I have tried to present an argument that looking at 'cosmopolitanisms' seems a well-matched analytic tool for critically approaching the "collapsing of distances," the broadening of the "outlines of communities", and the reframing of the sources of individual and social selves that are claimed to accompany the globalization of today. In addition to looking at contemporary instances, comparative education scholars can also productively examine different historical instances of actually existing vernacular cosmopolitanisms.[6]

While these arguments may be appealing to those who are disgusted by the raw distinction between local and global, each definition of multiple forms of existing cosmopolitanism may be confronted with the question of what are the normative and analytical distinctions between them, and how can they be represented in the global context of political interactions and more importantly in the diverse values invested in the world's diverse civilizations. Is there a need for a unifying force to bring together all these cosmopolitan traditions to make them effective?

The Challenge of World Governance

Some concepts focus on a world system with a world citizenship, bringing to the fore the idea of world government, a concept that has percolated in the academic literature and particularly in philosophy for quite some time.[7]

World government is related to the concept of world federalism.[8] Attempts have been made to focus on the viability of global governance rather than a world government—for instance, the controversial 1992 Commission on Global Governance, which was chaired by Swedish Prime Minister Ingvar Carlsson and former Commonwealth Secretary-General Shridath Ramphal.[9] In practice, ". . . 'global governance' is merely a descriptive term signifying the existing level of international cooperation and coordination, through the United Nations and other organizations in coping with global problems."[10]

Some form of global governance has been assigned to the United Nations, with its limited power and scope of operation, but important indeed in the context of international catastrophes such as the growing number of refugees leaving war zones (e.g., Syria at the time of writing this chapter), or the need for military intervention in a given region by an alliance of countries under the platform of the United Nations Blue Berets to prevent a genocide.

There are many scholars who have argued that there is in practice some form of concerted global governance being reinforced by the progress of globalization in the midst of nation-states. For instance, in the 1980s there was much discussion about the Washington consensus in which several financial and trade institutions (e.g., the World Bank, IMF, US Treasury Department,

Import-Export Bank, which were themselves located in close proximity in Washington) could have restructured economic policies by creating a model of economic reform based on trade liberalization, tax reform, fiscal policy discipline, privatization of state enterprises and economic restructuring. With the Washington consensus neoliberalism had finally found strong advocates in the global financial system.

Similar arguments are made about such dominant role in trade of the World Trade Organization in Geneva, or in financing of the IMF, the World Bank or the European Central Bank, or the role of the Organization for Economic Co-operation and Development, which has replaced the technical contributions of the World Bank with their technical models, pushing its educational loans for a new and more dominant intellectual perspective around the Program for International Student Assessment or PISA-OECD. The question of global governance is not a passing fad. It has certain and important implications in public policy, governability and educational policy in particular—more so, if, as many neo-institutionalists believe, there is a growing convergence of policies, practices and institutions into a global culture.

The Challenge of Paradoxes and Conundrums

There are then a number of paradoxes built into the implementation of global citizenship education. One of them could be discussed as the *Theseus paradox,* an ancient thought experiment asking the question of whether an object (in this case national citizenship) that has had all (or almost all) of its components replaced (by global citizenship) remains fundamentally the same object or is completely transformed. This paradox intrigued many political philosophers, particularly Thomas Hobbes and John Locke, and in some form or shape has caught the attention of many of the audiences to whom I have delivered these topics in my lectures.

I left this particular subject in the background, but I want to point out a simply logical implication that is revealed in the political philosophical scenarios discussed. There has already been intense debate about two Western theoretical models of citizenship—the republican citizenship civic tradition and the liberal democratic citizenship tradition.[11] Assuming that there is some overlapping between the two of them despite their important differences, one may ask about the emerging global citizenship tradition, which as many have documented, is not at all new.[12] These three traditions cannot be so different that we may confront logical fallacies. One of them is the fallacy of composition—inferring that if something is true of the whole, then it could also be true for any part of the whole. Another is the fallacy of hasty generalization—disregarding the nature of the sample, one could generalize about a population that the sample itself is not representative of.

Despite my enjoyment of logical arguments and counter-arguments, which I am sure philosophers will rekindle promptly, this book has mostly focused on the challenges for the enabling requirements for Global Citizenship Education—the topic of the next section.

11.1 Enabling Requirements for Global Citizenship Education. Missing Links in the Current Status and Practice of Citizenship Education. Priority Tasks and Conundrums

This book has offered an interpretation of what is at stake in the discussion about global citizenship education building. There are important semantic and conceptual challenges of clarification of what GCE is, and we have settled, for the moment, that GCE is a framework for action. Adding my own perspective, I have defined GCE as an intervention in search of a theory.

We defined the bare essentials for any model of citizenship education, and we have linked them to the practice of civic virtues. The agents, principles and institutional recognition of the concept are quite clear and do not require further elaboration. But all of these approaches are controversial, as is controversial the role of the UN in the world or the implications of a cosmopolitan democracy as solid bedrock for global citizenship education.

This book did not discuss how to implement teaching methods and curriculum to deal with the demands of global citizenship education, but we have pointed to a number of resources, particularly the work of APCEIU in Korea and the conceptual work of UNESCO. In the last four to five years the institutional recognition and its assemblage in the UN circuits has grown enormously and is deeply impacting similar circuits in governments and NGOs.

We highlighted some of the great tensions that will not go away, quickly imperiling concretization of global citizenship education as a worldwide project. One of the missing links is how to deal with tensions in human rights well exemplified by rabid nationalism and its counterpart of extreme religious radicalism, undermining any project of 'cosmopolitanism' however defined.[13]

There are tensions between globalism as a model of hegemony and social justice education as a model of democratic cosmopolitanism. There is plenty of bibliography talking about globalism as a model projected worldwide through multiple layers of globalization and reflecting the power of corporations as well as some of the governments who are world powers in a multipolar global system. Needless to say, the tensions between globalism as a model of capital accumulation and global social justice education as a model aiming at interrupting inequality cannot be ignored for long. The losers of globalization, or the discontents with globalization, to put it mildly, are letting us know their views and they do so in the voting booths, supporting groups, individuals and political parties that represent different ultra-nationalist perspectives.

Another important missing piece is immigration. The current waves of immigration are pushing the limits of systems perhaps as never before in the last half-century, and also pushing the actual strength of the implementation of human rights regimes. One could metaphorically say that immigration is like a small 'metatarsalgia' of multiple globalizations.

There are intractable yet pressing issues in citizenship building. For instance, what can and cannot be reconciled, including linguistic differences, epistemological differences, religious differences, community ownership differences, differential impacts of the model of the state and welfare, or whether the concept of 'glocalization' has any analytical meaning. Another tension that will never go away is the tension between individual rights (as represented in the human rights regime) and cultural rights (as represented in the history and culture of millenarian cultures and practices).

In this book I have highlighted priority tasks in the construction of global citizenship education, though I would emphasize that they apply *in toto* to the construction of citizenship building per se.

What is needed to implement global citizenship education, including missing links, priority tasks and dilemmas or conundrums? What follows is a selective summary of key arguments developed in the previous chapters.

11.2.   *An Agenda for Theoretical and Empirical Research as Well as Teaching in Global Citizenship Education*

The goal of this section is to highlight some of the central components in building a research and teaching agenda in Global Citizenship Education.

These goals include:

Promoting education as cognitive holistic democracy. This means to *promote education as cognitive democracy*, that is education as a cognitive, emotional, ethical, aesthetic, moral and as a political experience, and not exclusively as human capital training

Reclaiming the concept of the 'public' in public schooling geared towards the public good, and social justice education as a global goal for a cosmopolitan global citizenship.

Global Citizenship Education should include higher education as a central component of citizenship building.

Adult education and lifelong learning should promote a multicultural critical media literacy. There is a very important role for UNESCO in this area.

Hybrid cultural identities and diasporic citizenship should be recognized as the trademark of the current process of globalization. As so many analysts have said, immigration is in the DNA of human beings.

Understanding *similarities and differences between* global education, civic education, global citizenship education and planetary citizenship may help clarify the tasks at hand.

Clarifying the interactions of citizenship and multiple processes of globalization seems to be an unavoidable theoretical task, including discerning the impacts of the neoliberal globalization, anti-globalizations, hybrid cultures, human rights, network and knowledge society, the war against terrorism and the globalization of terrorism.

Policy makers and educators should be cognizant of the fact that a model of cognitive and holistic democracy may question some of the crucial *measurement issues and metrics*: How do we measure improvements in citizenship building, in civics, in changes in values, attitudes, skills, dexterities and capabilities of individuals in their lifeworlds and their practices over time?

In the curriculum area, the *dilemma of liberal democracies* should be addressed despite its complexities. That is to note that citizenship building as a concept started with a focus on rights and responsibilities of individuals to exercise their identities as citizens in a given city. Liberal democracy in the emerging Western liberal tradition was deployed to question the absolute power and legitimacy of kings.

Since the 18th century, thanks to the Enlightenment, societies moved from the concept of subject to the concept of the national-state citizen. Now the arguments are moving to global citizenship. Beside the theories of citizenship embedded in this conversation, there is also the question of theories of democracy, including definitions of alternative forms of democracy impacting citizenship building—for instance, the forms of representative democracy (liberal democracy, participative democracy) versus delegative democracy[14] and virtual democracy.[15]

Educators and policy makers and also civil society institutions and individuals should continuously pose the question of what is the *value added* of global citizenship, and question how to overcome tensions with rabid nationalism and/or models of religious fundamentalism operating through extremist violence.

It is imperative to *decouple human rights politics from imperialism*. Multiple examples of intervention and conversely the lack of intervention in genocide prevention, one of the most cosmopolitan responsibilities of the United Nations, should be discussed. Many interventions seem to have been connected to the interests of the dominant powers in a specific region of the globe, such as the First Gulf War in 1991, interventions in the former Yugoslavia's wars and ethnic conflicts (1991–2001) including Slovenia, Croatia, Bosnia and the Kosovo wars. Conversely, the lack of intervention in Rwanda for months that cost half a million human lives, and the current situation in Syria merit serious debate of what actually constitutes prevention of genocide and how this should be implemented as part of the global citizenship responsibilities of the UN and the world.

Global Citizenship Education as a new Framework for Action may also become a *paradigmatic change* of the discourse in education, moving from a dominant technocratic discourse to a holistic and humanistic discourse as predicated by the great documents of UNESCO that I have cited throughout this book as well as the work of many authors.[16]

Chapter 9 presented some reflections about the *role of lifelong and adult learning* in addition to basic classroom instruction. It is a most serious mistake to restrict global citizenship education to schooling and classroom activities.

Chapter 10 speaks of Global Citizenship Education as a new social movement. The proposal is a new social movement, or an amalgamation or partnership of multiple social movements, particularly when many of them are transnational. The idea is the creation of a new partnership between the nation-state, UN institutions, communities and social movements into a *new global social compact.*

There is, as I have explained in previous works, a 'citizenship debt' of social movements. They are usually able to veto initiatives or policies and/or challenge the action and/or inaction of the state in several policy domains. Unfortunately, as I have argued in Chapter 10, most social movements fail to promote a model of citizenship building that will embrace the majority of the population, that is a citizenship model that is workable ethically, politically and procedurally in constitutional terms.

11.3. The Model of Collaboration: UCLA-UNESCO in Global Citizenship Education: Our New Partnership and Agenda for the Future

As it has been explained throughout this book, many questions remain regarding the nature and possibility of education that can foster global citizenship. Answering these questions requires more research and policy orientations.

The UCLA UNESCO Chair research and policy works to further Global Citizenship Education using participatory action research to conduct empirical fieldwork worldwide.

Our studies will explore the global relevance and impacts of GCE as a new global narrative. As explained in this book, our agenda builds upon both the UN Decade for a Culture of Peace and Non-Violence for the Children of the World, and the UN Decade of Education for Sustainable Development in conjunction with the Sustainable Development Goals (2015–2030).

Our work will identify and compare innovative GCE approaches and good practices internationally, including models orienting teacher training more toward international issues. We will investigate how GCE policies, curriculum and pedagogical practices are developed, implemented and contextualized locally while being developed globally and vice versa. Our studies will also create avenues and provide recommendations for nurturing the consciousness of GCE as a new theoretical and methodological global narrative for students, teachers and policy makers, and also for the common citizen and their communities. Identifying and applying good practices of GCE worldwide will be a central goal of the UCLA UNESCO Chair agenda.

We agree with Ulrich Beck when he asked, "What is enlightenment? To have the courage to make use of one's cosmopolitan vision and to acknowledge one's multiple identities—to combine forms of life founded on language, skin color, nationality or religion with the awareness that, in a radically insecure world, all are equal and everyone is different." In essence, what Beck is talking about is global citizenship education.[17]

Furthering global citizenship education requires principles of human rights, liberty and equality for all, including the 'rights of hospitality' in the Kantian sense, a formidable and pressing need in this challenging age of global migration.

The UNESCO UCLA Chair, in the spirit of the scholarship presented in this book, sees global citizenship as being marked by an understanding of global ties, relations and connections, and a commitment to the collective good. We assume that furthering Global Citizenship Education is one of the most powerful tools we have to interrupt inequality in this growingly unequal global world.

In Summary

- Global Citizenship Education will help to refocus on a new learning strategy worldwide.
- It will help to rethink the dominant narrative in education that has grown too technocratic in terms of policy strategies of how to enhance educational environments.
- It will help to rethink educational outcomes (and the concept of quality of education) with its focus almost exclusively on learning cognitive outcomes to the detriment of affective, spiritual, ethical, moral, peace-based, aesthetic and artistic outcomes.
- It will help to situate an ethics of caring—a key principle of articulation of GCE—in the growing interpenetration of societies and cultures in this phase of multiple globalizations.
- It will help to define a concept of holistic education that provides the foundation for this new strategy and learning approach.
- Global Citizenship Education will help to promote a culture of academic rigor, discernment and struggle against injustices.
- Global Citizenship Education will work in creating a new generation of critical thinkers who are aware of global inequalities, and who will start during their learning sojourns to think about structural solutions, not only social entrepreneurship efforts, good and sublime as they may be. These new critical thinkers need to be educated early on in elementary and high school rather than waiting for them to reach the higher echelons of academia. Moreover, there is absolutely no reason why the new 'public intellectuals' of the 21st century cannot emerge from the ranks of our middle and high school classrooms rather than mass media and universities.
- But above all, Global Citizenship Education constitutes a most valuable tool to interrupt inequality.

Let me conclude this book with the closing comments in my keynote to the meeting that we organized on February 8, 2016 at UCLA a propos of the inauguration of the Chair, welcoming a large group of researchers from many continents:

We formally inaugurated the UNESCO UCLA Chair in the same year we celebrate the 500th anniversary of Thomas More's famous work, *Utopia*, a book which marked the understanding and deliberations of the nascent political science as a discipline, and governance as its practice. I hope that 500 years from now, someone will remember how a group of enthusiastic educators and people of goodwill congregated on this day at UCLA to deliberate academically and launch the UCLA UNESCO Chair in Global Learning and Global Citizenship Education. We are here today because we are convinced that one of the most effective ways to interrupt inequality is the struggle to implement global citizenship education worldwide. From the bottom of my heart, I want to thank to all of you for being here with us and for sharing the dream. And now, let us begin our long journey.

Notes

1. Alexander Wendt, "Why a World State Is Inevitable", *European Journal of International Relations*, volume 9, number 4 (2003), pp. 491–542, p. 493.
2. Ibid., p. 491.
3. "Now that populist rebellions are taking Britain out of the European Union and the Republican Party out of contention for the presidency, perhaps we should speak no more of left and right, liberals and conservatives. From now on the great political battles will be fought between nationalists and internationalists, nativists and globalists. From now on the loyalties that matter will be narrowly tribal—Make America Great Again, *this blessed plot, this earth, this realm, this England*—or multicultural and cosmopolitan. Well, maybe. But describing the division this way has one great flaw. It gives the elite side of the debate (the side that does most of the describing) too much credit for being truly cosmopolitan."
   Ross Douthat, "The Myth of Cosmopolitanism". www.nytimes.com/2016/07/03/opinion/sunday/the-myth-of-cosmopolitanism.html?_r=0
4. Douthat, ibid.
5. Noah Sobe "Rethinking 'Cosmopolitanism' as an Analytic for the Comparative Study of Globalization & Education", *Current Issues in Comparative Education*, volume 12, number 1 (2009), pp. 6–13.
6. Ibid., p. 13.
7. Yunker, 2011.
8. See for instance Frederick L. Schuman, *The Commonwealth of Man: An Inquiry into Power, Politics and World Government*. New York: Alfred A. Knopf, 1952.
9. www.gdrc.org/u-gov/global-neighbourhood/
10. Yunker, Op cit., 2011, p. 85.
11. www.academia.edu/1162380/Liberal_and_Republican_Conceptualizations_of_Citizenship_A_Theoretical_Inquiry
12. William Gaudelli, 2016.
13. Though the idea of an ISIS caliphate is nothing less than a model of global citizenship propelled by a specific view of Islam.

14. Guillermo O'Donnell, "Delegative Democracy?", http://kellogg.nd.edu/publications/workingpapers/WPS/172.pdf

15. https://cybersocialstructure.org/

16. www.un.org/en/development/desa/population/migration/publications/wallchart/index.shtml. The arguments presented in this book about global commons defines from a meta-theoretical perspective global citizenship education as a framework for action. There is important work from a theoretical perspective. At this level global citizenship education may be challenging the technocratic features of educational discourse. In this context, Professor Lynette Shultz argued in a recent workshop conducted at UCLA, that Global Citizenship Education is an opportunity to challenge patriarchy, male dominance and sexism; the Eurocentrism of most theories in vogue in academia; and to adopting a post-colonial stance, which will help confront the explicit narratives but also the subtexts of racism and homophobia. From an empirical perspective, not only a new agenda for research is needed but also innovative policies to implement this new framework for action.

17. Ulrich Beck, 2006.

18. https://sustainabledevelopment.un.org/content/documents/8521InformalSummary-UN Summit

Appendix
A Peace Education Manifesto and the Role of WCCES

"I am not impartial or objective; not a fixed observer of facts and happenings. I never was able to be an adherent of the traits that falsely claim impartiality or objectivity. That did not prevent me, however, from holding always a rigorously ethical position. Whoever really observes, does so from a given point of view. And this does not necessarily mean that the observer position is erroneous. It's an error when one becomes dogmatic about one's point of view and ignores the fact that, even if one is certain about his or her point of view, it does not mean that one's position is always ethically grounded."

—Paulo Freire

Our age of global interdependence is being marked not only by the dialectics of the global and the local that we will discuss in Beijing, but also by the dialectics of terrorism and anti-terrorism. I am writing to you as president of WCCES but also as a victim of state terrorism in Argentina that forced me into exile. I would like to invite the WCCES to a dialogue about our moral responsibilities.

Paulo Freire taught us that domination, aggression and violence are intrinsic parts of human and social life. He argued that few human encounters are exempt from one type of oppression or another. By virtue of race, ethnicity, class and gender, people tend either to be victims or perpetrators of oppression. Thus, for Freire, sexism, racism and class exploitation are the most salient forms of domination. Yet exploitation and domination exist on other grounds including religious beliefs, political affiliation, national origin, age, size and physical and intellectual abilities, to name just a few. His vision was prophetic.

We are a professional organization with multiple goals including enhancing global understanding, improving access and quality of education and operation of the educational systems. Most of us are interested in developing and applying models, methods and theories for the field of comparative education to serve the betterment of children, youth and adults as well as communities and nations.

I have spent my whole academic life developing theories and analyses or conducting empirical research to promote global citizenship education working from critical theory in the politics of liberation. However, we cannot dialogue with violence. We cannot tolerate systematic violence against human rights and our existing civilizations, against common people in the streets, going to a market in Lebanon, returning home to Russia after vacation or massacred in restaurants, hotels and theaters like in Paris and Bamako.

Violence and terrorism are being inextricably connected with politics and religion in this globalized world, violence that exists from Lebanon to a plane downed in the Sinai Desert or to Paris, the city of which Thomas Jefferson, a strong supporter of the French Revolution, argued that every citizen in the world has two capitals, their own and Paris.

There is violence infecting us from Israel to Gaza, to Libya, Chad, Egypt, Tunisia, Afghanistan, Mali, Yemen, Turkey, Belgian and various regions of Middle East, North Africa, Sub-Saharan Africa and Central Asia; the violence that is gaining ground in America with the tragedy of students being slaughtered in Mexico, people being the subject of street violence in Brazil and Argentina, and in Central America, home of many of the most violent cities in the world; and gang terror, with black lives that seem not to matter to some in the US—not to mention the violence against our environment. The list is long.

Violence should stop and peace should prevail. The recent terrorist acts that shocked the globe in Lebanon, the Sinai Peninsula, Nigeria, Paris and Bamako are simply another culmination of a long list of terrorist actions against democracy, humanism, pluralism, multiculturalism and the reign of reason. These violent acts should move us deeply both professionally and in terms of human interest. I convoke all of you today to react with a unanimous voice, even though I am sure there are different perspectives and different analyses of what is going on. Hence I do not expect people to agree wholesale with my analytical and normative perspective. But we should find a minimum common denominator to protect peace in the world. As comparative educators we have no other choice.

There are many faces of globalization, but particularly two that apply to this discussion: the globalization of anti-terrorism and terrorism going global. There is a manifestation of globalization, which extends beyond markets, and to some extent is against human rights. It is *globalization of the international war against terrorism.* This new form of globalization has been prompted in large part by the events of September 11, 2001—which were interpreted as the globalization of the terrorist threat—and the reaction of the United States to the event. This form of globalization is represented by the anti-terrorist response, which has been militaristic in nature, resulting in two coalition wars led by the US against Muslim regimes in Afghanistan and Iraq, under the auspices of the Global War on Terror. Islamophobia is also a theme of this globalization. Terrorism and the terrorist threat were made synonymous with Islam and Muslims, and became a global norm. Yet, the overall theme of this process was not only its military flavor, but also the emphasis on security and control of borders, people, capital and commodities—that is, the reverse of open markets, high-paced commodity exchanges and international understanding of "the other." Security as a precondition of freedom is a key theme of this form of globalization.

There is another form of globalization, namely the globalization of terrorism, which is well represented by the decaying Al Qaida network, with terrorist actions of many kinds, and the more virulent examples of ISIS and Boko Haram and their attempt to move the world to an apocalyptic war of unexpected proportions as a new crusade. Examples of these actions include Boko Haram's kidnapping of 300 girls from a Christian school in Nigeria, forcing them to convert to Islam and marry fighters. Another example is the growing consolidation of ISIS in the Middle East, providing a platform, a kind of sacred fire for youth who are disaffected and marginalized with modernity and Western practices. Thousands of youths have flown to Iraq and Syria to fight for what they believe is their sacred cause of social change, leading to the establishment of a new caliphate in the Levant and Middle East. Through a fatalistic and violently narrow interpretation, ISIS attempts to constitute and represent a global Islam, which makes them difficult to contain in a particular territory, as it has been the logic of counter-terrorism of the Obama administration. The motto of terrorism is probably best defined in the following terms: Only chaos will bring about freedom.

We must repudiate all acts of terror being made in the name of politics, religious fundamentalism or any other of the multiple reasons why human rights are violated in the whole world. On the one hand, to invoke the name of God to conduct indiscriminate killings and barbarian beheadings is blasphemous. On the other, states need to be held responsible for violent retribution through military campaigns and exclusionary domestic policies. Furthermore, people throughout the world must maintain tolerance and mutual respect for those who are different rather than placing blame on the whole. Yet, we are reaching a point in which the world democratic system should act, and do so forcefully and efficiently.

If the intention of a religious fundamentalist project is to build a global caliphate to oppress, dominate and exploit, and to build their dream at any cost with blatant disregard for the dreams of others, and for human lives, this project should be democratically but also forcefully confronted and stopped. Terrorists from any sign should be hunted, captured, prosecuted and must pay their dues to justice.

As a critical theorist I understand some of the roots of ISIS and other contentious groups' dissatisfaction with the world as it exists today. First and foremost is the imperialism and colonialism of Western powers that for centuries have parceled out human societies and remade them into countries in their own image. Imperial projects attempted to magically integrate and exploit diverse groups within imagined polities and assumed

the system would work properly—or least would protect their imperial strategic interests. Second, the workings of predatory capitalism are
undermining some of the most central ethical, mythical components of
civilization and its new incarnation in neoliberalism, which Freire characterized as the new evil of our times. Third, male chauvinism, which has
not only affected the process of liberation of women for centuries, but also
perpetuates the homophobic ideology that discriminates against the non-
heterosexual. And last, there is the celebratory logo-centrism and exploitation of resources and people of the European civilizations and Global
North, condemning the rest of the world, particularly the Global South, to
subordinate positions, and thus, producing the culture of silence that has
been forced upon the subaltern.

To explain the roots of today's dissatisfaction with modernity, we have
theories, and profess them in our classrooms. Alas, we cannot legitimate
and argue that the barbarism and horror of the past justifies the barbarism
and horror of the present. There is no logical and ethical justification other
than religion fundamentalism and fundamentalist nationalism for the acts
of terror we have witnessed.

A Great Conversation about Education for Peace at WCCES

> "Peaceful and just societies are a necessary precondition for sustainable de
> velopment; many conflicts are driven by poverty, hunger and hopelessness."

> "It was acknowledged that strong institutions, based on the rule of law, and
> not on rule by law, are essential for building peaceful societies where people
> live free from fear and want. A culture of justice needs to be created, and
> upheld, to empower all people, including the most marginalized."[18]

The UN Assembly in 2015 formulated a consensus built by all nations of the
globe. As a UNESCO-associated NGO, we need to relate more closely our
work to UN models of peace education, education for sustainable development and global citizenship education, recognizing the importance of the
2030 Sustainable Development Agenda with 17 goals and 169 targets and
implementing its symbolic five dimensions including people, planet, prosperity, peace and partnership.

Therefore I propose to WCCES to begin the great conversation about
education for peace in the context of the 2030 Sustainable Development
Agenda. To carry out this conversation, I hope we may reach out to our
societies and our modest international structure as well as our standing
committees, bringing our work more closely aligned with the politics of the
UN and UNESCO. What follow are some key principles for discussion.

First, although France's violent retribution is already in motion, we must
not resort to the failures of the past. We must use this opportunity for a
better world with alternative approaches to conflict resolution and peace.

Though war might be inevitable (it is after all one of the responsibilities of the nation-states as defined by Western political philosophy), we must organize against and stop the perpetual visions of foreign policy and economies that thrive on war. We must pressure governments to seek political and diplomatic solutions to global problems. But if ideologies, like Nazism in its time, cannot be persuaded to give up their global ambitions, the world's democracies should organize a reasonable response, avoiding as much as possible civilian casualties.

Second, we must build global solidarity movements that are founded on the premises to counter racism, Islamophobia and extremist ideologies. Groups need to be established to educate communities about mutual respect, empathy, various privileges, histories of marginalized groups, and community and socially responsible entrepreneurship.

Third, we should host an Angicos-type World Social Forum conference in North Africa and Southwest Asia that brings together various scholars, civil society organizations, youth leaders and activists and other people to address and organically and inclusively create new peaceful ideologies and social policies that resonate with indigenous structures and beliefs that challenge violence.

Fourth, pressure all governments and the UN to conduct war crimes procedures for those responsible for atrocities on all sides of the political spectrum.

Fifth, build spaces for disenfranchised and marginalized youth throughout the world, listen to their grievances, empower them to participate in society, provide tools for conflict resolution and have them contributing to addressing social issues. Make sure that we use the power of reason and education to prevent further radicalization of youth following radical religious and nationalistic perspectives, giving meaning to lives that find no meaning otherwise. But most of the important, intense conversations about violent interpretations of Islam should take place throughout the world, conducted by Islamic scholars who should answer these radical interpretations responsible, as well for the internecine wars between Islamic faith groups.

Sixth, challenge governments' adoption of neoliberal-based policies. Seek out economic alternatives that are more inclusive and less socially and environmentally destructive.

Seventh, convey to UNESCO that they need to double their efforts to bring dialogue about conflict and peace in the world system into our governments, community organizations, social movements, political parties and world citizens. We need to feature in our mass media more dialogue about peace, global citizenship and education for sustainable development. We should offer our services to promote peace at any cost. Only in this way might we be able to promote life, liberty and the pursuit of happiness. Peace is a treasure of humanity and we should preserve it at any cost.

Eighth, to seek these goals, we should immediately begin an institutional conversation among ourselves about how we can help in the promotion of world peace. This dialogue should take a central role in the World Congress that we will hold in Beijing. I suggest that our Standing Committees take the lead and among them propose an agenda for dialogue on peace within WCCES and to be discussed in our Beijing Congress as well.

Ninth, as members of the WCCES community, it is our duty to help educators complicate their understanding of diversity, and subsequently create a more inclusive learning environment for all students. Helping educators to expand student identities toward a more global and interconnected framework is essential in deconstructing the marginalizing and divisive discourses that often permeate our educational institutions.

Nobody is free of fear. Nobody is free if we cannot meet; enjoy a coffee or a meal in a restaurant; congregate in a public place to enjoy music, a movie or theater; go to the market; or gather together to deliberate about the human condition, knowledge, the arts or business in peace. What happened most recently in Nigeria, Lebanon, France, Mali and the Sinai Peninsula could happen anywhere else, and more often than we may expect.

We cannot remain silent facing these civilizational crises. We cannot remain neutral at a moment of moral crisis. We cannot remain unmoved by carnage, violence and blood baths of civilians. We cannot simply go on with business as usual in our profession. If we do so, we are accomplices to barbarism.

Yours in peace,

Dr. Carlos Alberto Torres, Distinguished Professor of Education, Graduate School of Education and Information Studies, University of California-Los Angeles (UCLA); UNESCO Chair in Global Learning and Global Citizenship Education; Director of the Paulo Freire Institute; and President of the World Council of Comparative Education Societies (WCCES).

Bibliography

Abdallah-Pretceille, M. 1999. *L'éducation Interculturelle*. Paris: PUF.

Alleman-Ghionda, C. 2009. "From Intercultural Education to the Inclusion of Diversity: Theory and Policies in Europe." In *The Routledge International Companion to Multicultural Education*, edited by J. A. Banks, 134–145. London: Routledge.

Altbach, P., ed. 2007. *Higher Education in the New Century: Global Challenges and Innovative Ideas*. Boston, MA: Center for International Higher Education.

Amselle, J.-L. 1998. *Mestizo Logics: Anthropology of Identity in Africa and Elsewhere. Mestizo Spaces*. Stanford, CA: Stanford University Press.

Apple, M. 2004. *Ideology and Curriculum*. 3rd ed. New York: Routledge Falmer.

Archibugi, D. and D. Held, eds. 1995. *Cosmopolitan Democracy: An Agenda for a New World Order*. Cambridge, UK: Polity Press.

Arnove, R. and C. A. Torres, eds. 2007. *Comparative Education: The Dialectics of the Global and the Local*. 3rd ed. Lanham, MD: Rowman and Littlefield Publishers.

Arnove, R., C. A. Torres, and Stephen Franz. 2013. *Comparative Education: The Dialects of the Global and the Local*. Lanham, MD: Rowman and Littlefield Publishers.

Atkinson, A. B., T. Piketty, and E. Saez. 2011. "Top Incomes in the Long Run of History." *Journal of Economic Literature*, 49(1): 3–71, www.aeaweb.org/articles. php?doi= 10.1257/jel.49.1.3

Austen-Smith, D., J. A. Frieden, M. A. Golden, K. O. Moene, and A. Przeworki, eds. 2008. *Selected Works of Michael Wallerstein: The Political Economy of Inequality, Unions, and Social Democracy*. New York: Cambridge University Press.

Ban Ki-moon. *The Global Education First Initiative*. www.unesco.org/new/en/education/global-education-first-initiative-gefi

Banks, J. A. 2009. *The Routledge International Companion to Multicultural Education*. London: Routledge.

Banks, J. A. and C. A. McGee Banks. 1995. *Handbook of Research on Multicultural Education*. New York: Macmillan.

Banting, K. and W. Kymlicka. 2013. "Is There Really a Backlash against Multiculturalism Policies? New Evidence from the Multiculturalism Policy Index." *Comparative European Politics*, 11: 577–598.

Bardhan, P., S. Bowles, and M. Wallerstein. 2006. *Globalization and Egalitarian Redistribution*. Princeton, NJ: Princeton University Press and Russell Foundation.

Barry, B. 2001. *Culture and Equality: An Egalitarian Critique of Multiculturalism*. Cambridge, UK: Polity Press.

Beck, U. 2002. "The Cosmopolitan Society and Its Enemies." *Theory, Culture & Society*, 19(1–2): 17–44.

Beck, U. 2006. *The Cosmopolitan Vision*. Cambridge, UK: Polity Press.

Bell, D. 1995. "Racial Realism—After We're Gone: Prudent Speculations on America on a Post-Racial Epoch." In *Critical Race Theory: The Cutting Edge*, edited by T. Delgado, 2–8. Philadelphia, PA: Temple University Press.

Benhabib, S. 2002. *The Claims of Culture: Equality and Diversity in the Global Era.* Princeton, NJ: Princeton University Press.

Benhabib, S. 2005. "Borders, Boundaries, and Citizenship." *Political Science and Politics*, 38(4): 673–677, www.jstor.org/stable/30044348.

Benhabib, S. 2011. *Dignity in Adversity: Human Rights in Troubled Times.* Cambridge, UK: Polity Press.

Boron, A. 2008. *Consolidando la explotación: La academia y el Banco Mundial contra el pensamiento critic* [Consolidating the Exploitation: The Academy and the World Bank against Critical Thinking]. Cordoba, Spain: Espartaco.

Bottani, N. 2001. "Usages et mésusages des approches comparatives dans un cadre politique." In *Autour du comparatisme en education*, edited by R. Sirota, 71–76. Paris: PUF.

Bouchard, G. and C. Taylor. 1999. *Building the Future: A Time for Reconciliation* [Report of the Consultation Commission of Accompdation Practices Related to Cultural Differences]. Montréal, Québec: Government of Québec.

Bourdieu, P. and L. Vacquant. 1999. "The Cunning Imperialist Reason." *Theory, Culture, Society*, 16(1): 41–58.

Bowles, S. and H. Gintis. 1986. *Democracy and Capitalism: The Contradictions of Modern Political Life.* New York: Basic Books.

Burbules, N. and C.A. Torres, eds. 2000. *Education and Globalization: Critical Analysis.* New York: Routledge.

Burke, P. J. and S. Jackson. 2007. *Reconceptualising Lifelong Learning: Feminist Interventions.* London: Routledge.

Carnoy, M. 1999. *Globalization and Educational Reform: What Planners Need to Know.* Paris: UNESCO/IIEP.

Carnoy, M. 2001. "El impacto de la mundialización en las estrategias de reforma educativa." *Revista de Educación*, (número extraordinario): 101–110.

Carnoy, M. and C. A. Torres. 1992. *Educational Change and Structural Adjustment: A Case Study of Costa Rica.* Monograph prepared for the UNESCO–ILO Interagency Task Force on Austerity, Adjustment, and Human Resources. Occasional Papers series. Paris: UNESCO.

Castells, M. 1996. *The Rise of the Network Society.* Cambridge, UK: Blackwell.

Castells, M. 1997. *The Power of Identity: The Information Age: Economy, Society and Culture.* Volume II. Oxford, UK: Blackwell.

Clifton, J. 2011. *The Coming Jobs War.* New York: Gallup Press.

d'Avray, D. L. 2010. *Rationalities in History: A Weberian Essay in Comparison.* Cambridge, UK: Cambridge University Press.

Dale, I. R. 2003. "Globalization and the Rescaling of Educational Governance: A Case of Sociological Ectopia." In *Critique and Utopia: New Developments in the Sociology of Education in the Twenty-First Century*, edited by C. A. Torres and A. Teodoro, 25–42. Lanham, MD: Rowman and Littlefield.

Dale, I. R. and S. L. Robertson. 2007. "New Arenas of Global Governance and International Organisations: Reflections and Directions." In *New Arenas of Education Governance: The Impact of International Organizations and Markets on Educational Policy Making*, edited by K. Martens, A. Rusconi, and K. Leuze, 217–228. Basingstoke, UK: Palgrave Macmillan.

de Sousa Santos, B. 2002. "Toward a Multicultural Conception of Human Rights." In *Moral Imperialism: A Critical Anthology*, edited by B. E. Hernàndez-Truyol, 39–60. New York: New York University Press.

Deudney, D. 1999. "Geopolitics and Change." In *New Thinking in International Relations Theory*, edited by M. Doyle and G. J. Ikenberry, 91–123. Boulder, CO: Westview Press.

Deudney, D. 2000. "Regrounding Realism." *Security Studies*, 10(1): 1–45.

Dewey, J. 1916. *Democracy and Education.* Carbondale, IL: Southern Illinois University Press.

Education Above All. 2012. *Education for Global Citizenship*. Doha, Qatar: Education Above All. http://bit.ly/1IQIrcM

Education for Global Citizenship. In press. *The Oxford Research Encyclopedia of Education (ORE)*.

Enders, J., J. File, J. Huisman, and D. Westerheijden, eds. 2005. *The European Higher Education and Research Landscape 2020*. Enschede, The Netherlands: Center for Higher Education Policy Studies.

Etzioni, A. 1995. *New Communitarianism Thinking: Persons, Virtues, Institutions and Communities*. Charlottesville, VA: University of Virginia Press.

European Council. 2008. *White Paper on Intercultural Dialogue: "Living Together as Equals in Dignity"*. Strasbourg, Germany.

Falk, R. 1993. "The Making of the Global Citizenship." In *Global Visions: Beyond the New World Order*, edited by J. Brecher, J. Brown Childs, and J. Kutler, 39–50. Boston, MA: South End Press.

Falk, R. 2002. "An Emerging Matrix of Citizenship: Complex, Uneven and Fluid." In *Global Citizenship: A Critical Introduction*, edited by N. Dower and J. Williams, 15–29. New York: Routledge.

Feenberg, A. and W. Leiss, eds. 2007. *The Essential Marcuse: Selected Writings of Philosopher and Social Critic Herbert Marcuse*. Boston, MA: Beacon Press.

Foucault, M. 1972. *The Archaeology of Knowledge and the Discourse on Language*. Trans. A.M. Sheridan Smith. New York: Pantheon Books.

Foucault, M. 1980. *Power/Knowledge*. Trans. C. Gordon, L. Marshall, J. Mepham, and K. Soper. New York: Pantheon Books.

Foucault, M. 2010. *El coraje de la verdad: El gobierno de sí y de los otros II*. Curso en el Collège de France (1983–1984) [Lectures at the College de France, 1983–1984]. Buenos Aires, Argentina: Fondo de Cultura Económica.

Fraser, N. 1997. *Justice Interruptus: Critical Reflections on the "Postsocialist" Condition*. New York: Routledge.

Freire, P. 1970. *Pedagogy of the Oppressed*. Trans. M.B. Ramos. New York: Continuum.

Freire, P. 1998. *The Politics of Education*. Los Angeles, CA: University of California.

Freire, P. 2007. *Pedagogy of the Oppressed*. 30th Anniversary ed. New York: Continuum.

Friedman, T. 2005. *The World Is Flat: A Brief History of the Twenty-First Century*. 1st ed. New York: Farrar, Straus and Giroux.

Fukuyama, F. Y. 2012. *The Future of History: Can Liberal Democracy Survive the Decline of Middle Class?* Accessed May 25, 2012. www.foreignaffairs.com/articles/136782/francis-fukuyama/the-future-of-history

Gadotti, M. 2004. *Os Mestres de Rousseau*. São Paulo, Brazil: Cortez Editores.

Galeano, E. 1993. *Las Palabras Andantes*. Buenos Aires, Argentina: Catalogos SRL.

Galissot, R., M. Kilani, and A. Rivera. 2000. *L'imbroglio Etnique Quatorze Mots Clés*. Lausanne, Switzerland: Editions Payot.

García Canclini, N. (1990). *Culturas híbridas. Estrategias para entrar y salir de la modernidad*. México City, Mexico: Grijalbo.

Gaudelli, W. 2016. *Global Citizenship Education: Everyday Transcendence*. New York: Routledge.

Gewirtz, S. 1998. "Conceptualizing Social Justice in Education: Mapping the Territory." *Journal of Education Policy*, 13(4): 469–484.

Giddens, A. 1994. *Beyond Left and Right: The Future of Radical Politics*. Stanford, CA: Stanford University Press.

Gitlin, T. 1995. *The Twilight of Common Dreams: Why America Is Wracked by Culture Wars*. New York: Henry Holt.

Global Citizenship Education. 2014. *Preparing learners for the challenges of the twenty-first century*. United Nations Educational, Scientific and Cultural Organization, 7, place de Fontenoy, 75352 Paris 07 SP, France

Gorski, P. 2006. "Complicity with Conservatism: The De-Politicizing of Multicultural and Intercultural Education." *Intercultural Education*, 17(2): 163–177.

Gramsci, A. 1971. *Selections from the Prison Notebooks of Antonio Gramsci.* Trans. Q. Hoare and G. N. Smith. New York: International Publishers.

Grant, C. A. and A. Portera. 2011. *Intercultural and Multicultural Education: Enhancing Global Interconnectedness.* London: Routledge.

Gruzinski, S. 1999. *La Pensée Metises.* Paris: Fayard.

Gundara, J. S. and S. Jacobs. 2000. *Intercultural Europe: Diversity and Social Policy.* Aldershot, UK: Ashgate.

Gutmann, A. 1987. *Democratic Education.* Princeton, NJ: Princeton University Press.

Habermas, J 1973. *Theory and Practice.* Trans. J. Vietel. Boston, MA: Beacon Press.

Habermas, J. 1991. (1962). *The Structural Transformation of the Public Sphere: An Inquiry into a Category of Bourgeois Society.* Cambridge, MA: MIT Press.

Habermas, J. 1992. "Citizenship and National Identity: Some Reflections on the Future of Europe." *Praxis International*, 12: 1–12.

Habermas, J. 2004. "Why Europe Needs a Constitution." In *Developing a Constitution for Europe*, edited by E. O. Eriksen, J. E. Fossum, and A. J. Menéndez, 19–34. London: Routledge.

Held, D., ed. 1991. *Political Theory Today.* Stanford, CA: Stanford University Press.

Herrera, L. and R. Sakr. 2014. *Wired Citizenship: Youth Learning and Activism in the Middle East.* New York: Taylor and Francis.

Hill, I. 2007. "Multicultural and International Education: Never the Twain Shall Meet." *Review of Education*, 53(2): 245–264.

Institut National de Recherche Pédagogique. 2007. *Dossier Interculturel. Approches Interculturelles en Education. Étude Comparative International.* Paris: Ed. O. Meunier.

Jung, C. G. 1968. *Analytical Psychology: Its Theory and Practice.* New York: Vintage Books.

Kymlicka, W. 2010. "The Rise and Fall of Multiculturalism: New Debates on Inclusion and Accommodation in Diverse Societies." In *The Multiculturalism Backlash: European Discourses, Policies and Practices*, edited by S. Wessendorf and S. Vertovec, 32–49. London: Routledge.

Ladson-Billings, G. 2004. "New Directions in Multicultural Education: Complexities, Boundaries, and Critical Race Theory." In *Handbook of Research on Multicultural Education*, edited by J. Banks and C. A. McGee Banks, 50–65. San Francisco, CA: Jossey-Bass.

Landson-Billings, G. and W. F. Tate. 1995. "Toward a Critical Race Theory of Education." *Teachers College Record*, 97(1): 47–68.

Lauder, H., P. Brown, J.-A. Dillabough, and A. H. Halsey, eds. 2006. *Education, Globalization and Social Change.* Oxford, UK: Oxford University Press.

Leicester, M. 1992. "Antiracism Versus New Multiculturalism: Moving beyond the Interminable Debate." In *Education for Cultural Diversity: Convergence and Divergence*, edited by J. Lynch and S. Modgil, 215–229. London: Farmer Press.

Luke, A. and C. Luke. 2000. "A Situated Perspective on Cultural Globalization." In *Globalization and Education: Critical Perspectives*, edited by N. C. Burbules and C. A. Torres, 275–297. New York: Routledge.

Marshall, T. H. (1950). *Citizenship and Social Class and Other Essays.* Cambridge, UK: Cambridge University Press.

Maxwell, B., D. I. Waddington, K. McDonough, A.-A. Cormier, and M. Schwimmer. 2012. "Interculturalism, Multiculturalism and the State Funding and Regulation of Conservative Religious Schools." *Educational Theory*, 62(4): 427–447.

McDonald, M. and K. Zeicher. 2009. "Social Justice Teacher Education." In *Handbook of Social Justice Education*, edited by W. Ayers, T. Quinn, and D. Stovall, 595–610. New York: Routledge.

McLaren, P. 1997. *Revolutionary Multiculturalism: Pedagogies of Dissent for the New Millennium*. Boulder, CO: Westview Press.

Mignolo, W. D. 2000. *Local Histories/Global Designs: Coloniality, Subaltern Knowledges and Border Thinking*. Princeton, NJ: Princeton University Press.

Milani, C. R. S. & R. N. Laniado. 2006. *Transnational Social Movements and the Globalization Agenda: A Methodological Approach Based on the Analysis of the World Social Forum*. Working Paper 5, December 2006. The Edelstein Center for Social Research. Accessed December 15, 2010, from www.edelsteincenter.org

Morrow, R. A. 2006. "Foreword—Critical Theory, Globalization, and Higher Education: Political Economy and the Cul-de-sac of the Postmodernist Cultural Turn." In *The University, State and Market: The Political Economy of Globalization in the Americas*, edited by R. A. Rhoads and C. A. Torres, xxvi–xxvii. Stanford, CA: Stanford University Press.

Morrow, R. A. 2008. "Paulo Freire, Indigenous Knowledge and Eurocentrics Critiques of Development: Three Prospectives." In *Social Justice Education for Teachers: Paulo Freire and the Possible Dream*, edited by C. A. Torres and N. Pedro, 81–100. Rotterdam, The Netherlands: Sense Publishers.

Morrow, R. A. and C. A. Torres. 1995. *Social Theory and Education: A Critique of Theories of Social and Cultural Reproduction*. Albany, NY: State University of New York Press.

Morrow, R. A. and C. A. Torres. 2013. "The State, Social Movements, and Educational Reform." In *Education: The Dialectic of the Global and the Local*. 4th ed., edited by R. Arnove, C. A. Torres, and S. Franz, 89–112. Lanham, MD: Rowman and Littlefield Publishers.

Nieto, S. 1996. *Affirming Diversity: The Sociopolitical Context of Multicultural Education*. 2nd ed. New York: Longman.

North, C. 2006. "More than Words? Delving into the Substantive Meaning(s) of 'Social Justice' Education." *Review of Educational Research*, 76(4): 507–535.

Nuhoglu Soysal, Y. 1994. *Limits of Citizenship: Migrants and Postnational Membership in Europe*. Chicago, IL: University of Chicago Press.

Offe, C. 2006. "Social Protection in a Supranational Context. European Integration and the Fates of the 'European Social Model'." In *Globalization and Egalitarian Redistribution*, edited by P. Bardhan, S. Bowles, and M. Wallerstein, 33–63. Princeton, NJ: Princeton University Press and Russell Foundation.

Peters, M. A. and T. Besley. 2014. "Islam and the End of European Multiculturalism?" *Special Issue of Policies Futures in Education*, 12: 1.

Piketty, T. 2014. *Capital in the Twenty First Century*. Cambridge, MA: Belknap Press.

Portelli. 1972. *Gramsci y el bloque histórico*. Mexico City, Mexico: Siglo XXI Editores.

Przeworski, A. 2003. *Capitalism, Democracy and Science*. Interview with Adam Przeworski. Conducted and edited by Gerardo L. Munck. February 24, 2003, New York. http://as.nyu.edu/docs/IO/2800/munck.pdf

Pusser, B., K. Kempner, S. Marginson, and I. Ordorika. 2012. "Introduction and Overview of the Book." In *Universities and the Public Sphere. Knowledge Creation and State Building in the Era of Globalization*, edited by B. Pusser, K. Kempner, S. Marginson, and I. Ordorika, 1–4. London: Routledge.

Rawls, J. 1971. *A Theory of Justice*. Cambridge, MA: Harvard University Press.

Rawls, J. 1993. *Political Liberalism*. New York: Columbia University.

Rawls, J. 2001. *Justice as Fairness: A Restatement*. Cambridge MA: Harvard University Press.

Reich, R. 1988. *Education and the Global Economy*. Washington, DC: National Education Association.

Reich, R. 1992. *The Work of Nations: Preparing Ourselves for 21st Century Capitalism*. New York: Vintage Books.

Rexhepi, J. and C. A. Torres. 2011. "Reimagining Critical Theory." *British Journal of Sociology of Education*, 32(5): 679–698.

Rhoads, R. A. and G. R. Rhoads. 2006. "Graduate Student Unionization as a Post-Industrial Social Movement: Identity, Ideology, and the Contested US Academy." In *The University, State, and Market: The Political Economy of Globalization in the Americas*, edited by R. Rhoads and C. A. Torres, 275–298. Stanford, CA: Stanford University Press.

Rhoades, G. and S. Slaughter. 2006. "Academic Capitalism and the New Economy: Privatization as Shifting the Target of Public Subsidy in Higher Education." In *The University, State and Market. The Political Economy of Globalization in the Americas*, edited by R. A. Rhoads and C. A. Torres, 103–140. Stanford, CA: Stanford University Press.

Rhoads, R. A. and C. A. Torres, eds. 2006. *The University, State and Markets: The Political Economy of Globalization in the Americas*. Stanford, CA: Stanford University Press.

Rhoads, R. A. and K. Szelényi. 2011. *Global Citizenship and the University: Advancing Social Life and Relations in an Interdependent World*. Stanford, CA: Stanford University Press.

Saenz, E. and T. Piketty. http://gmond.parisschoolofeconomics.eu/topincomes.

Sandel, M. 1982. *Liberalism and the Limits of Justice*. Cambridge, UK: Cambridge University Press.

Santos, B. D. S. 2012. "Public Sphere and Epistemologies of the South." *Africa Development*, 38(1): 43–67.

Santos Regò, A. M. and S. Nieto. 2000. "Multicultural/Intercultural Teacher Education in Two Contexts: Lessons from the United States and Spain." *Teaching and Teacher Education*, 16(4): 413–427.

Sassen, S. 1998. *Globalization and Its Discontents*. New York: New Press.

Sassen, S. 2002. "The Repositioning of Citizenship: Emergent Subjects and Spaces for Politics." *Berkeley Journal of Sociology*, 46: 4–25.

Schirru, G. 2010. *Antonio Gramsci e os problemas da educação*. Paper presented to the III Seminario Internacional de Educação, Pesquisas em Educação no Brasil e no Mundo, November 23–26, in Uninove, São Paulo, Brazil.

Schugurensky, D. 1994. *Global Economic Restructuring and University Change: The Case of the University of Buenos Aires*. Ph.D. diss., University of Alberta.

Semali, L. and L. J. Kincheloe. 1999. *What Is Indigenous Knowledge? Voices from the Academy*. New York: Falmer Press.

Sen, A. 1992. *Inequality Reexamined*. Oxford, UK: Oxford University Press.

Shultz, L., A. Abdi, and G. Richardson, eds. 2011. *Global Citizenship Education in Post-Secondary Institutions: Theories, Practices, Policies*. New York: Peter Lang.

Slaughter, S. and G. Rhoades. 2004. *Academic Capitalism and the New Economy*. Baltimore, MD: John Hopkins University Press.

Slaughter, S. and L. L. Leslie. 1997. *Academic Capitalism: Politics, Policies, and the Entrepreneurial University*. Baltimore, MD: John Hopkins University Press.

Sleeter, C. E. 1996. *Multicultural Education as Social Civism*. Albany, NY: State University of New York Press.

Sleeter, C. E. and C. A. Grant. 1999. *Making Choices for Multicultural Education: Five Approaches to Race, Class, and Gender*. 3rd ed. Upper Saddle River, NJ: Merrill Publishing Company.

Soetendorp, Rabbi A. http://charterforcompassion.org/node/6564

Solow, R. July 12, 1987. "We'd better watch out." *New York Times Book Review*: 36.

Song, S. 2012. "The Boundary Problem in Democratic Theory: Why the Demos Should Be Bounded by the State." *International Theory*, 4(1): 39–68, doi:10.1017/ S1752971911000248, http://polisci.berkeley.edu/sites/default/files/people/u3868/ Song%20-%20Boundary%20Problem%20in%20Democratic%20Theory.pdf

Soysal, Y. 1994. *Limits of Citizenship: Migrants and Postnational Membership in Europe.* Chicago, IL: Chicago University Press.

Stiglitz, J. E. 2002. *Globalization and Its Discontents.* New York: W. W. Norton.

Suarez-Orozco, C., M. M. Suarez-Orozco, and I. Todorova. 2008. *Learning in a New Land: Immigrant Students in American Society.* Cambridge, MA: Harvard University Press.

Suárez-Orozco, M. and C. Sattin-Bajaj, eds. 2010. *Educating the Whole Child for the Whole World: The Ross School Model and Education for the Global Era.* New York: New York University Press.

Tarozzi, M. 2005. *Cittadinanza Interculturale: Esperienza Educativa Come Agire Politico.* Firenze, Italy: La nuova Italia.

Tarozzi, M. 2015. *Dall'intercultura alla giustizia sociale. Per un progetto pedagogico e politico di cittadinanza globale.* Milano, Italy: Franco Angeli.

Tarozzi, M., and C. A. Torres. (2016). *Global Citizenship Education and the Crisis of Multiculturalism: Comparative Perspectives.* London & Oxford, Bloomsbury Publishing.

Tarrow, S. 1998. *Power in Movement: Social Movements and Contentious Politics.* Cambridge, UK: Cambridge University Press.

Taylor, C. 1992. *Multiculturalism and the Politics of Recognition.* Princeton, NJ: Princeton University Press.

Teodoro, A. 2003. "Educational Policies and New Ways of Governance in a Trans-nationalization Period." In *The International Handbook on the Sociology of Education,* edited by C. A. Torres and A. Antikainen. Lanham, MD: Rowman & Littlefield.

Teodoro, A. 2008. *Tempos e andamentos na politicas de educação: Estudos Iberoamericanos.* Brasilia, Brazil: Liber Livro Editora, CYTED.

Teodoro, A., ed. 2010. *A educação superior no espaço iberoamericano: Do elitismo á trasnacionalização.* Lisbon, Portugal: Edições Universitárias Lusófonas.

Tönnies, F. and C. P. Loomis. (1872) 1957. *Community, Society.* East Lansing, MI: Michigan State University Press.

Torres, C. A. 1992. *The Church, Society and Hegemony: A Critical Sociology of Religion in Latin America.* (Trans. R. A. Young). London: Praeger.

Torres, C. A. 1998a. *Education, Democracy and Multiculturalism: Dilemmas of Citizenship in a Global World.* Lanham, MD: Rowman and Littlefield Publishers.

Torres, C. A. 1998b. *Democracy, Education, and Multiculturalism: Dilemmas of Citizenship in a Global World.* Lanham, MD: Rowman and Littlefield Publishers.

Torres, C. A. 2002. "Globalization, Education, and Citizenship: Solidarity Versus Markets?" *American Educational Research Journal,* 39(2): 363–378.

Torres, C. A. 2009a. *Globalizations and Education: Collected Essays on Class, Race, Gender, and the State.* Introduction by M. W. Apple, Afterword by P. Demo. New York: Teachers College Press, Columbia University.

Torres, C. A. 2009b. *Globalizations and Education: Collected Essays on Class, Race, Gender, and the State.* New York: Teachers College Press.

Torres, C. A. 2009c. *Education and Neoliberal Globalization.* New York: Routledge.

Torres, C. A 2011. "Public Universities and the Neoliberal Common Sense: Seven Iconoclastic Theses." *International Studies in Sociology of Education,* 21(3): 177–197.

Torres, C. A. 2013a. *Political Sociology of Adult Education.* Rotterdam, The Netherlands: Sense Publishers.

Torres, C. A. 2013b. "Neoliberalism as a New Historical Bloc: A Gramscian Analysis of Neoliberalism's Common Sense in Education." *International Studies in Sociology of Education,* 23(2): 80–106.

Torres, C. A. 2013c. "Comparative Education: The Dialectics of Globalization and Its Discontents." In *Comparative Education: The Dialectics of the Global and the Local.* 4th ed., edited by R. Arnove, C. A. Torres, and S. Franz, 459–483. Lanham, MD: Rowman and Littlefield Publishers.

Torres, C. A. 2014. *First Freire: Early Writings in Social Justice Education.* New York: Teachers College Press.

Torres, C. A. 2015a. "Global Citizenship and Global Universities. The Age of Global Interdependence and Cosmopolitanism." *European Journal of Education*: 262–279.

Torres, C. A. 2015b. *Neoliberalism, Globalization Agendas and Banking Educational Policy: Is Popular Education an Answer?* Paper prepared for the Max Weber Foundation Meeting in New Delhi, India, February 13–16, 2015.

Torres, C. A. 2015c. *Global Citizenship Education and Global Peace Opportunities in Achieving Peace through GCED.* Paper presented to the 2nd UNESCO Forum on Global Citizenship Education: Building Peaceful and Sustainable Societies–Preparing for post-2015, UNESCO Headquarters in Paris, January 28–30, 2015.

Torres, C. A. and P. Noguera. 2009. *Social Justice for Teachers. Paulo Freire and Education as a Possible Dream.* The Hague, The Netherlands: Sense Publishers.

Torres, C. A. and R. A. Rhoads. 2006. "Introduction: Globalization and Higher Education in the Americas." In *The University, State, and Market*, edited by R. Rhoads and C. A. Torres, 3–37. Stanford, CA: Stanford University Press.

Torres, C. A. and R. V. Heertum. 2009. "Globalization and Neoliberalism: The Challenges and Opportunities of Radical Pedagogy." In *Re-reading Education Policies: A Handbook Studying the Policy Agenda of the Twenty-First Century*, edited by M. Simons, M. Olssen, and M. A. Peters, 150–151. Rotterdam, The Netherlands: Sense Publishers.

Touraine, A. 1968. *Le Comunisme Utopique: Le Mouvement de Mai 1968.* Paris: Seuil.

Touraine, A. 1988. *Return of the Actor: Social Theory in Postindustrial Society.* Minneapolis, MN: University of Minnesota Press.

Touraine, A. 1997. *Puorrons-nous Vivre Ensemble? égaux et Différentes.* Paris: Libraire Arthéme Fayard.

UCLA Global Strategic Priorities. 2014. *Change the World; Lead the World.* Document for comments, unpublished.

UN Department of Economic and Social Affairs. 2013. *International Migration Wallchart.* Accessed June 8, 2015.

UNESCO. 2005. *Towards Knowledge Societies.* Paris: UNESCO World Report.

UNESCO. 2–4 December 2013. *Concept Note UNESCO Forum on Global Citizenship Education: Preparing Learners for the Challenge of the 21st Century.* Bangkok, Thailand.

UNESCO. 2015. *Global Citizenship Education: Topics and Learning Objectives.* Paris.

United Nations. 1–12 December 2014. *Ministers and Heads of Delegation Attending the UN Climate Change Conference 2014—COP20.* Lima, Peru.

Urry, J. 1998. "Contemporary Transformation of Time and Space." In *The Globalization of Higher Education*, edited by P. Scott, 1–17. London: Society for Research into Higher Education and Open University.

Velasquez, M., C. Andre, T. Shanks, and M. J. Meyer. *The Common Good.* www.scu.edu/ethics/ethics-resources/ethical-decision-making/the-common-good/

Vertovec, S. and S. Wessendorf. 2010. *The Multiculturalism Backlash: European Discourses, Policies and Practices.* London: Routledge.

Wieviorka, M. 2001. *La différence: Identités culturelles: enjeux, débats et politiques.* Paris: Balland.

Wintersteiner, W., H. Grobbauer, G. Diendorfer, and S. Reitmair-Juárez. 2015. "Global Citizenship Education. Citizenship Education for Globalizing Societies." In cooperation with the Austrian Commission for UNESCO Klagenfurt, Salzburg, Vienna.

World Bank. 2014/2015. *Ending Poverty and Sharing Prosperity*. Global Monitoring Report. www.worldbank

Yunker, J. A. 2011. *The Idea of World Government: From Ancient Times to the Twenty-First Century*. New York: Routledge.

Index

Made in the USA
San Bernardino, CA
22 January 2020